IMAGES
of America

WOODSTOCK

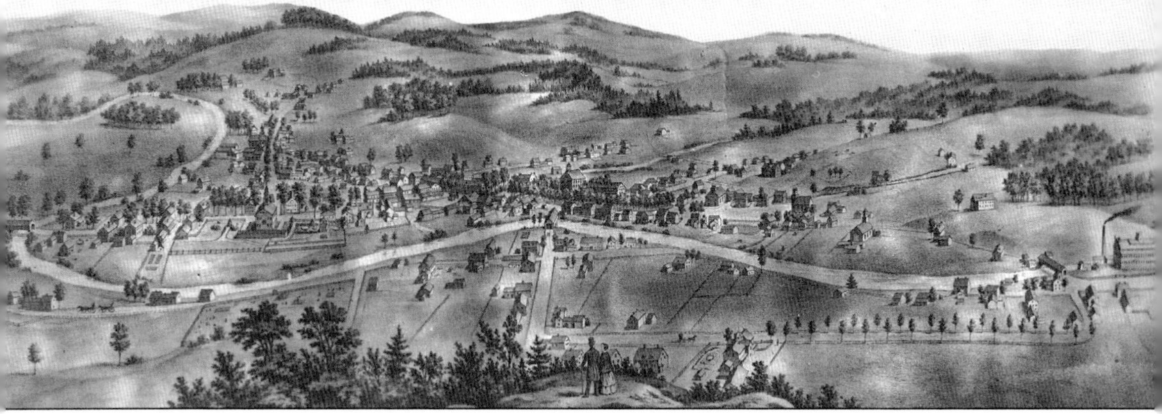

Looking southeasterly down from Mount Tom, this c. 1860 lithographic view shows Woodstock Village. In the center are the Windsor County Courthouse and the Woodstock Green, and to the right is the road to West Woodstock and beyond into the Green Mountains. The Ottauquechee River is in the foreground, and all three of the village's covered bridges are shown. (Courtesy of Jireh Billings.)

On the Cover: Vermonters have long been known for their uniquely subtle and dry sense of humor; however, the circumstances concerning this obviously posed May 1889 image are apparently lost to history. In the background is the stone Cabot Block that, to this day, still faces the square on Elm Street. Perhaps the nattily attired Woodstock Village wags are protesting the poorly drained condition of Elm Street in front of the Woodstock Post Office. (Courtesy of the Woodstock History Center.)

IMAGES
of America

WOODSTOCK

Frank J. Barrett Jr.

ARCADIA
PUBLISHING

ISBN 978-1-4671-2598-7

Published by Arcadia Publishing
Charleston, South Carolina

Printed in the United States of America

Library of Congress Control Number: 2017933994

For all general information, please contact Arcadia Publishing:
Telephone 843-853-2070
Fax 843-853-0044
E-mail sales@arcadiapublishing.com
For customer service and orders:
Toll-Free 1-888-313-2665

Visit us on the Internet at www.arcadiapublishing.com

To Frank J. Barrett: father, architect, artist, historian, and teacher from whom I learned to love the history of buildings, people, and the landscape. And that has made all the difference.

Contents

ACKNOWLEDGMENTS

This project first began as a casual conversation with Woodstock resident Roland H. Moore and then spread to a meeting in Pauline Gillingham Billings's living room with her son Jireh S. Billings, Roland, and representatives of the Woodstock History Center. Woodstock is indeed fortunate that, since the earliest days of photography, the town has been well photographed by professionals and amateurs alike. And much of that important record has come to be permanently housed within the extensive archives of the Woodstock History Center. Additionally, the written record of Woodstock's earlier history has been well transcribed by at least one very notable author in 1889, Henry Swan Dana, who was a descendant of some of Woodstock's first settlers.

Unless otherwise noted, all of the images used in compilation of this book are from the archives of the Woodstock History Center.

The text that introduces and accompanies all of these images has been largely culled from the extensive archives and library of the Woodstock History Center, as well as from several related volumes in the author's own personal library.

The author is very grateful for the continued support of this project from the Billings family, Roland Moore, and the Woodstock History Center, including executive director Matthew Powers and staff. And, as in the past when working with Arcadia Publishing, I am grateful for the editorial support, technical and otherwise, of Erin Vosgien and Stacia Bannerman. Unfortunately for the purposes of this volume, the rich treasure trove of important and colorful historic images made available to me was far in excess of what could realistically fit within the pages of this book. As a result, some painful choices concerning images and subject matter had to be made. Nonetheless, it was my goal from the beginning that the final product will both delight and inform the reader, as well as also provide a substantive overview of the varied and many individual aspects that over the past 200-plus years have contributed to make Woodstock such a uniquely rich community of history, architecture, culture, and natural beauty.

INTRODUCTION

Woodstock, Vermont, is a community long known for its rich regional beauty that uniquely combines and embraces both the natural landscape and the built environment. However, as unique as the environs of Woodstock might be, the story of the town's origins and founding were indeed common with many of the towns in western New Hampshire and much of the Green Mountain State of Vermont—a story that begins in the mid-18th century, if not earlier.

Almost since the time of its inception on the banks of the Piscataqua River in the 1620s, what was to become the Royal Colony of New Hampshire quickly became overshadowed, and at times often ruled, by its far larger neighbor to the south, the Massachusetts Bay Colony. While fearing God, Massachusetts Puritans expressed little fear toward the tiny struggling colony of New Hampshire to the north, or its territorial rights. After more than a century of continued interference by the Bay Colony, an aging King George II (1683–1760) took steps in 1741 to settle several long-troubling issues. First, he established the southerly and easterly boundaries between New Hampshire and Massachusetts at their present-day locations (the present-day state of Maine was then a territory of Massachusetts), and he appointed a new royal governor, Benning Wentworth (1696–1770), to govern the province of New Hampshire. Wentworth was of a long-established Portsmouth family loyal to the crown, and unlike the troublesome Congregationalists of the Bay Colony, Wentworth was a staunch Anglican, so on the surface he was loyal to both church and state. But note that Benning Wentworth had no small amount of ego and nerve.

Unfortunately, at that time, the king ignored the question of the colony's westerly boundary. Massachusetts claimed much of the upper Connecticut River valley, and New York believed its easterly boundary was at the Connecticut River. Wentworth claimed the westerly boundary was aligned with the westerly boundaries of Massachusetts and Connecticut, 20 miles east of the Hudson River. Therefore, in 1749, Wentworth chartered the town of Bennington, in present-day Vermont, as an act of putting the two neighboring colonies on notice and marking his territory, 20 miles east of the Hudson River. Despite howls of protest to the king from authorities in New York, over the next five years Governor Wentworth went on to charter 16 additional towns across the lower spine of the Green Mountains and up the west side of the Connecticut River into the area of Bellows Falls.

At that time, the region of present-day Vermont remained a disputed territory not only between the three competing English colonies but also between the British and French empires, both of whom had long been competing for control of the North America continent. Once again, as had happened over the past 100 years or more, fighting broke out between the two European rivals in 1754 that would decide the matter in Great Brittan's favor with the defeat of French forces on the Plains of Abraham at Québec in September 1760.

With the conquest of Canada by Great Britain, Governor Wentworth once again began aggressively chartering new towns on both sides of the upper Connecticut River valley and west all the way into the Lake Champlain basin. And once again, New York authorities cried foul to the king's government in London. The elderly King George II had never gotten around to deciding the location of the boundary between New Hampshire and New York and died in 1760. That same year, his young grandson George III ascended to the throne, but it was not until July 1764 that the new king ruled that the division line between the two competing colonies was the westerly bank of the Connecticut River. However, by that time, as far as New York was concerned, the damage had been done because west of the Connecticut River, Wentworth had successfully chartered 138 towns and, in the process, had acquired great amounts of land and fees for both himself and those in government close to him in the colonial capital of Portsmouth, New Hampshire.

In the summer of 1761, Wentworth issued the first round of new town charters, including that for the Town of Woodstock, in the name of King George III, dated July 10. Wherever possible, the governor's surveyors used an increment of six miles square to layout the boundaries of a new township. The governor believed that a township of about that size would enable all the inhabitants to travel to and from the all-important annual town meeting. The charter for the Town of Woodstock laid out a rectangular tract of land 7.5 miles by 5.5 miles of 24,960 total acres. Wentworth named the new town after Woodstock in Oxfordshire, England, in homage to George Spencer, the 4th Duke of Marlborough.

The charter establishing Woodstock was in the same format as all of the charters issued by Wentworth, and even used the same preprinted form with the appropriate blanks filled in and the individual proprietors names listed. Of those individual proprietors who each had a share, there were 62, and little appears known of them other than that they were probably all from Connecticut or western Massachusetts. As was also typical, Governor Wentworth took two shares for himself, and one share each was given to the Incorporated Society for the Propagation of the Gospel in Foreign Parts, the Glebe for the Church of England as by Law Established, the first settled minister in the town, and one share for the benefit of the town's school district. In total, there were 68 equal shares, however, the governor took his two shares as a contiguous 500-acre plot of land located within the very northeasterly corner of the new township.

Although it was expected that the division of land into individual lots and settlement would therefore begin and move forward in a timely manner, for the next almost nine years, only minimal settlement was undertaken in Woodstock, as well as in many of the other newly chartered towns west of the Connecticut River. The problem was the great confusion and uncertainty with New York and the question of valid land titles caused by the king's ruling in favor of New York in 1764. In spite of the king's stern edicts from London, New York authorities considered the New Hampshire land titles void and became increasingly heavy-handed and greedily demanded that new fees be paid to them and more. By July 2, 1777, the matter of land titles and the "Yorkers" actions reached such a breaking point that on that day, at a convention held in nearby Windsor, the free and independent Republic of Vermont was declared.

As to Woodstock, after some number of years, expense, and considerable effort by a small handful of individuals, the controversy with New York became resolved, and an entirely new charter was issued on February 5, 1772, reestablishing the Town of Woodstock in Cumberland County, within the Province of New York. Woodstock was better able to settle its differences with New York than many of the towns west of the Connecticut River, and so finally, permanent settlement began.

One

Patterns of Rural Life

During the years of controversy with New York, there did occur some small amount of settlement within the vast and dense wilderness that was Woodstock. Timothy Knox, a squatter really, in 1765 erected a crude hut beside Kedron Brook north of present-day South Woodstock. Here for the next three years, he went about hunting, fishing, and trapping. He was the first and only white inhabitant in Woodstock until June 1768, when Andrew Powers properly acquired 400 acres of land bordering on the Pomfret town line, immediately west of the 500-acre so-called Governors Lot at present-day Taftsville. The land secured by Powers prompted settlement by family members and others within this immediate area and at several other scattered locations within Woodstock. By early 1771, a census ordered by the governor of New York found that there was a total of 42 inhabitants settled in the town, 10 of whom were heads of families, and 19 under the age of 16.

The town continued to be divided up into individual lots as more settlers moved in, and in addition to clearing land for agriculture, sawmills and gristmills were constructed, roads were laid out, local town government was organized, and school districts were established. Gradually, what had been a continuous dense wilderness of upland hardwoods and coniferous trees along lowland areas of brooks, streams, and swamps gave way to a pattern of individual farms spread across the face of the land. The broader lands of the Ottauquechee River valley were the most prized for cultivation, and the rolling hillsides provided area for upland pasture, maple sugar orchards, and woodlots.

Over time, the rural working landscape of Woodstock acquired a beauty and a sense of place that came to define Vermont. Throughout much of the 19th century, sheep, raised for their wool, grazed upon much of Woodstock's upland pasturelands. The introduction of dairy farming replaced sheep and wool, remaining the economic back bone of Vermont well into the late 20th century—much to the scenic delight of Woodstock visitors and photographers alike.

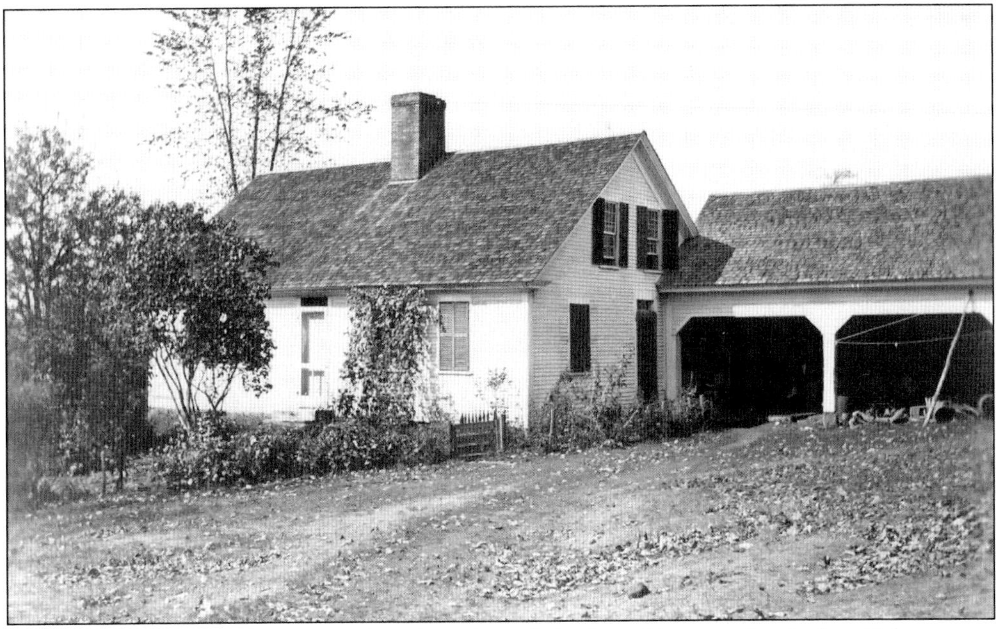

The first settlers in Vermont erected crude and simple log huts. However, by the late 18th century, so-called Cape-style homes started to dot the rural landscape, like this early example erected in Woodstock. Named for the simple and efficient fisherman cottages of Cape Cod, this building type with its central chimney and connected sheds proved ideal for the Vermont farmer making a livelihood on the region's rugged hillsides.

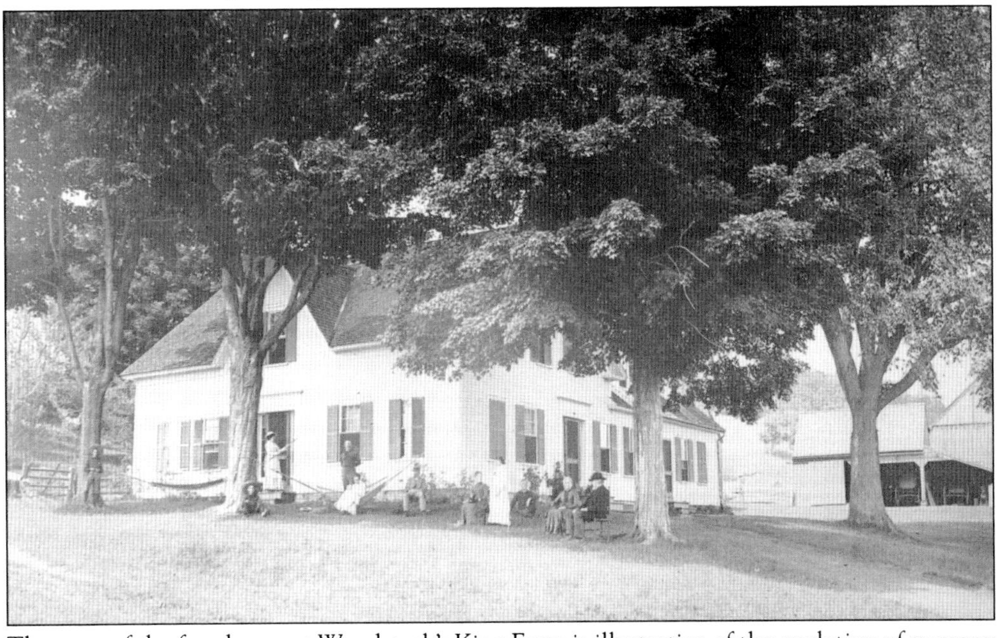

The story of the farmhouse at Woodstock's King Farm is illustrative of the evolution of so many of the region's early rural homes. First erected in 1793 as a very simple and compact Cape with low eaves and a center chimney, the house was extensively remodeled and enlarged around 1862. As was typical for that time, fashionable Greek Revival–style features were added to the building's exterior.

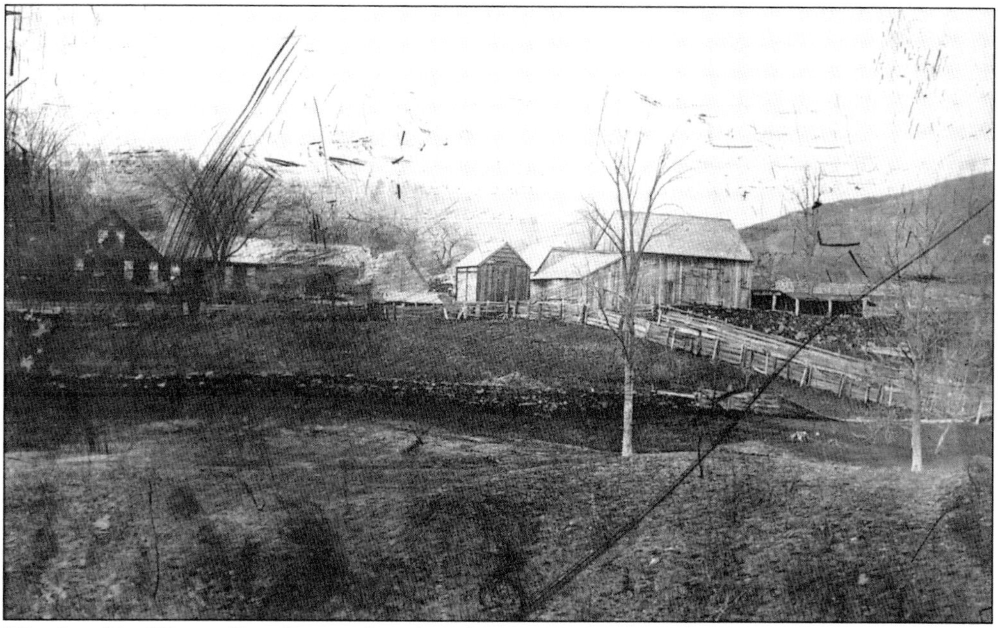

Woodstock's 157-acre King Farm is listed in the National Register of Historic Places and is richly descriptive of Vermont's hillside farms. First established by Jesse Williams in 1792, the property became owned by Jabez King by 1807 and remained in that family until 1985. This c. 1860 image of the farm shows many of the original buildings while it was still raising sheep, before the change to dairy.

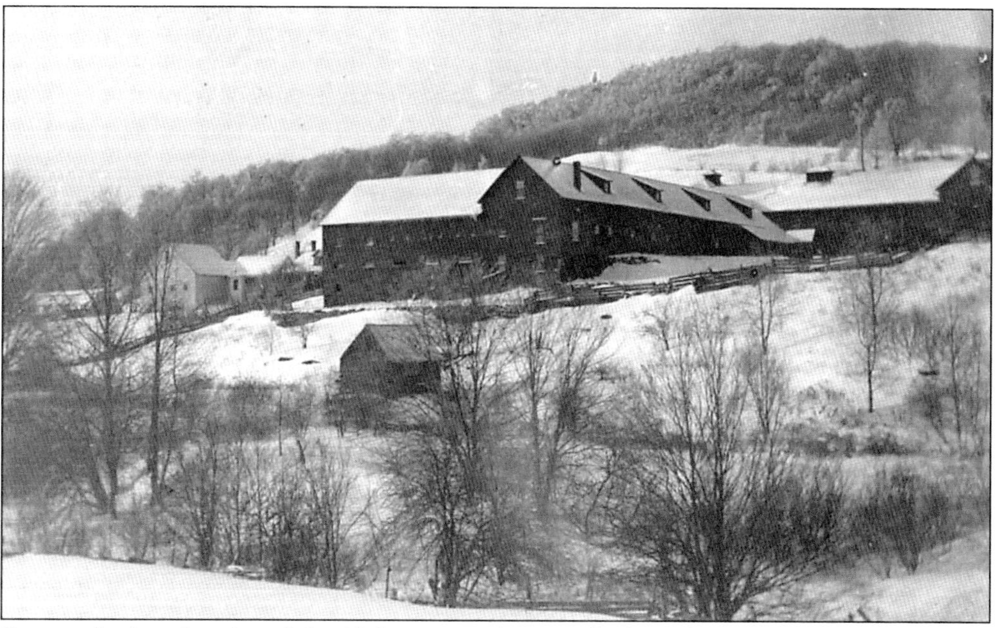

During the last decades of the 19th century, large-scale dairy farming was becoming more common in Vermont. This 1909 view of Cloudland Farm near Woodstock illustrates the great complex of buildings necessary to support such a large operation. Unlike sheep, dairy cows needed to be stabled and milked and fed twice a day, meaning great amounts of feed had to be stored throughout much of the year.

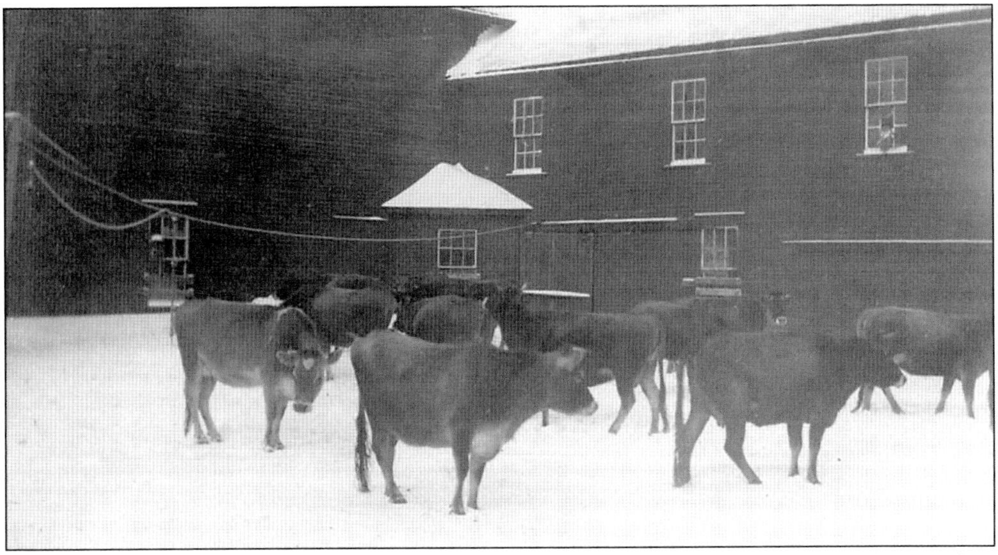

The Billings Farm in Woodstock was the first in Vermont to import Jersey cattle, and soon after, other farms followed. By 1909, when this image was made of some of the large herd of Jerseys at the Cloudland Farm near Woodstock, two of the finest herds of Jerseys in the state were in Woodstock at the large and successful Billings and Cloudland farm operations.

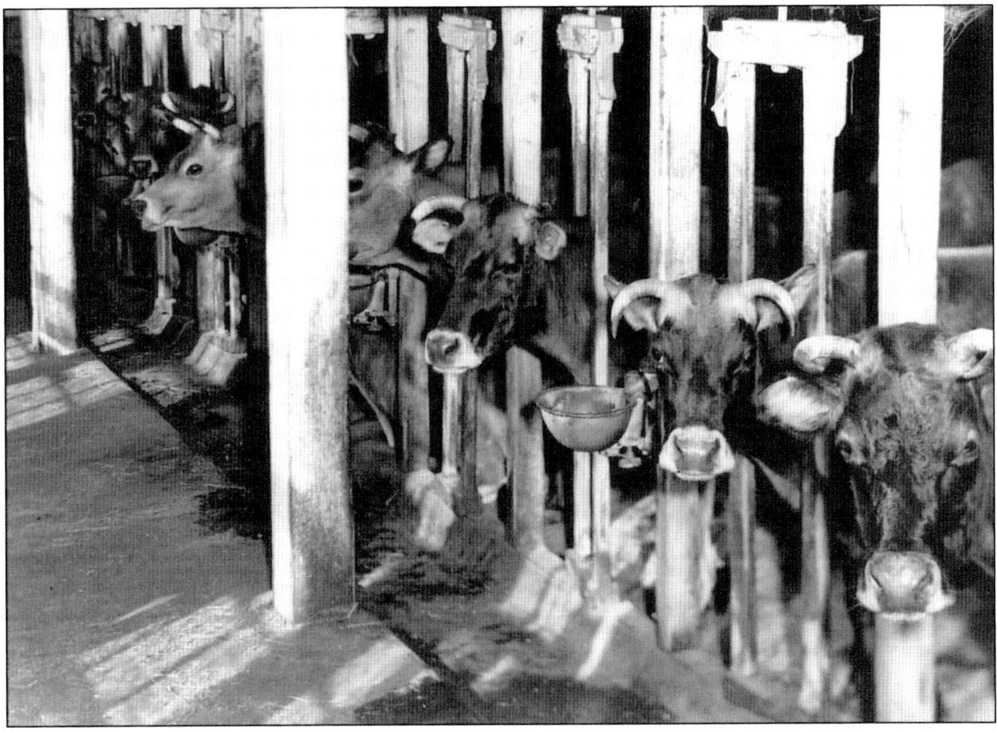

Jersey cows are seen waiting to be fed at the Cloudland Farm near Woodstock in 1909. Originally bred on the Isle of Jersey in the English Channel, Jerseys are good foragers well suited to grazing on Vermont's hillside terrain. Although smaller than other breeds, Jerseys became popular for the high butterfat content of their milk, lower maintenance costs due to a lower body weight (880 to 1,100 pounds), and genial dispositions.

Dairy farming means milking the cows twice a day—at dawn and dusk. And after the milk was gathered, it had to be strained to remove any foreign matter as it was poured into standardized steel milk cans for shipment to processing plants. This quintessential Vermont view is of a young man believed to be working at the Nelson farm in Woodstock in the 1940s.

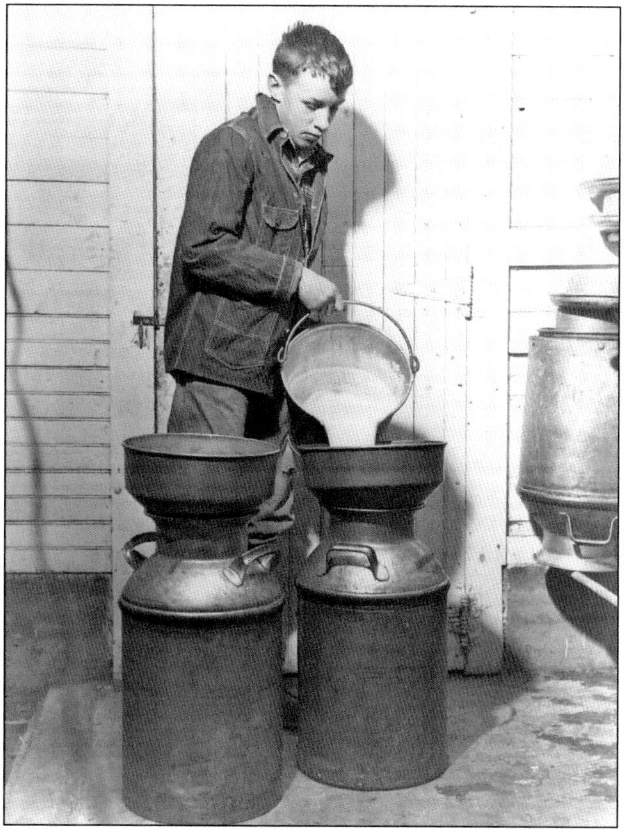

After the milk was placed into cans for shipment, it had to be brought to the local creamery or nearest railroad siding for shipment to large processing plants. The eventual destination for much of the milk produced in Vermont was urban markets in southern New England. Pictured in the 1940s is a Woodstock farm's pickup truck heading out with a load of milk cans on board.

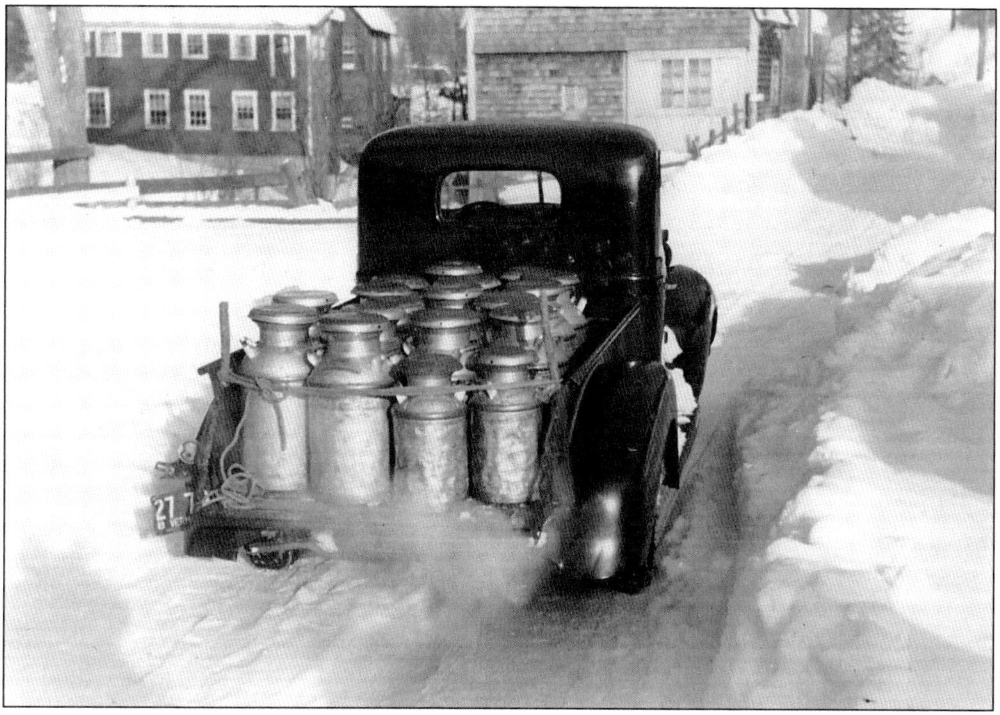

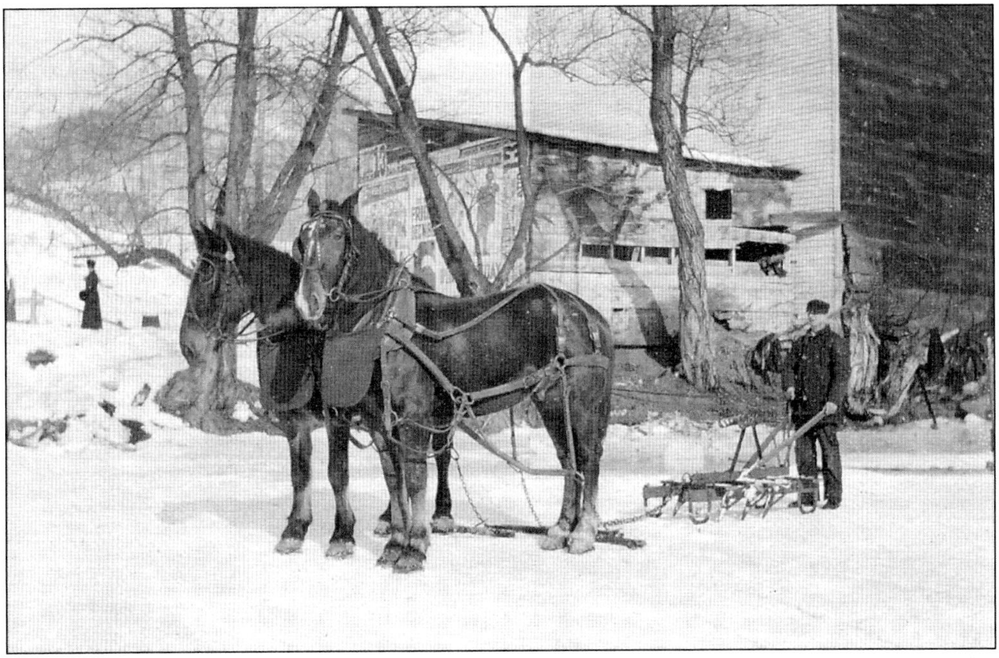

Before the advent of mechanical refrigeration in the 1920s, blocks of ice were harvested from the frozen surface of Woodstock's ponds and the Ottauquechee River during the winter months. The first task was to clean snow off of the ice to be cut, using teams of horses, and then the surface of the ice was scored into a series of grids.

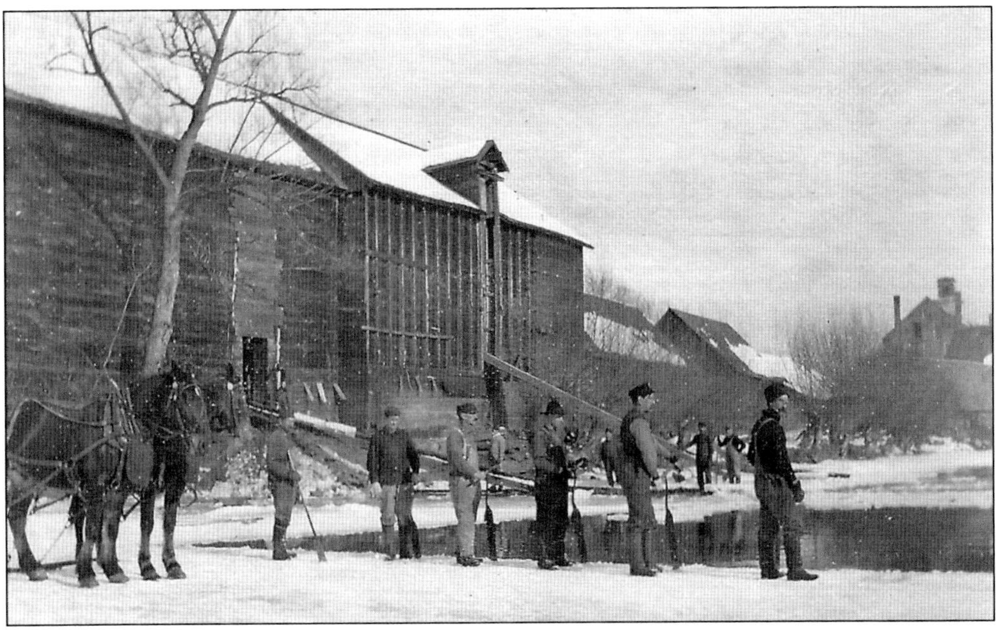

After the ice was scored into a grid, men using long saws, which were made for cutting the ice, sliced it into rectangular chunks. This view shows a large icehouse beside the millpond on the Ottauquechee River west of Woodstock Village, where ice was packed in sawdust and stored until used in the summer. Most farms had individual icehouses as well. Note the two conveyors going up into the icehouse.

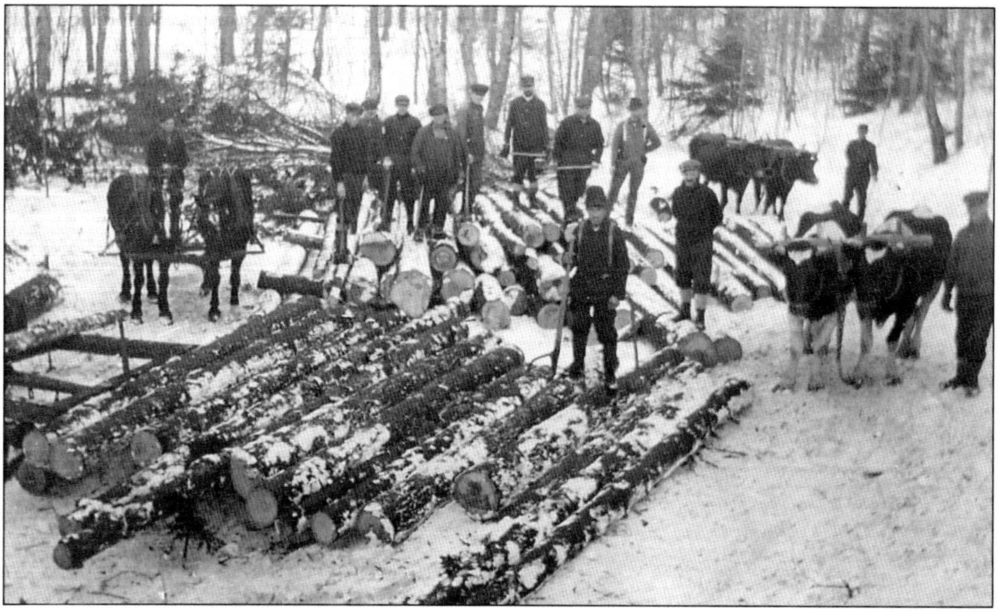

It was not unusual for larger farms to engage in logging operations during the winter months, harvesting timber from upland woodlots that was utilized for sawlogs and firewood. In 1909, the large Cloudland Farm used both teams of horses and oxen to get the harvested timber out of the woods, as seen in this view taken at the log landing.

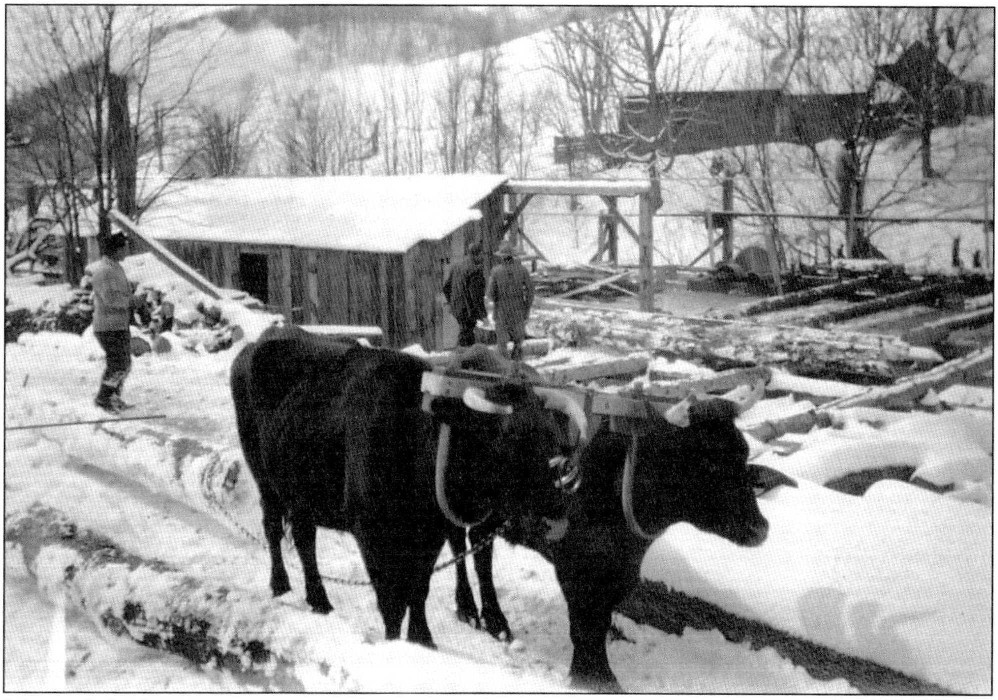

Many of the larger farms also maintained seasonal sawmill operations that, during the winter months, processed lumber from their own upland woodlots. Pictured in 1909 is the sawmill at the Cloudland Farm. Teams of horses were typically faster and more maneuverable although tiring sooner, while oxen were a bit slower and more cumbersome in tight areas but had longer stamina.

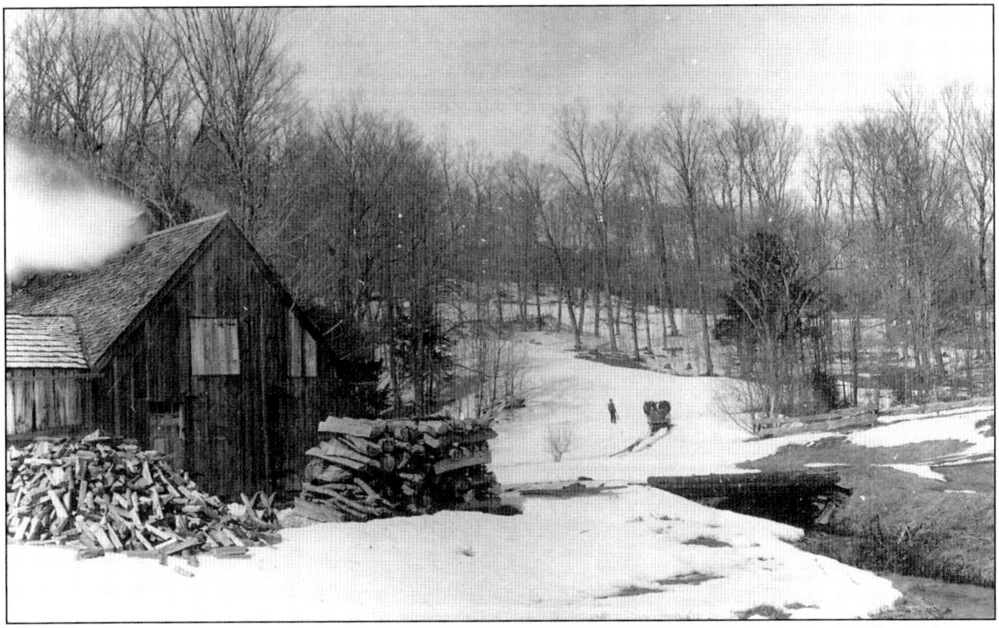

Native peoples first developed the craft of making maple syrup by boiling the sap collected from sugar maple trees. Vermonters and others in the Northeast developed that craft into a major annual agricultural product early each spring. Woodstock had many sugaring operations; seen here, a working sugarhouse is boiling the sap into sugar as an assistant heads back out into the sugar bush to gather more sap.

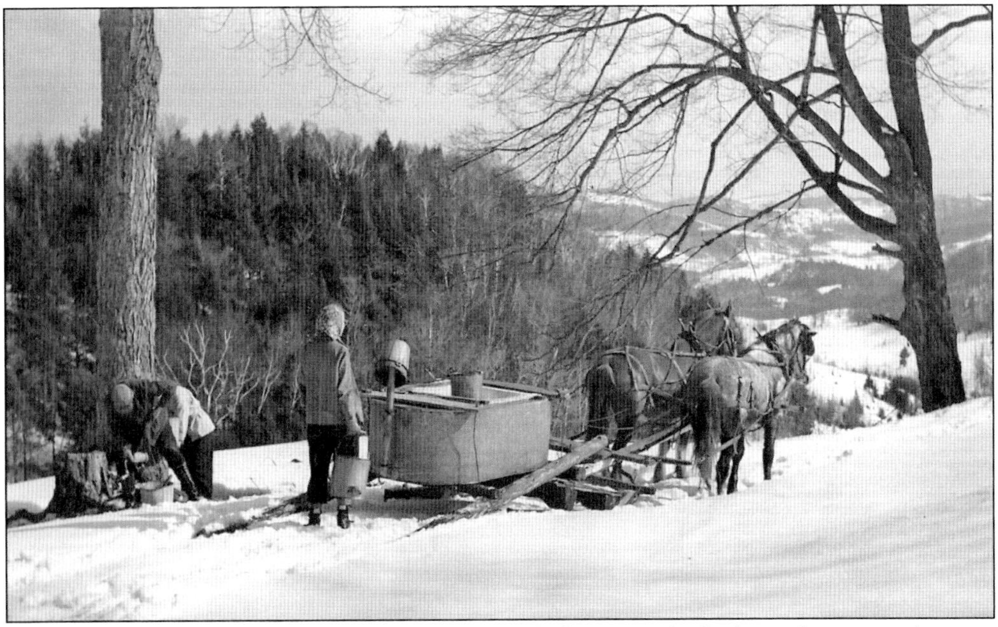

Teams of horses and oxen were used to pull the sleds upon which the gathering tanks were mounted through the upland maple sugar orchards in the early spring throughout sugaring season. Here, in this upland hillside scene overlooking the Ottauquechee River valley below, a Woodstock couple is emptying tin sap buckets, which were hung on tapped sugar maple trees, into the gathering tank.

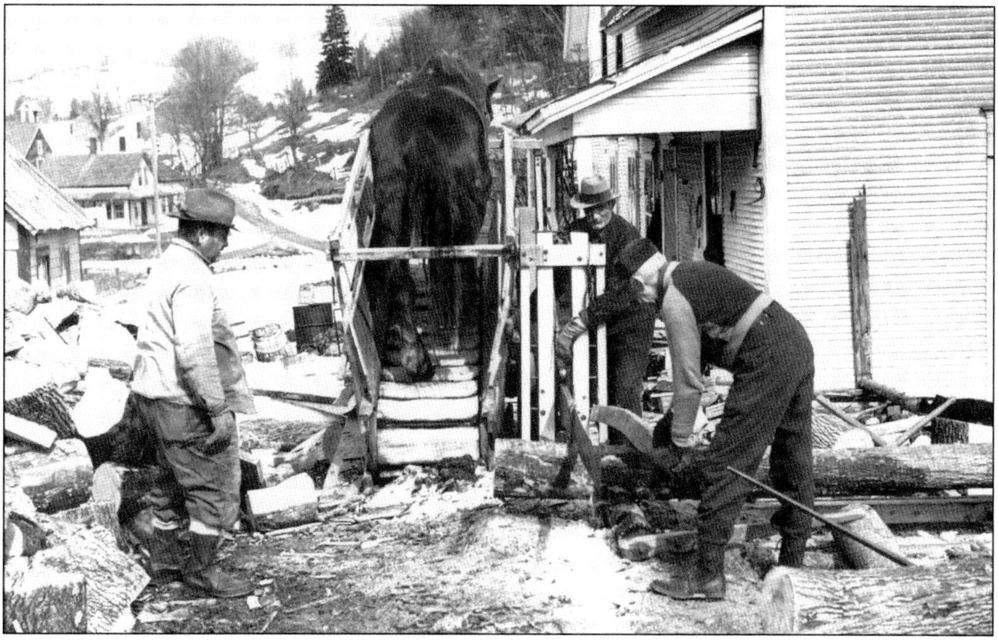

Judging by the snow still left on the ground, it looks to be very early spring, and these three Woodstock men are sawing and splitting firewood. Note the horse working the treadmill that is in turn powering the saw. At one time, using horses to power treadmills that operated labor-saving equipment was a common sight in rural Vermont. It was labor saving for the farmer but not for the horse.

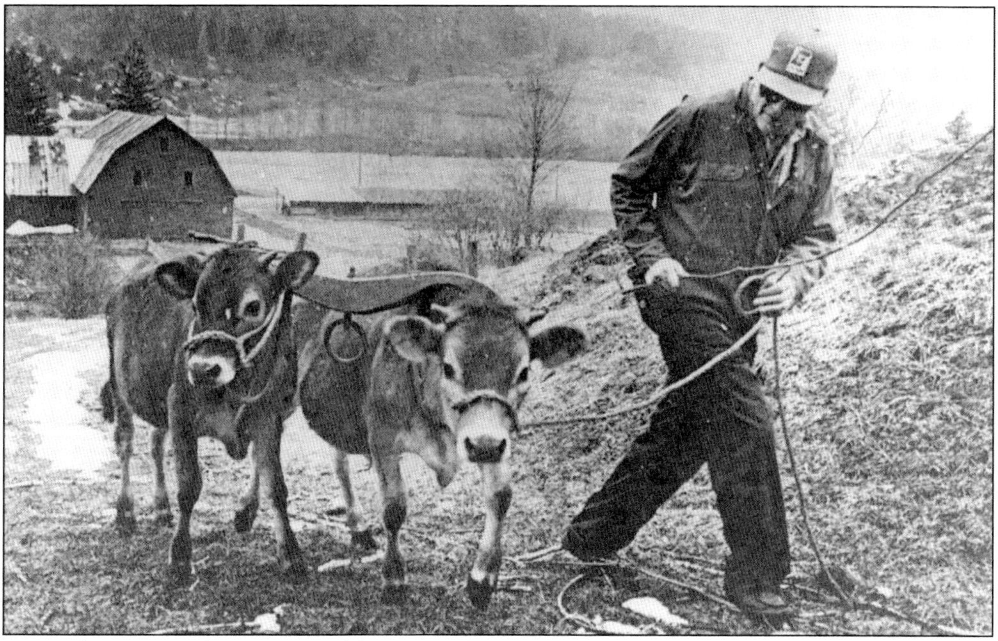

Long after teams of oxen stopped being used as work animals on Vermont farms, many farmers still enjoyed developing teams for pulling contests at local and county fairs, and for some light chores around the farm. Pictured, Al Conklin is working with a young team of Jersey oxen on his Woodstock farm; he is training them for future exhibition work when they become full grown.

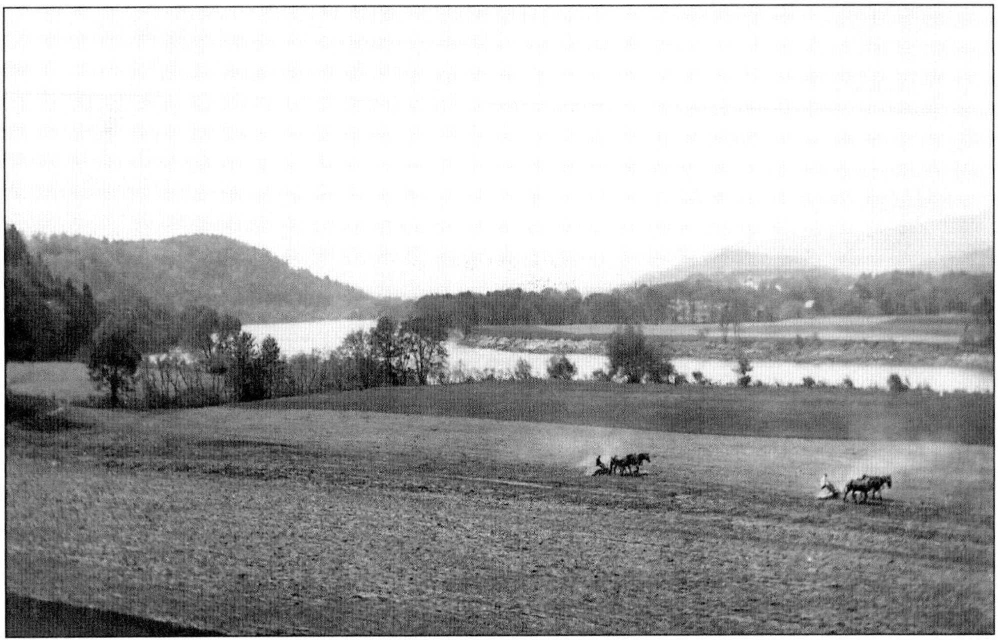

This c. 1900 photograph, taken at the Billings Farm, depicts late-spring plowing of the rich meadowlands along the Ottauquechee River. Although the farm tractor had by this time been in use for several decades on big midwestern farms, many Vermont farms still relied upon teams of horses to handle most farm chores well into the 1920s and later.

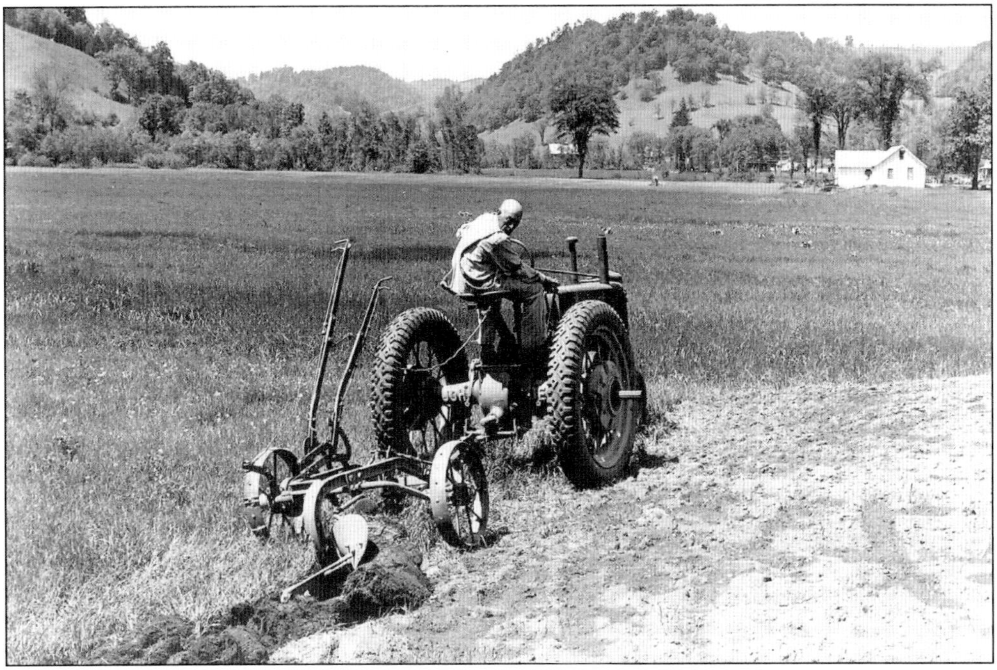

Just as he did with automobiles, it was Henry Ford who, in 1916, made the farm tractor a compact, reliable, and affordable piece of equipment suitable for smaller Vermont farms. Between 1920 and 1950, the number of farm tractors in Vermont increased from 444 to over 10,000 in use. This 1950s view shows a tractor beginning to plow a field at the Nelson farm in Woodstock.

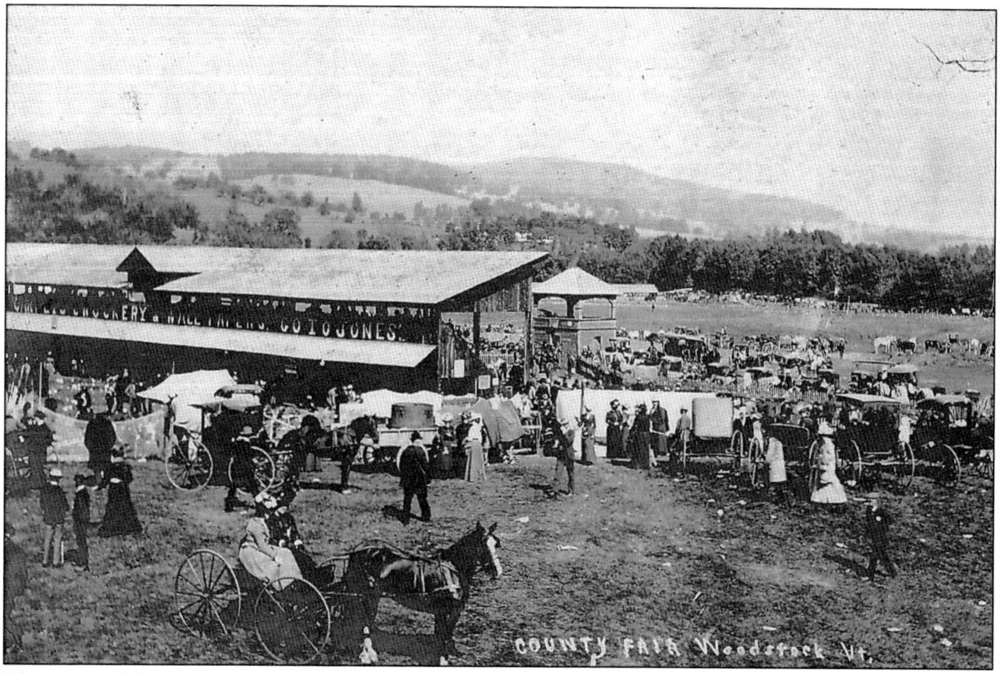

The turn of the 20th century was the golden age of county fairs across Vermont. In Woodstock, the Windsor County Agricultural Society (1846–1932) owned large fairgrounds on the outskirts of the village, adjacent to the Billings Farm, complete with a racetrack and grandstand, as shown in this c. 1900 view. As popular and much anticipated as this annual fair was, by the early 1930s it was no more.

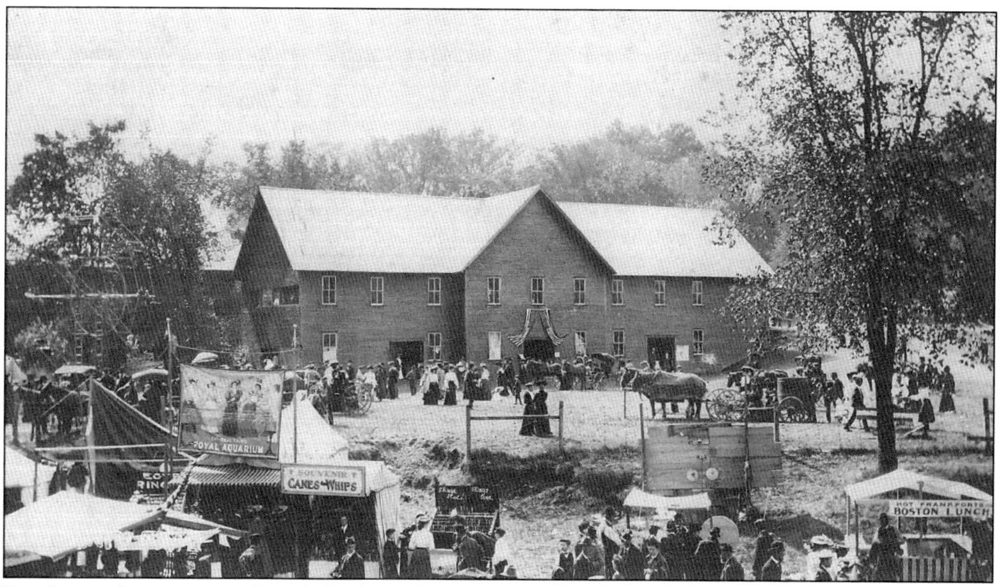

Food, socializing, agricultural displays, demonstrations, and competitions mixed with games of chance and horse-trotting events were all part of the annual county fair experience. This c. 1900 photograph shows one of the main buildings on the grounds of the Windsor County Fair. In the foreground are several vendors' booths and a traveling amusement act from some faraway place.

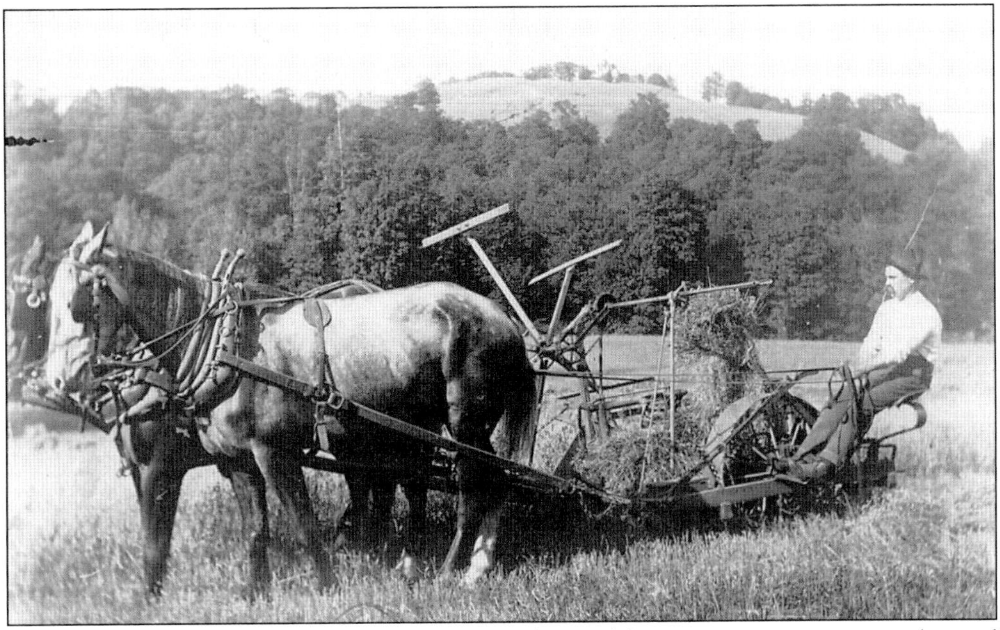

Because of the hilly terrain, it took longer for mechanized farm equipment to come to be used on Vermont farms than in the flat midwestern parts of the country. However, greater industrial production, standardization, and availability of cost-effective agricultural equipment were changing farm practices by the 1890s. This 1909 shows part of a grain-harvesting operation at the large Cloudland Farm in Woodstock.

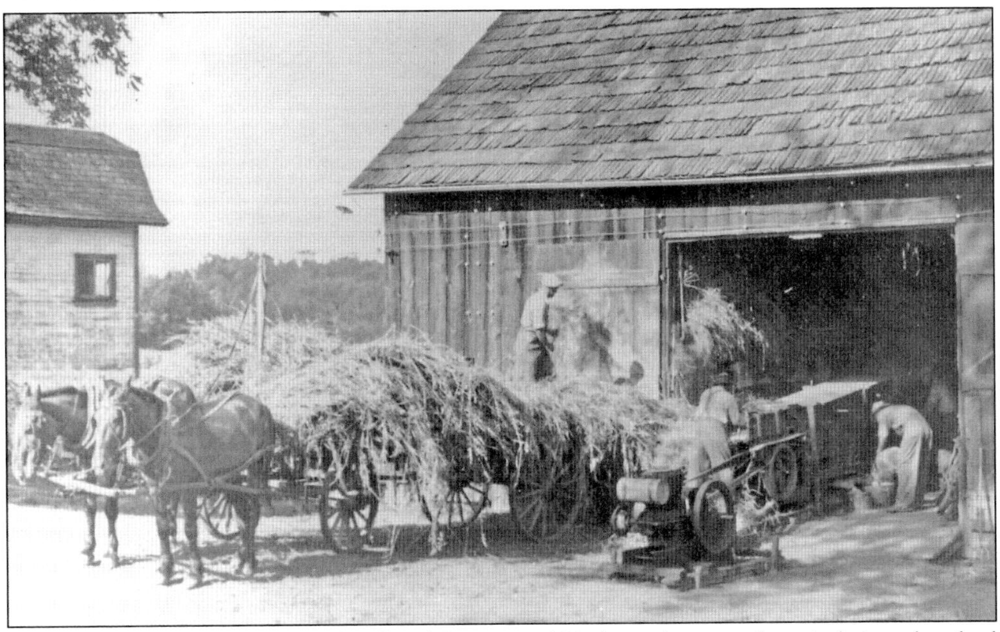

Another view of work at the Cloudland Farm in 1909 shows harvested grain being threshed with the aid of mechanized equipment, powered by a "one-lunger" stationary gas engine. The economically priced, commercially available gasoline-powered stationary engine was a tremendous boost to work efficiency on Vermont's hillside farms, and even came to power small individual electric-generating plants before the age of widespread rural electrification.

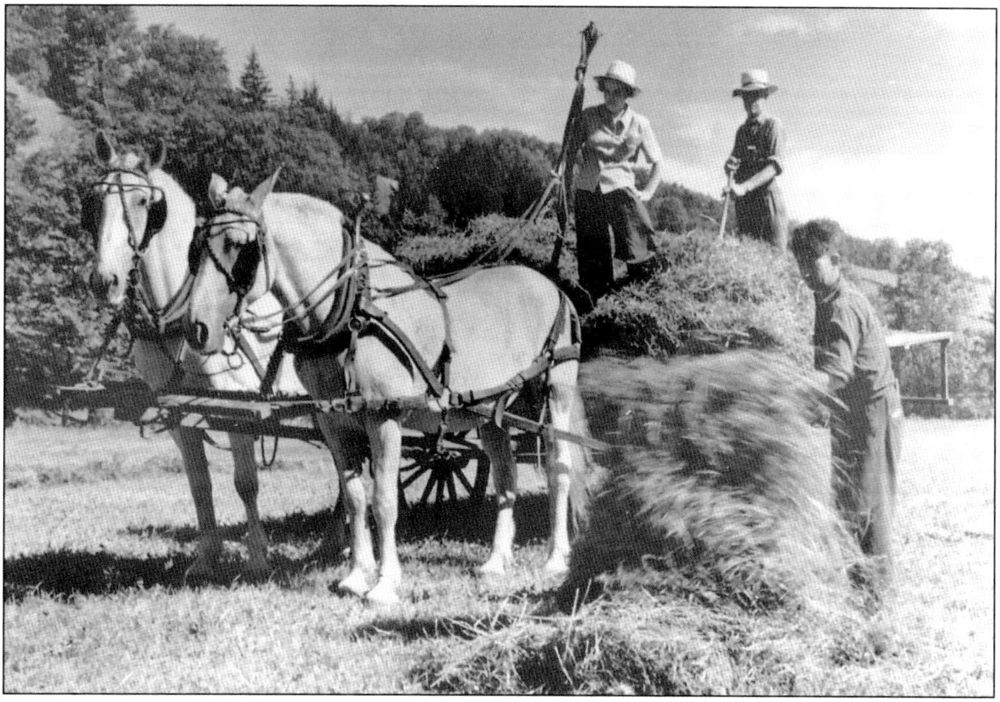

Cutting and loading hay on the steeper hillsides of Vermont farms was still a hand operation well into the earlier decades of the 20th century. In time, mechanized tractors, sickle bars, and baling machines would change that. Here, hay is being hand loaded at the Cloudland Farm in 1909. Horses were still the overwhelmingly primary source of motive power on Vermont farms.

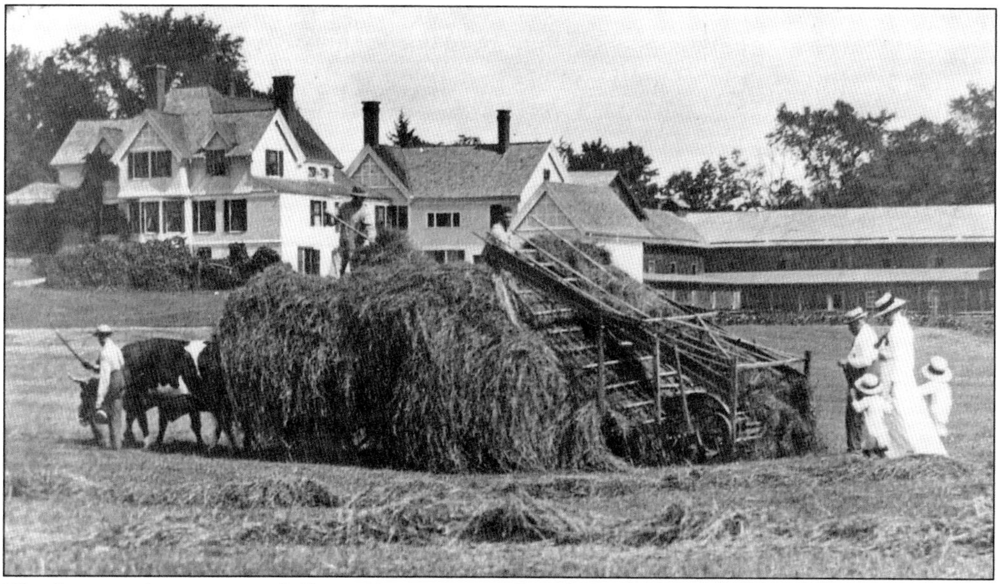

The large and prosperous Billings Farm in Woodstock, located along the flat meadowlands of the Ottauquechee River, afforded greater opportunity for early mechanized farm equipment. The Billings farmhouse is in the background. Here, a powerful team of oxen is shown pulling a flatbed wagon and a hay-loading machine, which is gathering up the cut hay—a substantial operation indeed for man, machine, and beast!

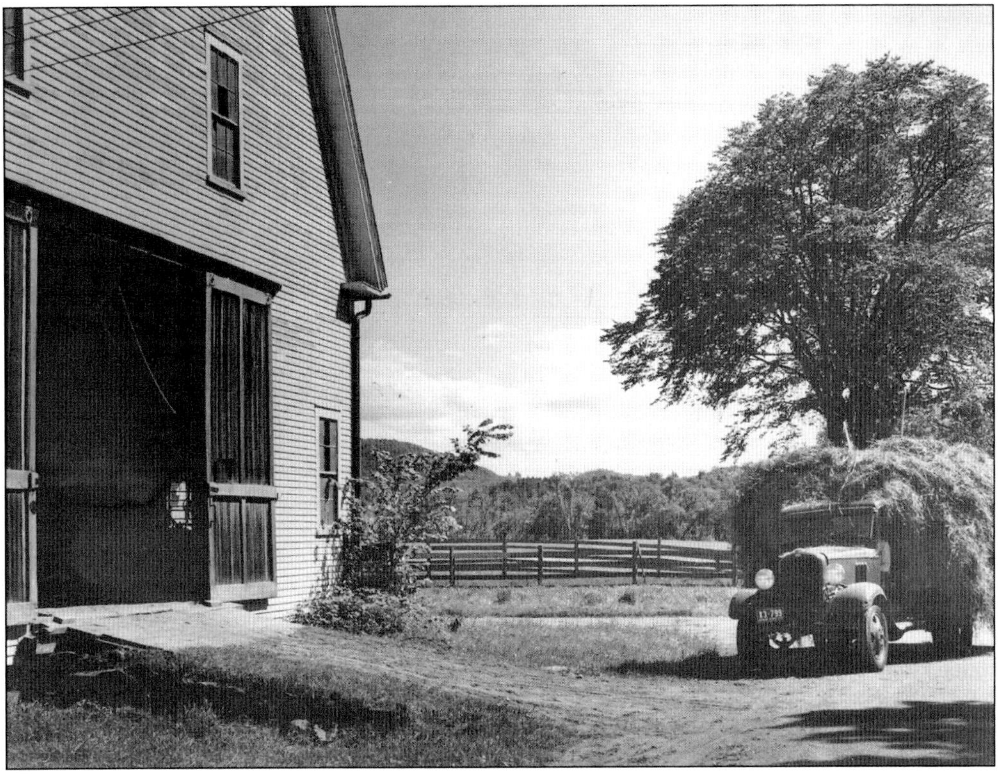

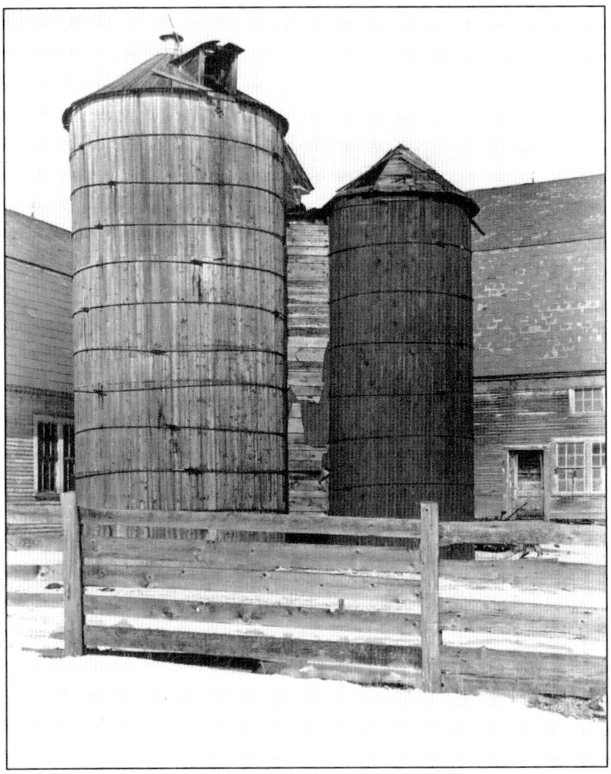

By the 1920s, trucks were becoming increasingly more common on the nation's roads, and in the decades to follow, older ones were often retired to farms to help with the chores, replacing the tradition of teams of horses. Pictured in the 1950s is an aging 1936 Chevrolet truck, loaded with unbaled hay, approaching the barn at the Conklin-Nelson farm in Woodstock.

By the turn of the 20th century, the ability to produce greater amounts of hay and grain on many of Vermont's bigger farms, and the availability of steam- or gasoline-powered engines to help move that material, prompted the use of silos for compact feed storage. These are the silos at the Cloudland Farm in Woodstock, purchased in kit form and assembled from specially pre-shaped wooden boards and steel hoops.

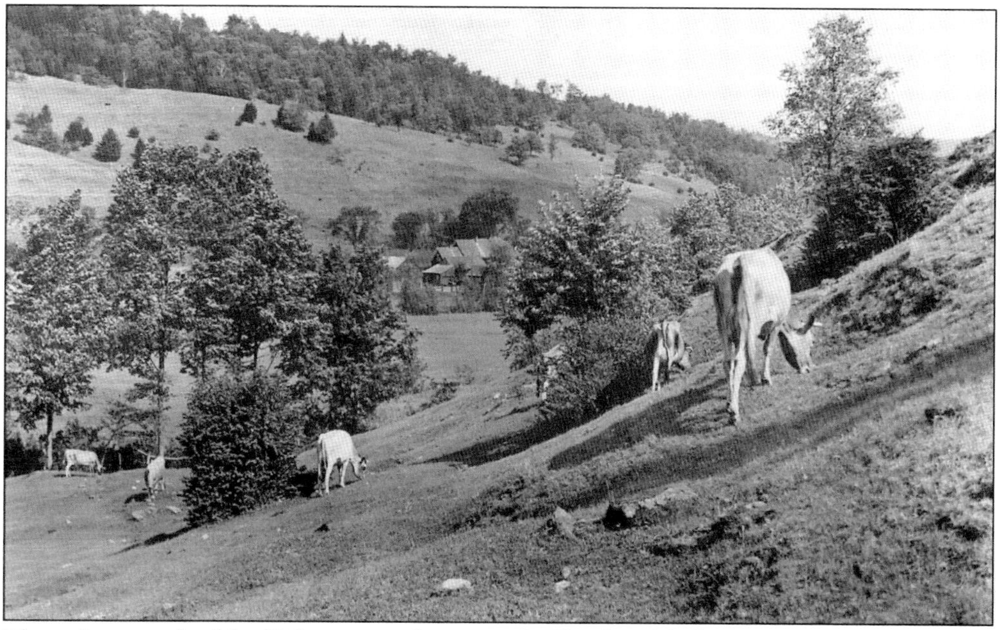

Throughout much of the 20th century, this view of a Woodstock hillside with Jersey cows grazing was typical of the Vermont landscape. On the far hillside, the once open land of the previous century is slowly beginning to grow back to forest again. In the foreground, the typical rockiness of the upland Vermont soil that always made farming difficult in the Green Mountains is evident.

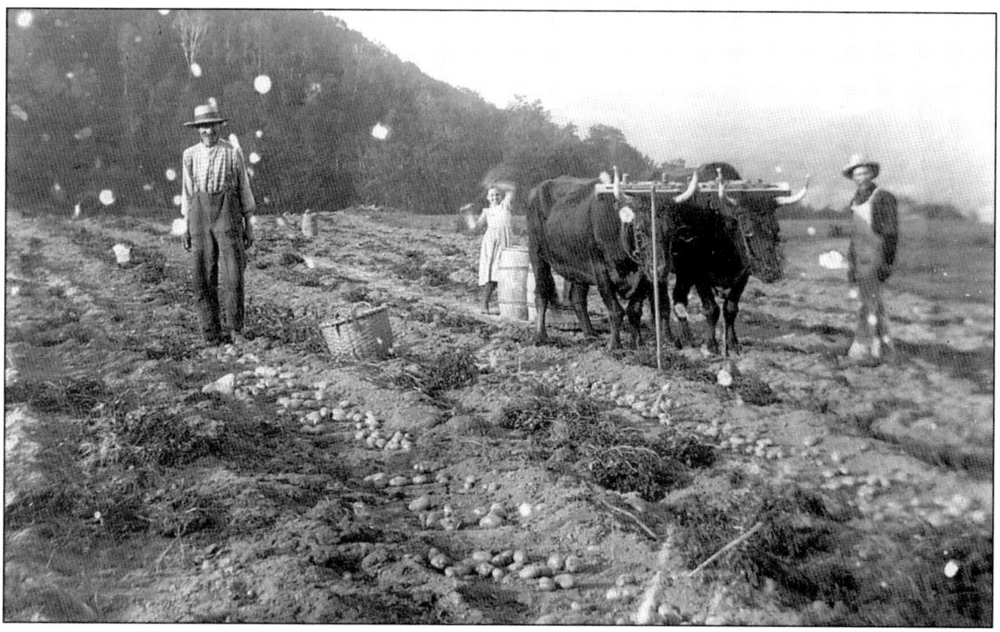

Potato farming was never a primary agricultural practice in Vermont; however, some farms were known to produce a harvest each year. Here, a 19th-century Woodstock farm family is gathering their fall potato crop with the aid of their team of oxen. Before the days of mechanical refrigeration, a root cellar at the farmhouse would preserve this and other food supplies through the long winter months.

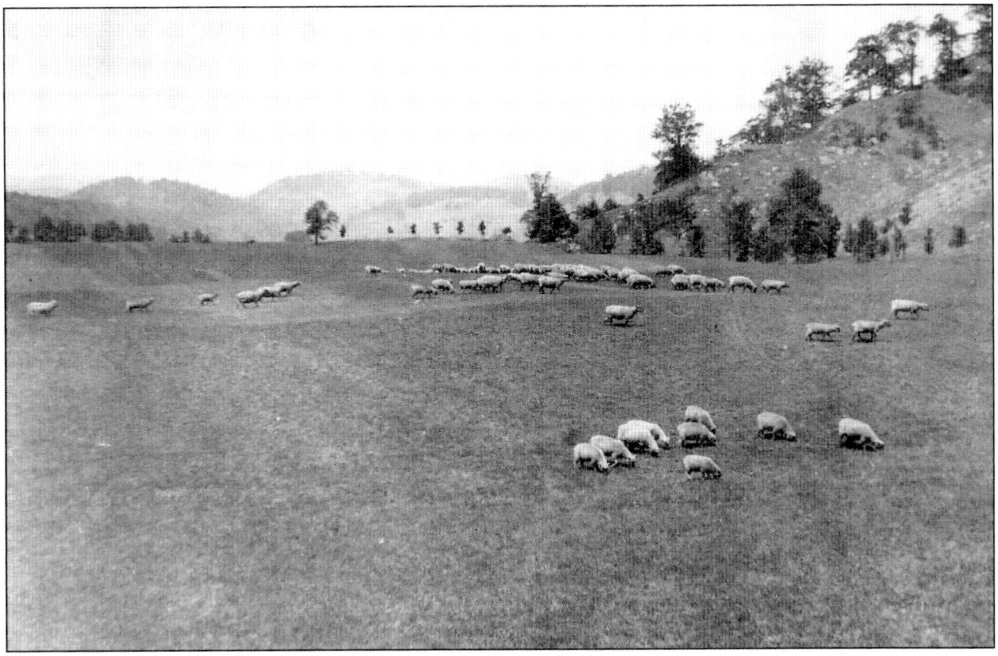

Prior to Vermont developing a dairy industry in the late 19th century, its major agricultural industry was sheep farming. The raising of sheep for the production of wool required far less labor and farm buildings and was ideal for rough upland pasture. Here, a flock of sheep from the Billings Farm spends the summer months grazing on the slopes of Mount Tom in Woodstock.

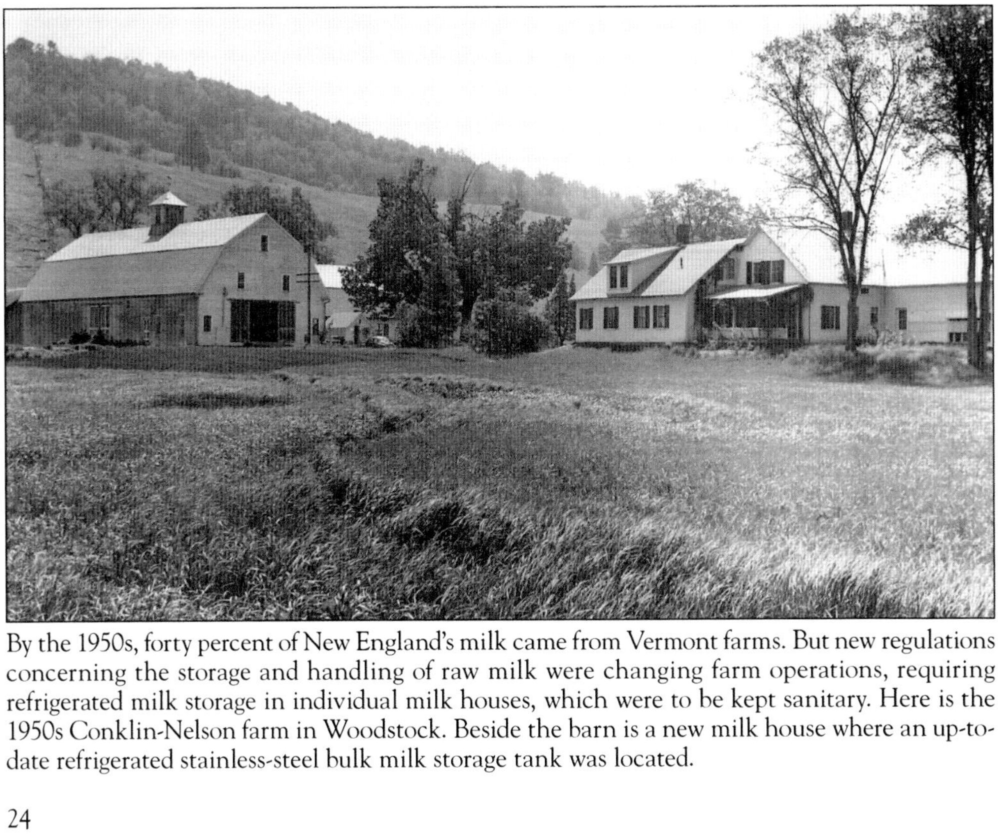

By the 1950s, forty percent of New England's milk came from Vermont farms. But new regulations concerning the storage and handling of raw milk were changing farm operations, requiring refrigerated milk storage in individual milk houses, which were to be kept sanitary. Here is the 1950s Conklin-Nelson farm in Woodstock. Beside the barn is a new milk house where an up-to-date refrigerated stainless-steel bulk milk storage tank was located.

Two

TAFTSVILLE AND SOUTH WOODSTOCK

When one thinks of Woodstock, it is Woodstock Village that first comes to mind. However, Woodstock is a township of land that extends far beyond Woodstock Village and includes the following three unincorporated village areas: Taftsville, South Woodstock, and West Woodstock. This chapter will take a look at those first two village areas, both of which are today individual historic districts listed in the National Register of Historic Places.

Both Taftsville and South Woodstock were areas of early settlement in the latter half of the 18th century, and both soon developed their own unique characteristics of services, manufacturing, and architecture. Both village areas were located on well-traveled highway routes that passed through the town, which in turn played a role in their subsequent development. But there perhaps is where the similarities end.

Taftsville, situated at the intersection of US Route 4 and Happy Valley Road, in the very northeasterly corner of Woodstock, became so named when Stephen Taft and his two brothers, originally of Uxbridge, Massachusetts, dammed the Ottauquechee River in 1793 and established mills and manufacturing shops. By virtue of the family's hard work and industrious nature, a busy little village came into being. The village became its own historic district in 2001.

South Woodstock is situated along the southern branch of the Ottauquechee River, more recently called Kedron Brook. South Street, also referred to as Branch Road, South Road, and Vermont Route 106, was laid out from the green in Woodstock Village to South Woodstock in 1787. Jabez Cottle and other family members were early settlers, and by 1781, they had sawmills and gristmills in operation around which a village area continued to grow. Like much of the town, the hills and valleys around South Woodstock provided for a strong rural agrarian economy to take hold.

The village's early-19th-century character has been maintained in part because it remained somewhat distant from the economically important Woodstock Railway, which affected the local economy until the 20th century, when road transport became more common. Today, the village of South Woodstock is a historic district, created in 1983.

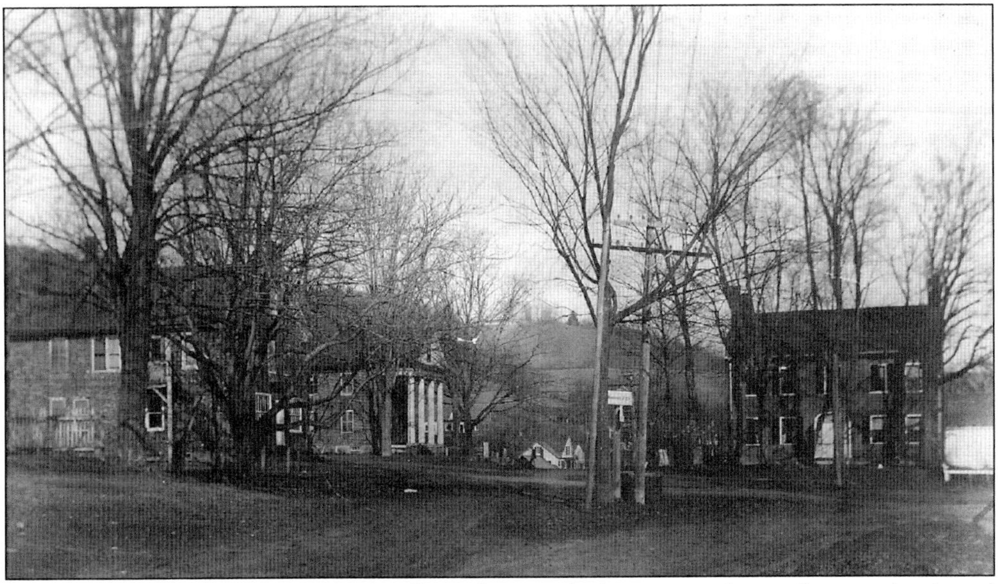

This early-20th-century image of Taftsville, with a view looking across the small triangular-shaped common, shows, from left to right, the general store (1840); the Pillars (1836), the residence of Owen Taft; and the Daniel Taft Jr. House (1826). Taftsville has long been recognized for its fine early-19th-century masonry architecture constructed of local brick.

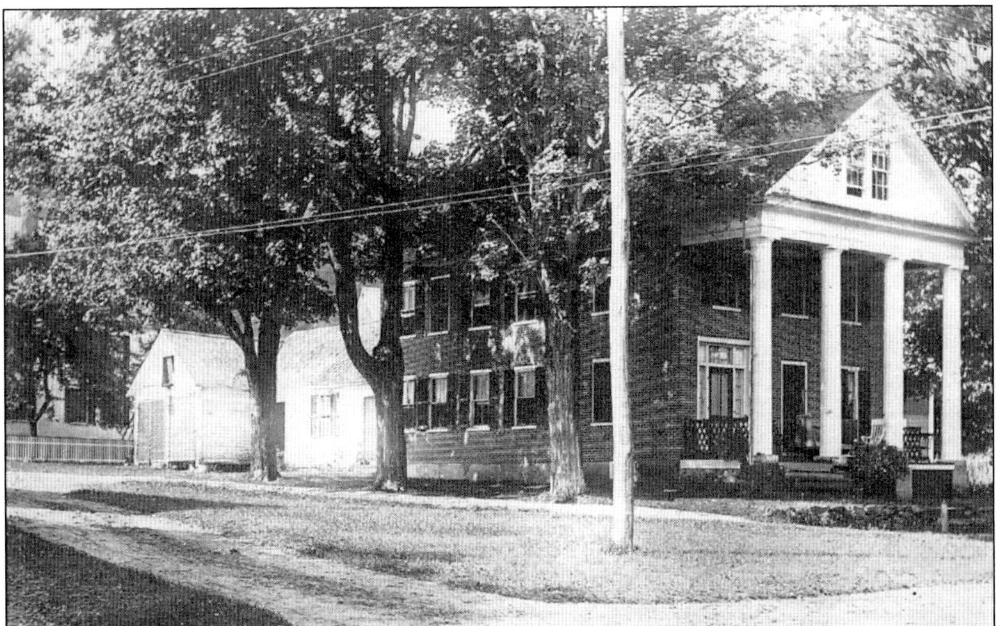

The Pillars, constructed in 1836 by Owen Taft, is a splendid example of antebellum Greek Revival architecture. The four columns were each made by turning a single straight hemlock tree trunk on a giant lathe, set up in the road while the house was under construction. The lathe was powered by a horse continuously walking on a treadmill.

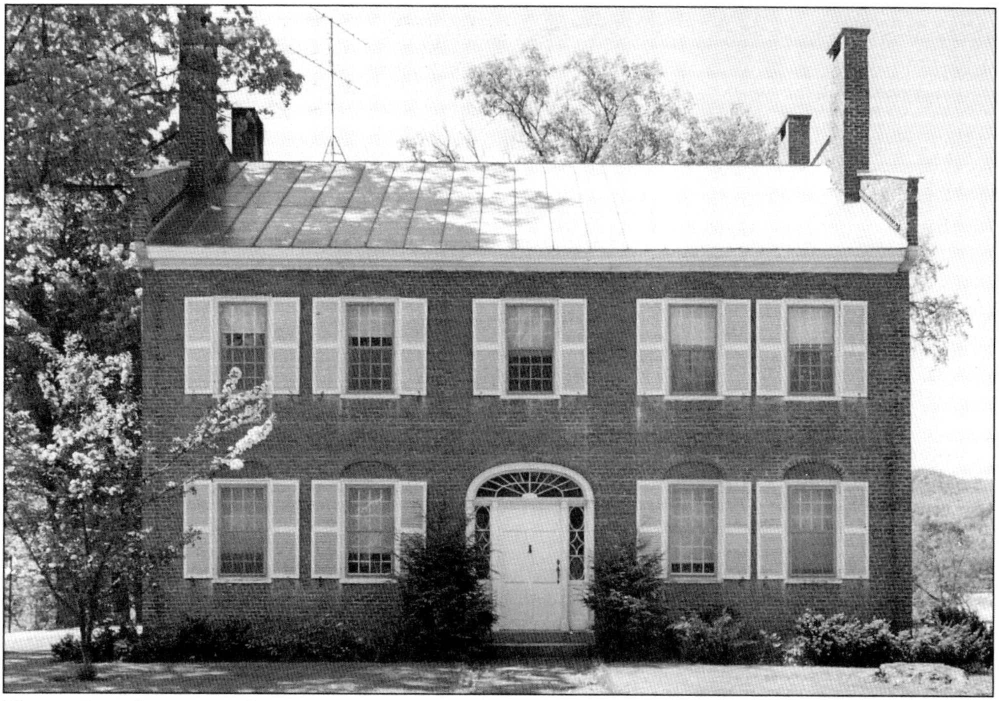

The earliest house on this site was a two-story wood-frame structure erected in 1805. In 1826, as Daniel Taft Jr. prospered operating his mills across the road on the edge of the Ottauquechee River, he moved the earlier building back and constructed this finely proportioned Federal-style brick home for his family. The earlier wood-frame building became the wing on the rear of the house.

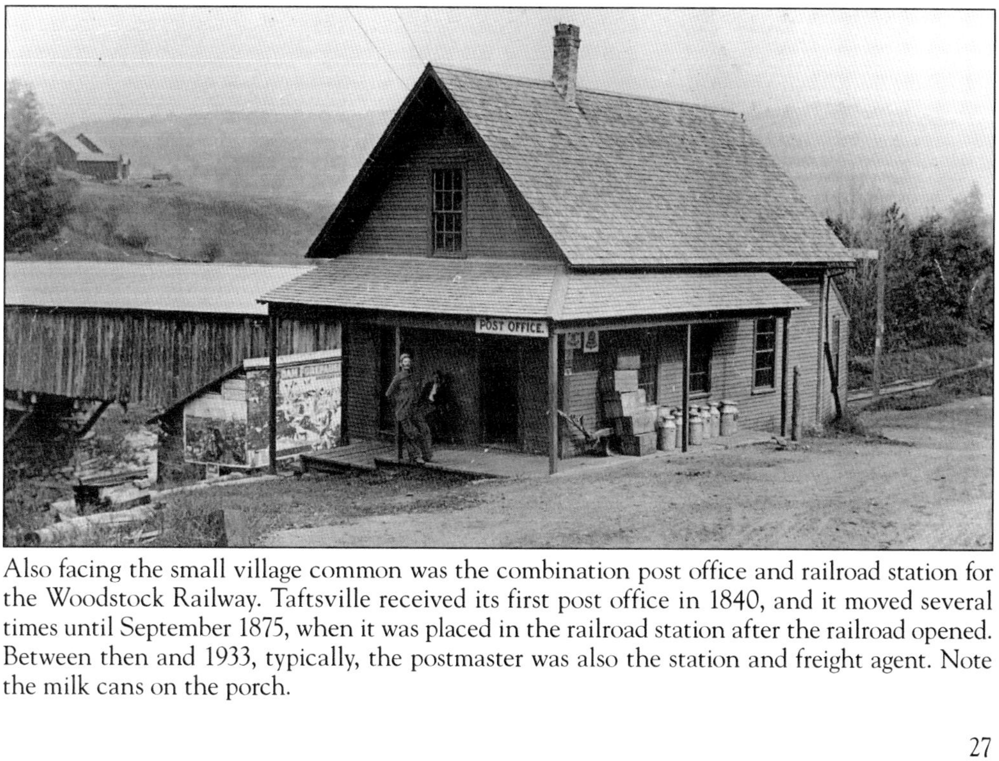

Also facing the small village common was the combination post office and railroad station for the Woodstock Railway. Taftsville received its first post office in 1840, and it moved several times until September 1875, when it was placed in the railroad station after the railroad opened. Between then and 1933, typically, the postmaster was also the station and freight agent. Note the milk cans on the porch.

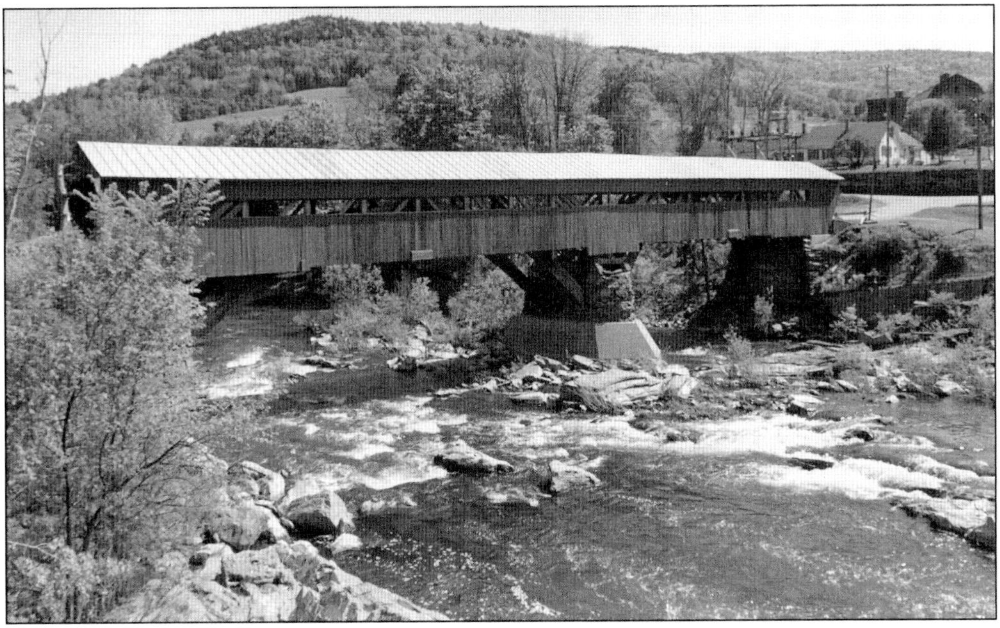

Around 1793, Stephen Taft threw a rough bridge across the Ottauquechee River at this location, and at least two more were constructed here until this structure was erected in 1836 at a total cost of $1,800. Builder Solomon Emmons III used a unique combination of modified multiple kingpost trusses and semi-independent laminated wooden arches. Today, the 189-foot-long wooden bridge it is one of the oldest in the country.

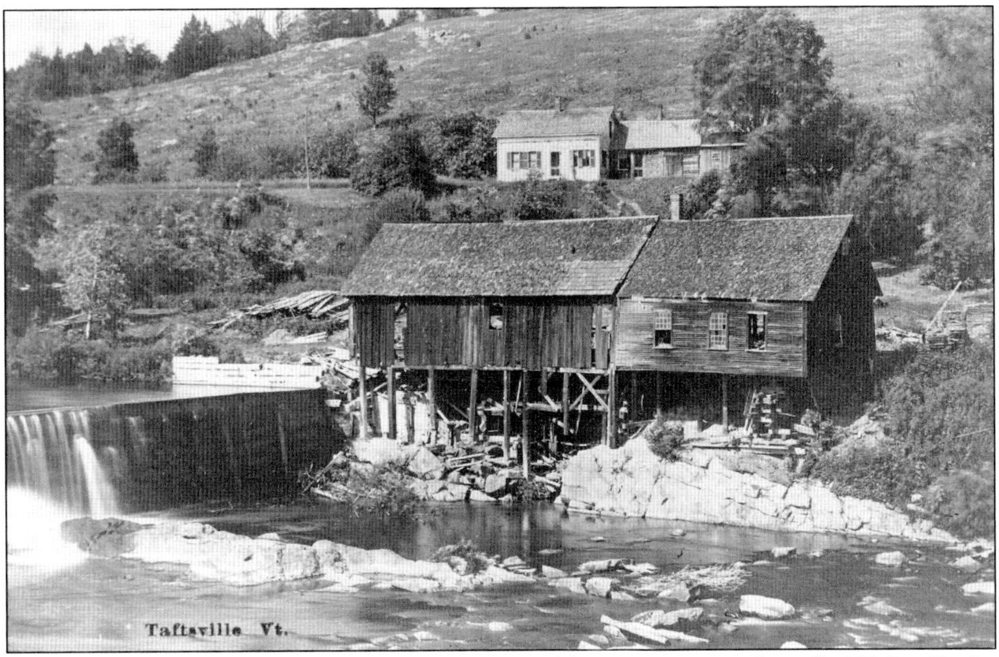

In 1793, when Stephen Taft first settled in what would in time come to be called Taftsville, he first constructed a footbridge across the Ottauquechee River and then a dam. By 1795, he and his younger brother Daniel, had succeeded in constructing a sawmill on the north bank of the river. Shown here almost 100 years later, the old sawmill, although still operating, is showing its age.

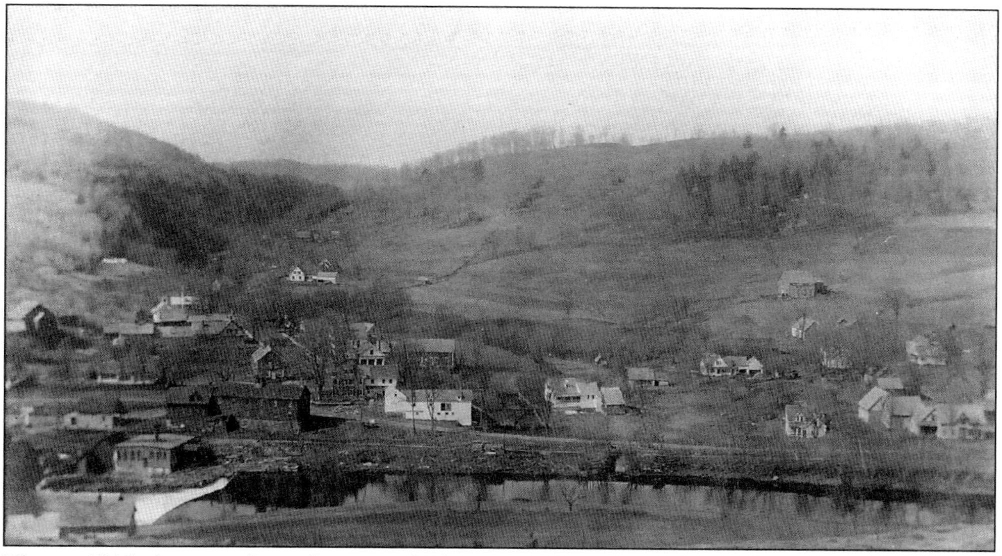

This c. 1915 photograph, with a view looking south upon Taftsville, shows the brick electric-generating powerhouse, erected in 1911, at the far left. Above it are the railroad station and the mill buildings erected by the Tafts. The village and Happy Valley Road and brook are beyond. The tracks of the Woodstock Railway are visible along the top of the south bank of the Ottauquechee River.

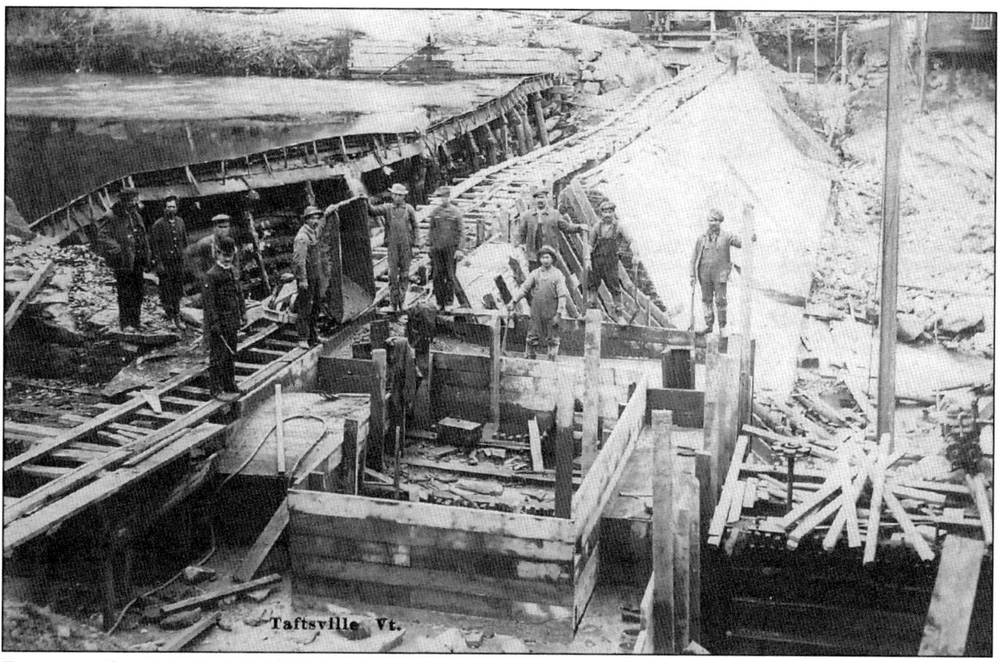

For more than 100 years, the original wood crib and stone dam constructed by the Tafts served well, with continued maintenance and repairs. In 1909, a new 192-foot-long concrete dam was constructed in front of the original dam, which was then removed. Here, work is progressing on the new dam and foundations for a new powerhouse. The old sawmill on the north bank was also removed.

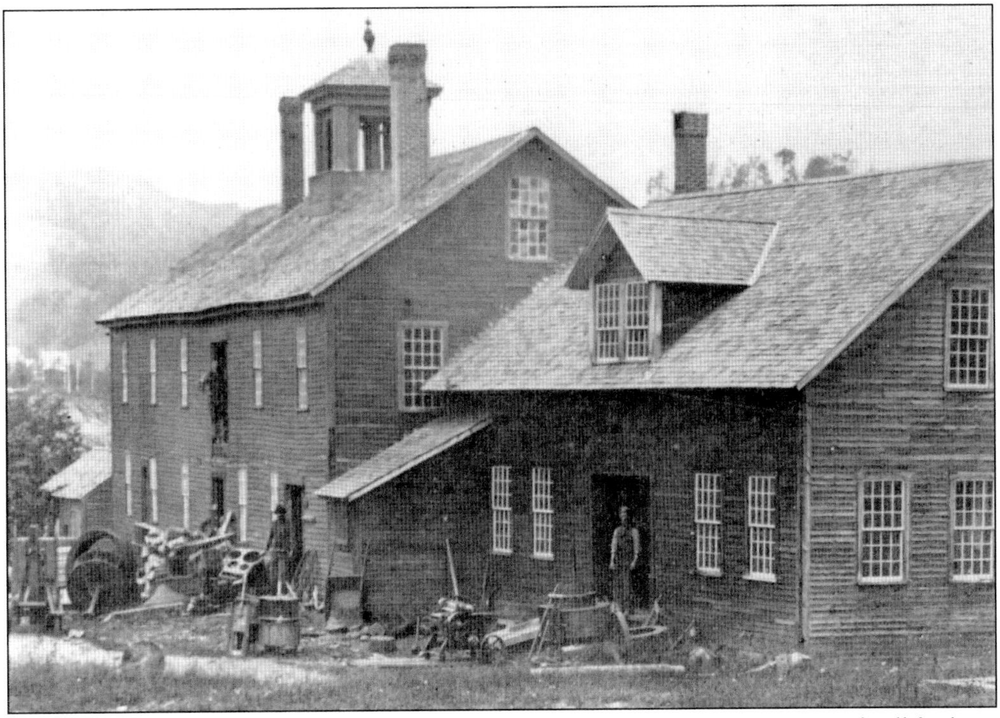

Shortly after constructing a dam and sawmill in 1795, the Tafts began construction of mill facilities on the south side of the river. The largest of these buildings, show here, dated from after 1811 and several earlier fires. Numerous cast metal products were manufactured, including plows and scythes. By the early decades of the 20th century, the buildings, once housing a very prosperous business, were mostly vacant and were later razed.

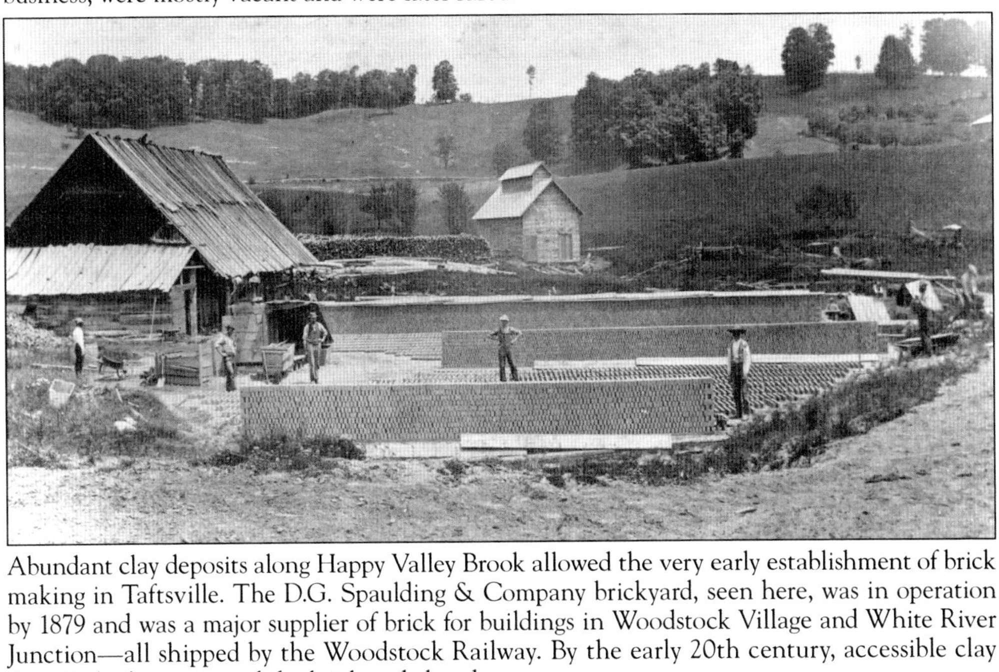

Abundant clay deposits along Happy Valley Brook allowed the very early establishment of brick making in Taftsville. The D.G. Spaulding & Company brickyard, seen here, was in operation by 1879 and was a major supplier of brick for buildings in Woodstock Village and White River Junction—all shipped by the Woodstock Railway. By the early 20th century, accessible clay deposits had run out and the brickyard closed.

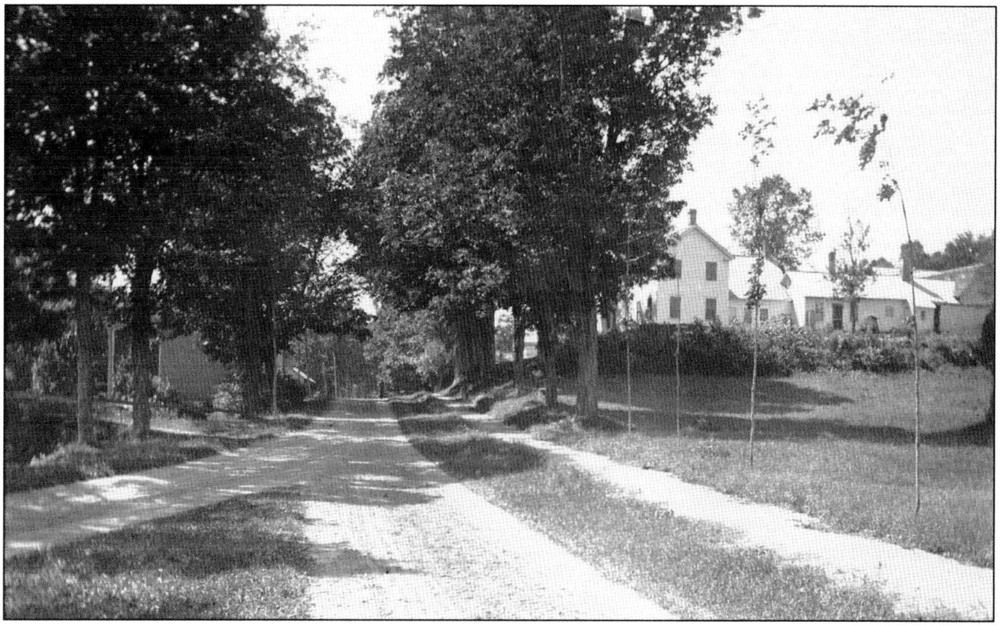

Looking south along the main street of South Woodstock, this c. 1915 view shows an early two-story village home, erected in 1798, on the right. On the left, partly obscured by trees, is the brick Orion Grange Hall No. 83, constructed in 1825 as the village's third schoolhouse. During the age of the automobile, the main street through the village came to be officially referred to as Vermont Route 106. (Courtesy of Mary McCuaig and the Green Mountain Perkins Academy and Historical Association.)

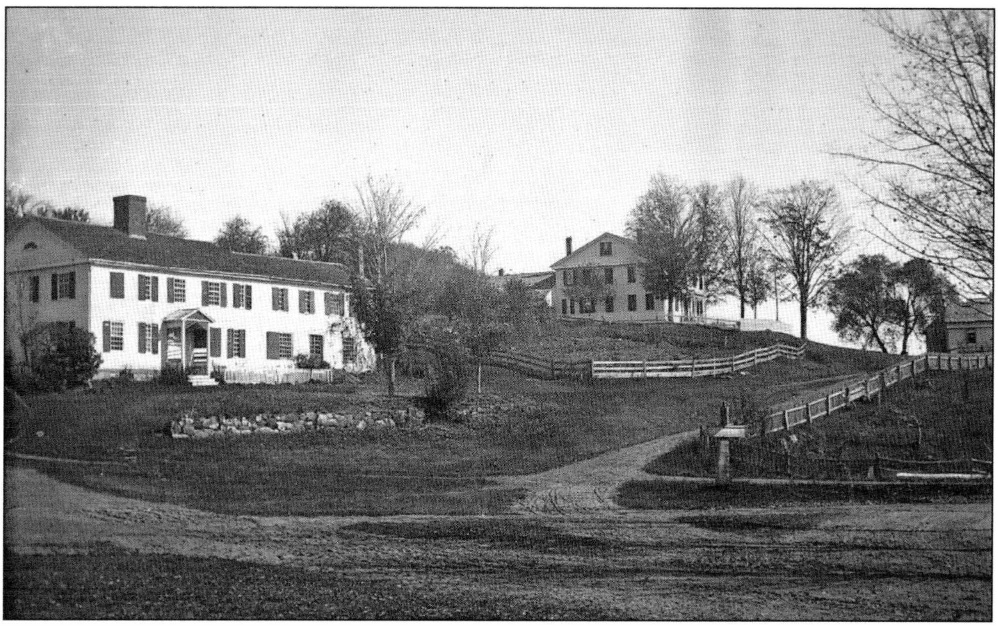

The large white building on the left-hand side of this early view of South Woodstock is believed to have been used as a boardinghouse for workers in the days when there were numerous lumber, furniture, starch, and other mills in the village. By about 1905, it was no longer needed and was taken down. The Kendall Homestead on the hill still stands today.

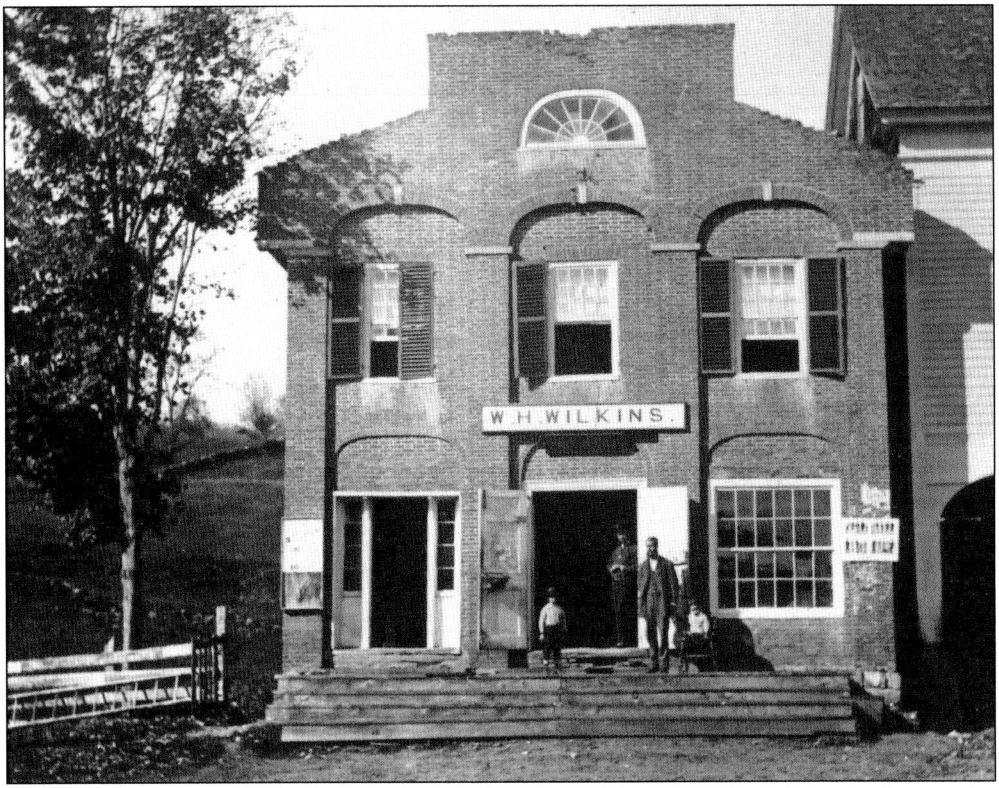

Richard Ransom Jr. was an enterprising merchant and, in 1822, constructed this brick store, his third in the village. Ransom referred to his business as the National Store, and over the years, it went by other names as different owners operated businesses therein. As originally designed, this building is indeed a delightful piece of Federal-style brick masonry architecture.

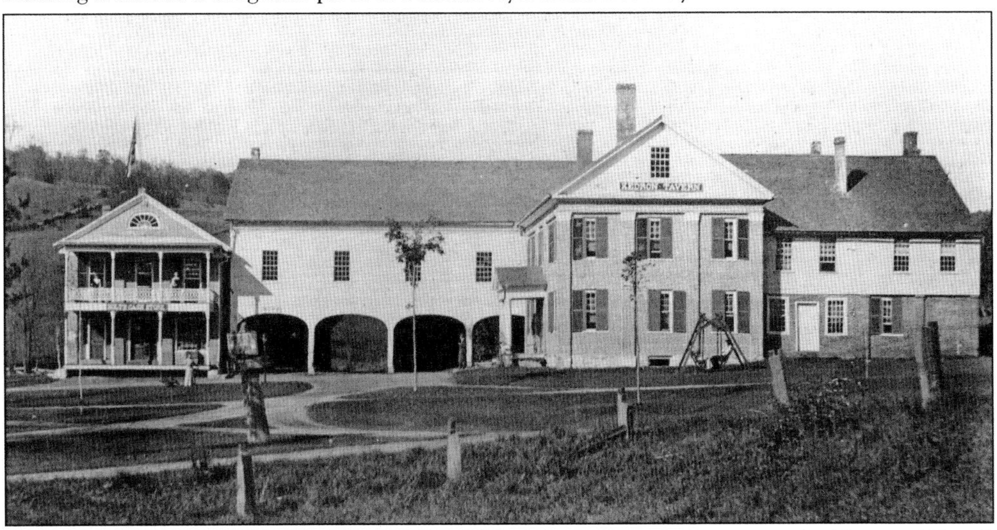

Richard Ransom Jr. and Richard Mather joined together in 1826 to construct the National Hotel, later known as the Kedron Tavern. At some time thereafter, a large wood-frame addition, with stables and a dance hall above, had joined the tavern stand with the store building, which had also been altered with a two-story front porch and rooms on the second floor.

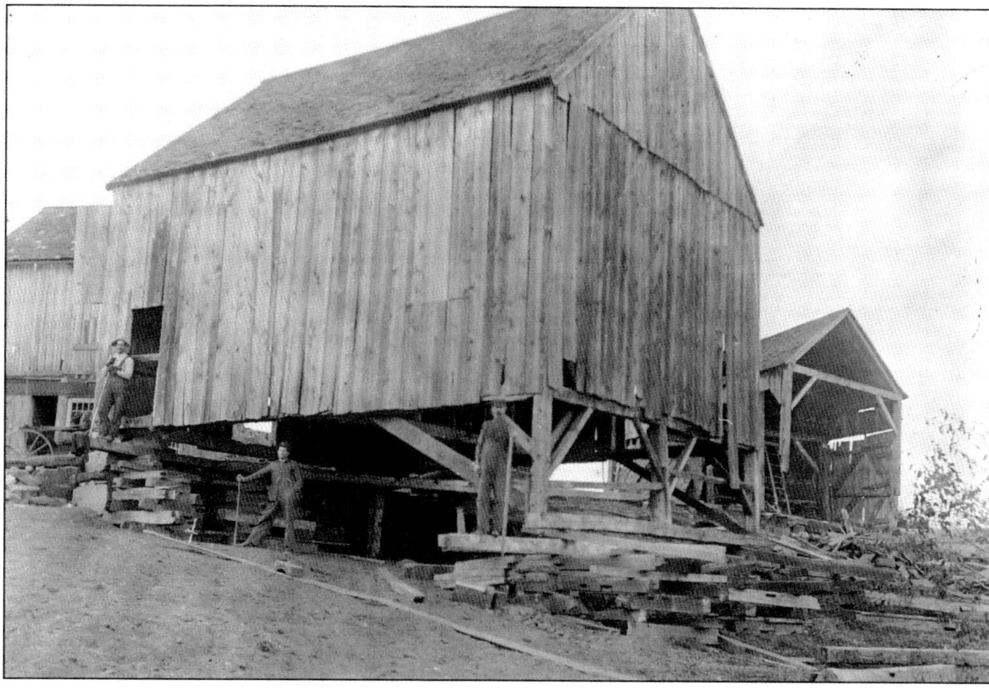

Because building materials were expensive and time consuming to produce, it was not unusual to move barns and repurpose them for other uses. Such was the case seen here around 1905 on the South Woodstock farm of Erwin and Ada Fullerton, who like many farmers in Vermont were changing from sheep, which required very little shelter, to dairy cattle, which required larger buildings for stabling and feed storage. (Courtesy of Mary McCuaig and the Green Mountain Perkins Academy and Historical Association.)

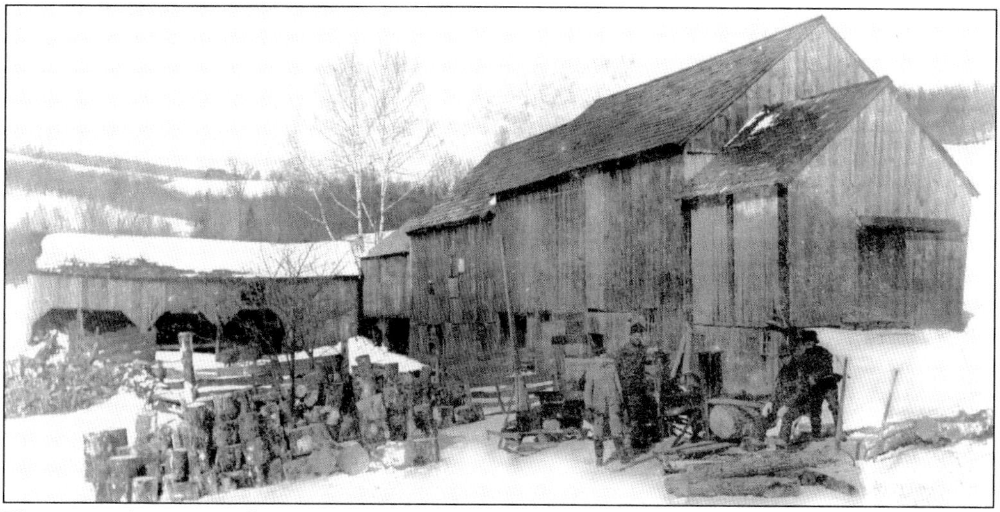

This view of George Fullerton's farm around 1905 shows not only a group of men sawing chunks of firewood that will then be hand split but also a series of connected farm buildings behind them. At least five individual structures can be counted, and perhaps some or all were moved from other locations to better fulfill changing needs. The saw rig appears to be powered by an early stationary gasoline engine. (Courtesy of Mary McCuaig and the Green Mountain Perkins Academy and Historical Association.)

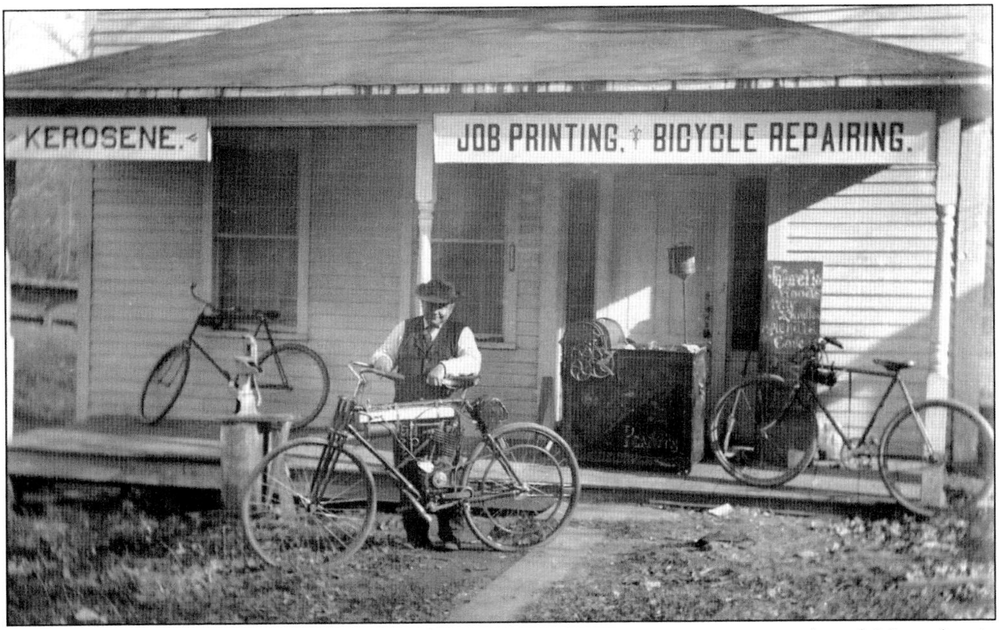

This South Woodstock fellow appears to have a very enterprising operation in hand. His eclectic business provides on-site printing; the sale of postcards, kerosene, and foodstuffs, like roasted peanuts; and lastly, bicycle repair services. Note the early motorcycle that he is justifiably proud to own and show off to the photographer around 1910. (Courtesy of Mary McCuaig and the Green Mountain Perkins Academy and Historical Association.)

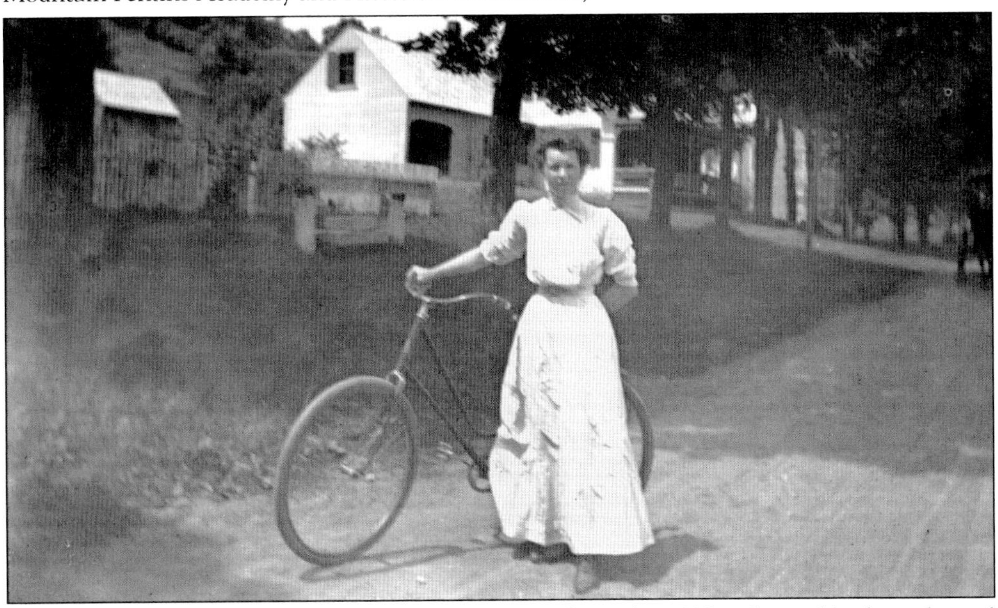

The common availability of the so-called safety bicycle in the 1890s, obtainable through mail order and delivered to the nearest railroad station by Railway Express, allowed people in rural areas, such as this South Woodstock young woman, greater mobility and freedom during the non-winter months. Bicycling was clearly not just a pastime for visiting urban folks staying five miles away at the fancy Woodstock Inn. (Courtesy of Mary McCuaig and the Green Mountain Perkins Academy and Historical Association.)

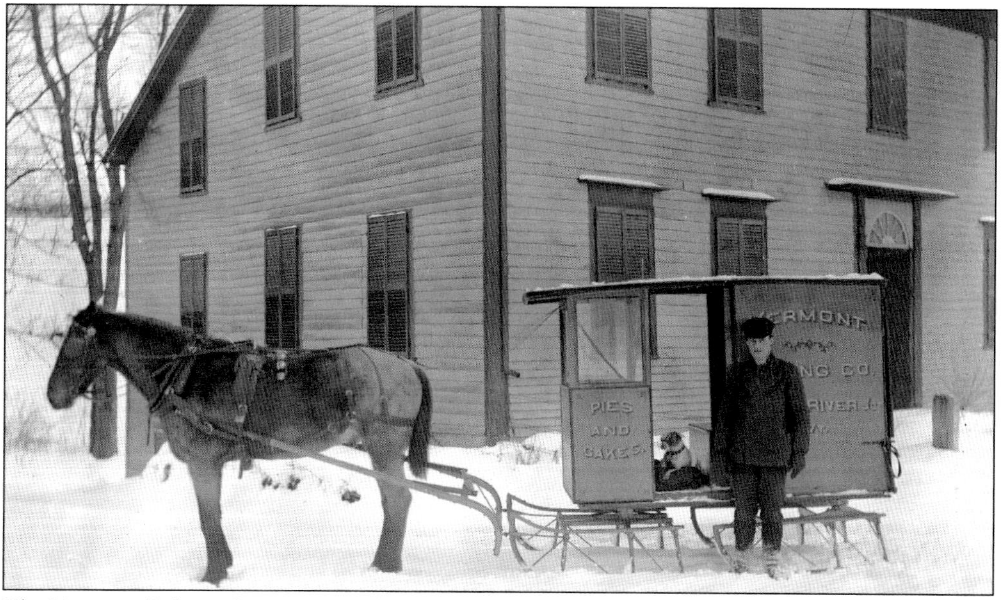

The Vermont Baking Company was located in White River Junction and distributed baked goods throughout the region. In this c. 1915 picture, a young man, his dog, and a small horse-drawn delivery van are making home deliveries of pies and cakes in South Woodstock. The goods probably first arrived at the Woodstock Railway station located five miles away. (Courtesy of Mary McCuaig and the Green Mountain Perkins Academy and Historical Association.)

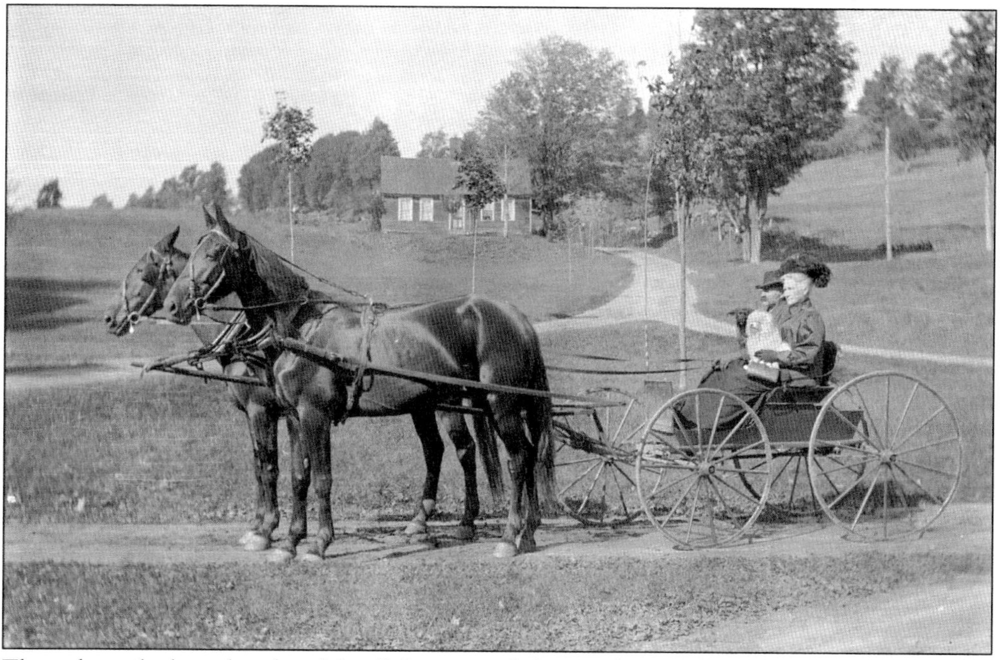

Throughout the later decades of the 19th century, lighter and more affordable horse-drawn buggies were becoming mass-produced in far-off locations and were made available to rural buyers by rail distribution. Here, a properly dressed South Woodstock couple is perhaps preparing to head into Woodstock for their weekly trip to the market, church, or the opera house, about 1915. (Courtesy of Mary McCuaig and the Green Mountain Perkins Academy and Historical Association.)

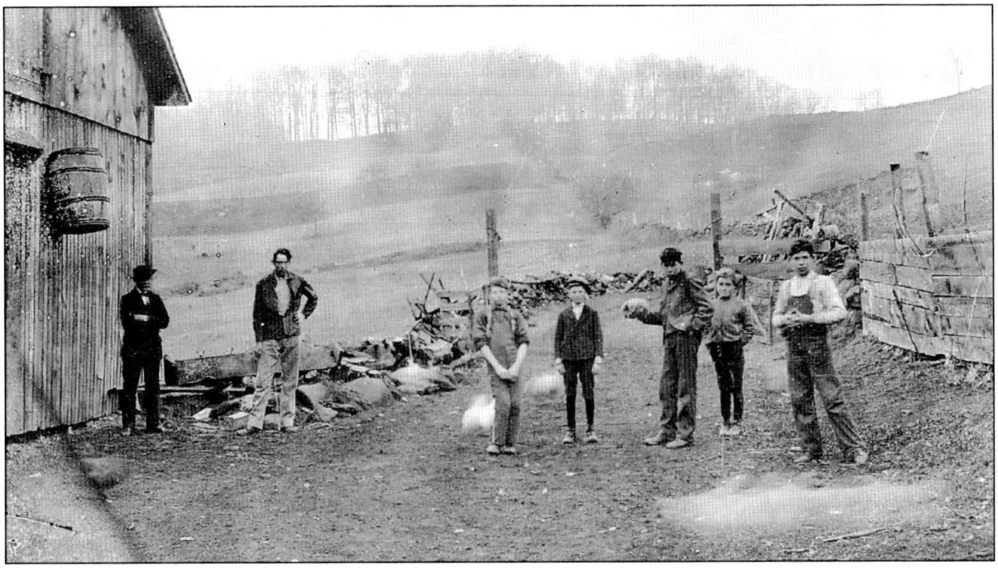

Utilizing peach baskets, the game of basketball was invented in Springfield, Massachusetts, in December 1891. Pictured about 1915, these South Woodstock farm boys had set up their own basketball court in a local farmyard and used a wooden barrel with the bottom removed. Clearly, Yankee ingenuity was alive and well in the Kedron Brook Valley of Woodstock, Vermont! (Courtesy of Mary McCuaig and the Green Mountain Perkins Academy and Historical Association.)

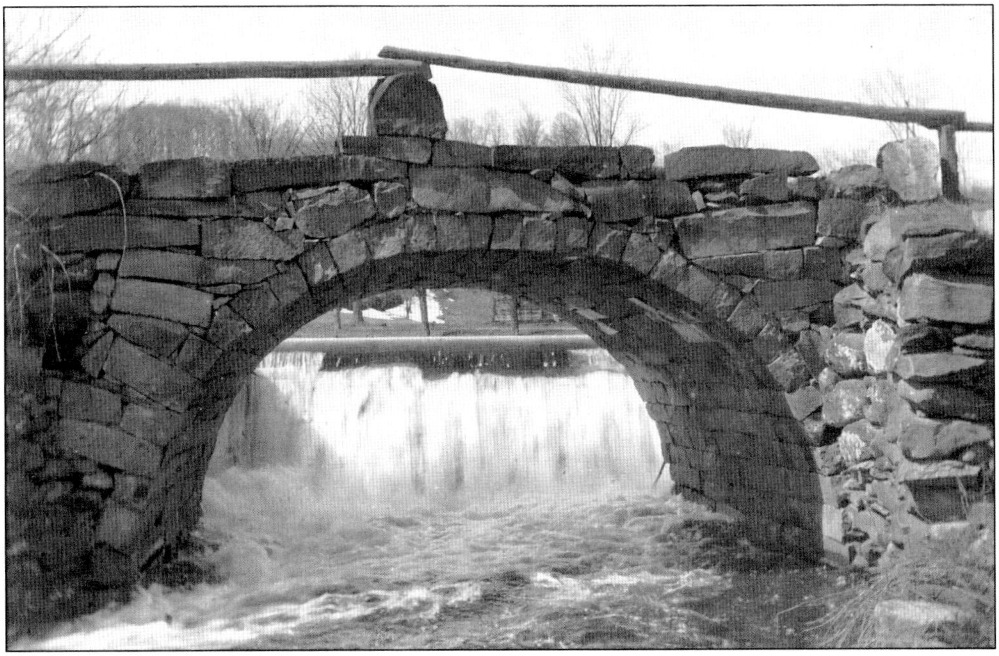

Located within the village of South Woodstock for many years, this stone arched bridge carried present-day Route 106 over Kedron Brook. A penstock from the dam seen beyond fed a gristmill located downstream. The bridge was a remarkable piece of 19th-century engineering utilizing dry laid stone masonry that did not require mortar to hold it together. To better accommodate 20th-century automobiles and trucks, the bridge was replaced in 1949. (Courtesy of Mary McCuaig and the Green Mountain Perkins Academy and Historical Association.)

Three

Woodstock Village

There never was an overarching plan to establish a village center at or near the present-day location of Woodstock Village, as did happen on occasion with some regional towns. At first glance, it just seemed to have happened that way—an organic settlement that just grew on its own free will. However, a closer reconsideration of the matter would suggest that there was indeed good reason why a thriving village center took root at this location after all—planned or not.

The earliest trail through the vast wilderness that would become Woodstock followed the Ottauquechee River westward into the Green Mountains. And the broad flatlands near the two primary tributaries of the Ottauquechee River, the north and south branches as they were often referred to, undoubtedly offered easier and better settlement than steeper and more remotely located terrain.

By 1772, when Joab Hoisington made a large purchase of land in the area that would become Woodstock Village, a sawmill was already established on the south branch of the Ottauquechee River; however, no homesteads were yet in the area. That spring, Hoisington erected a simple log house on the site of the present bank building, at the end of the common, thus becoming the first settler in what would soon become a thriving village. By the spring of 1774, a gristmill was added along the brook, and additional settlers made the area their home. The Vermont General Assembly in 1786 designated Woodstock as the shire town for Windsor County. To serve the needs of the rapidly growing village, Capt. Israel Richardson opened a tavern stand in 1792, and four years later, Elisha Taylor opened a second such facility. About 1801, two new turnpike roads, the Royalton and Woodstock and the Windsor and Woodstock, linked up at the square within the heart of the village. By this time, the village area of Woodstock was rapidly gaining in importance as a shire town, a growing commercial center, and as a junction point along the early network of turnpike roads that crossed Vermont.

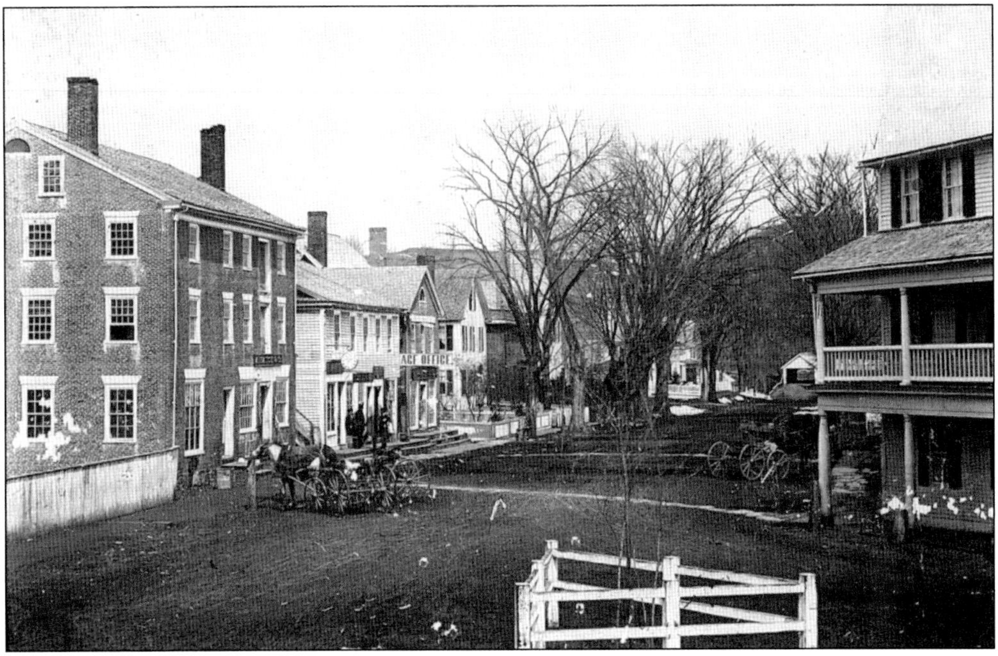

An 1859 view looking from the square northward along Elm Street shows the bridge over the Ottauquechee River in the far distance; however, the Congregational church is obscured behind the trees. To the right are the front porches of Barker's Hotel, and to the left is the brick building that today is the home of F.H. Gillingham and Sons.

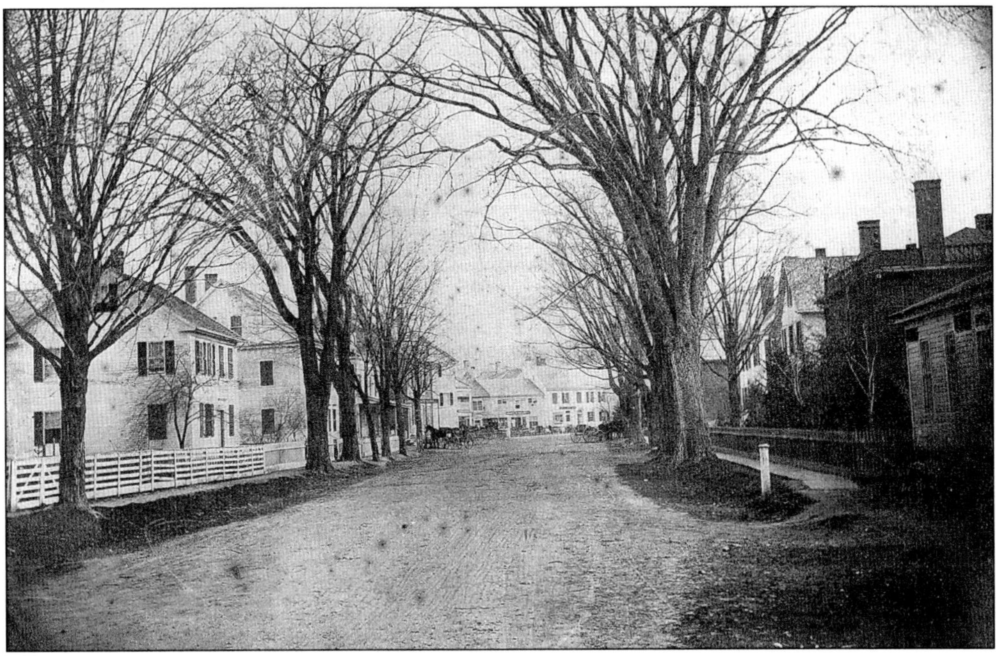

Elm Street is pictured around 1860 in a view looking south toward the square from about in front of the Congregational church. In the center distance is the stone Edson's Block, and slightly to the left are the porches of Barker's Hotel. Elm Street was originally part of the very southerly end of the important Royalton and Woodstock Turnpike.

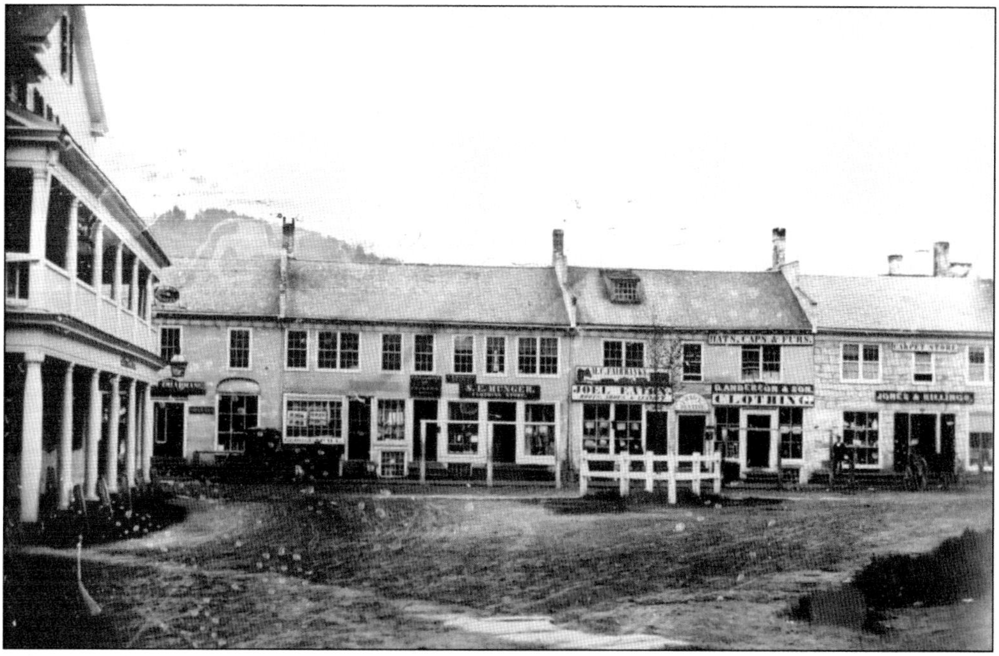

Sylvester Edson acquired a large block of land on the south side of Central Street in 1814, and by 1820, he had erected the first section of a row of connected commercial buildings that came to be known as Edson's Row, shown here in an 1857 photograph. While not housing Woodstock's first businesses, Edson's Row helped to further establish the village as a vibrant trading center.

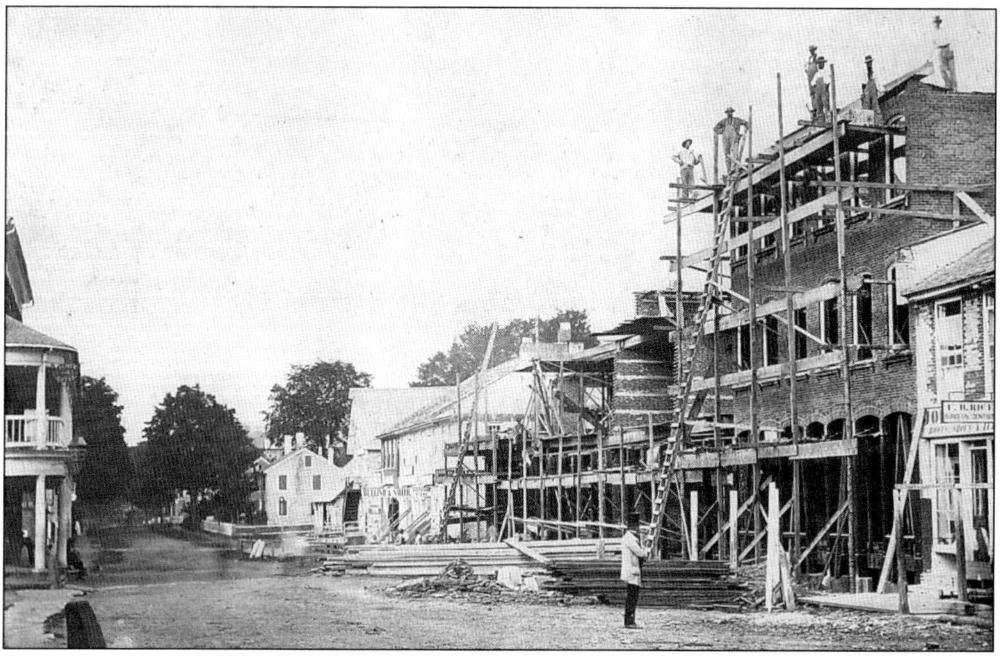

On the morning of February 10, 1860, all but the westerly end of Edson's Row burned, impacting 25 businesses and causing $30,000 of loss. That summer, the Phoenix Block, shown here under construction and, at the time, described as "scarcely surpassed by anything of the kind in Vermont," literally rose from the ashes of the former structure.

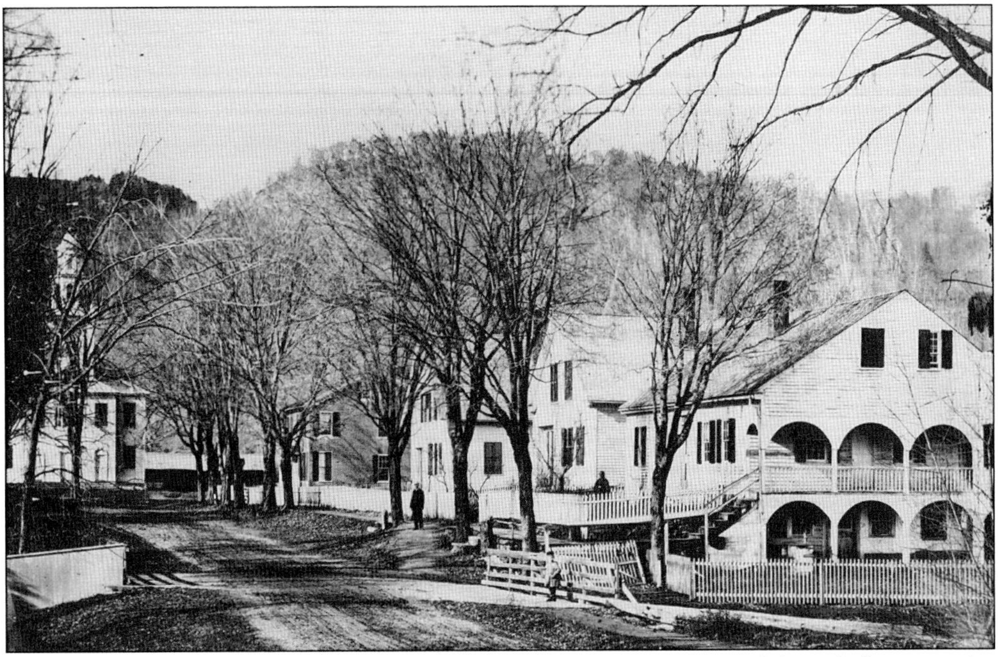

Pleasant Street was first opened in 1807 and included a bridge across the south branch (known today as Kedron Brook) of the Ottauquechee River, as seen in the westerly looking view around 1870. The area had numerous early dams and small millsites because of the brook. The Congregational church in the background was erected in 1808.

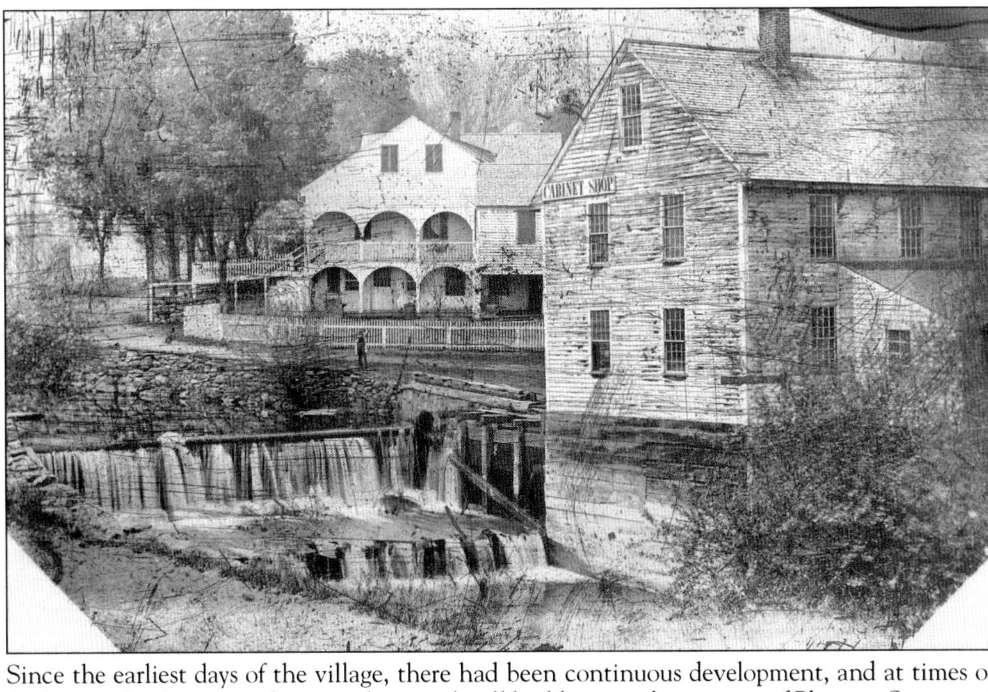

Since the earliest days of the village, there had been continuous development, and at times of freshets, redevelopment of various dams and mill buildings in the vicinity of Pleasant Street and the mouth of south branch, or Kedron Brook as it is now called. This mid-19th-century view shows Benson's cabinet shop and dam, located adjacent to the west side of Pleasant Street.

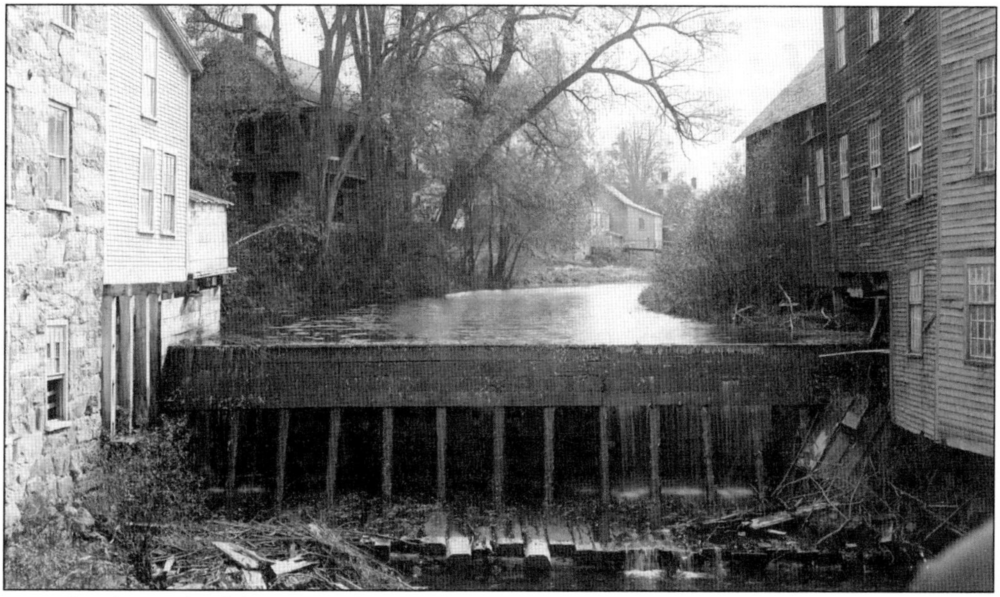

Immediately south of the point where Kedron Brook flows under Central Street, Jacob Wilder first established a mill to make linseed oil in 1792, and so it thrived for many decades under the ownership of numerous proprietors. The stone mill building on the east bank of the brook is believed to have been constructed in the 1840s and is still in place today, although no longer a mill facility.

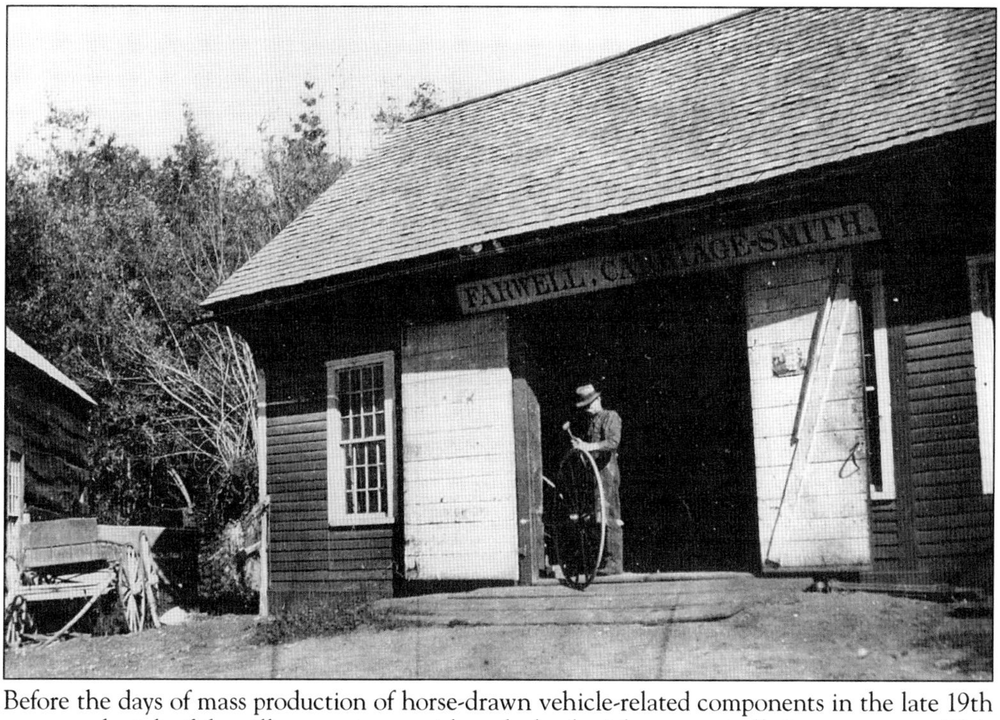

Before the days of mass production of horse-drawn vehicle-related components in the late 19th century, the job of the village carriage-smith and wheelwright was a vitally important one. This view is of Farwell's carriage and wheelwright shop in Woodstock. The gentleman in the doorway is making repairs to a carriage wheel, perhaps installing a new steel rim.

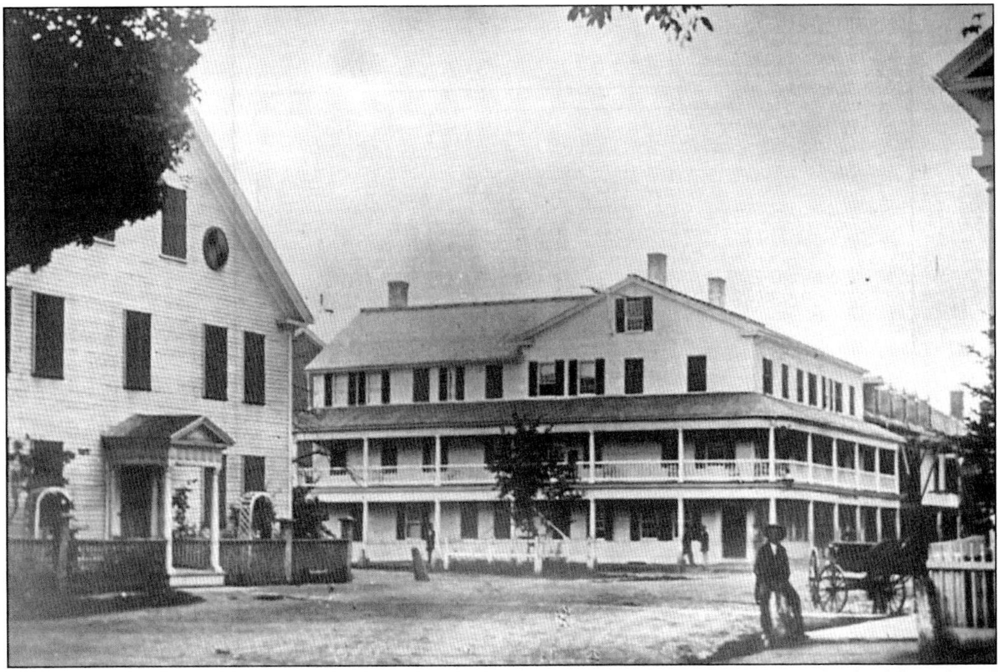

The Village Hotel was opened for business by Elisha Taylor in December 1796. The building faced the square and Central Street in the center of the village for 71 years, until its destruction by fire. Through various ownerships, it remained an important hospitality center offering food and lodging for travelers or rural folks in town for routine marketing and trading.

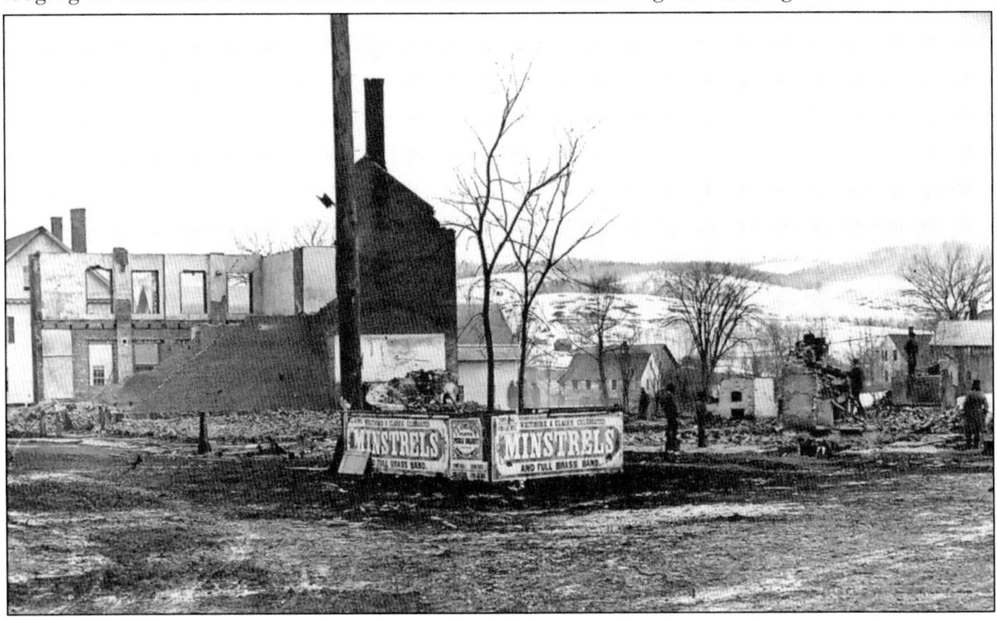

During the night of March 23, 1867, a fire started in the second-story hayloft of the stable behind the hotel. Within three hours, Henry's Hotel, as it was then called, was completely destroyed, and so were many adjacent buildings and businesses, including the county jail. This view looks from the square northeasterly across the burned site. It is not known if the advertised minstrel show was scheduled to be held in the destroyed hotel.

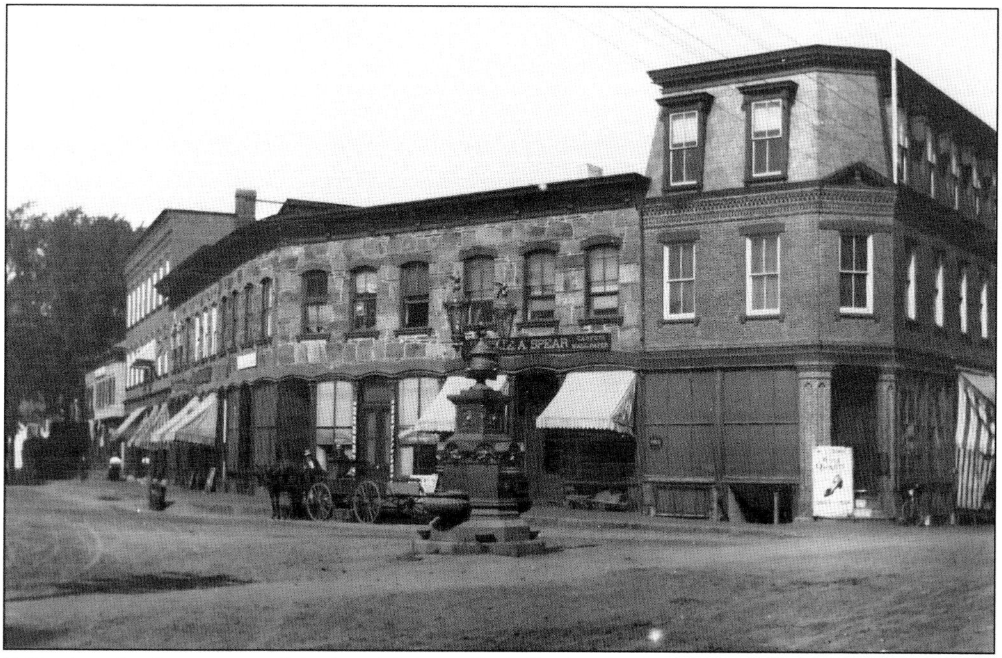

Following the destruction of the hotel, Morris Cady Fairbanks constructed the block often referred to in later years as the "Fruit Store" building with its mansard, or "French-style," roof. Beside it, the stone Cabot Block was constructed in 1869. For many years following the Civil War, the local GAR (Grand Army of the Republic) hall was upstairs in the Fairbanks Building.

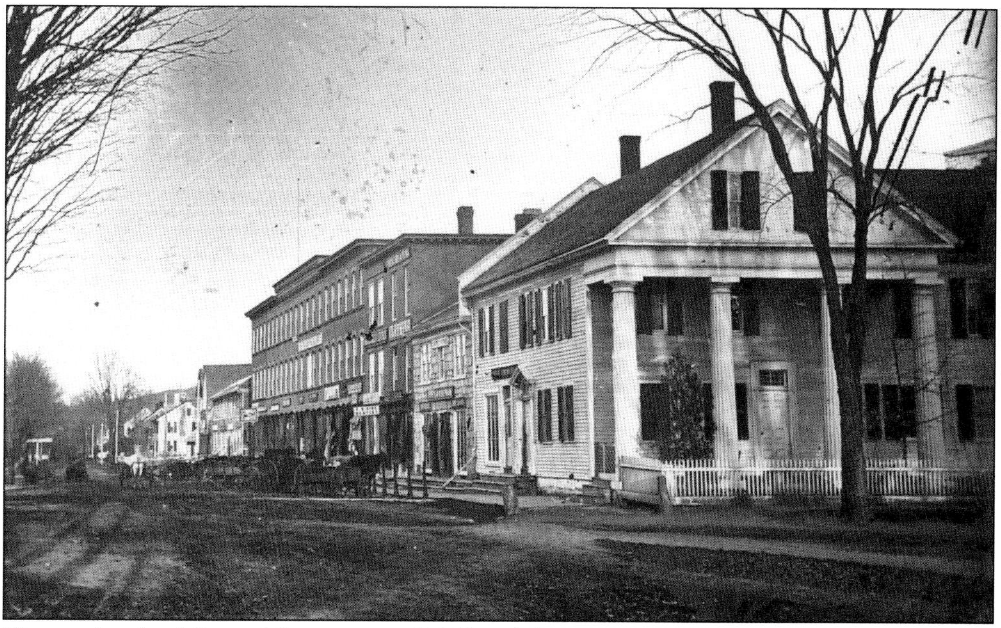

The south side of Central Street around 1865 and the impressive new Phoenix Block are shown here. In the foreground is the so-called Churchill house, constructed in 1793 on the site of the first log hut erected in the Woodstock Village area by Jacob Hoisington in the early spring of 1772. Hoisington's hut was also the first tavern in Woodstock. Visible beside the house is the remaining section of the former Edson Row block.

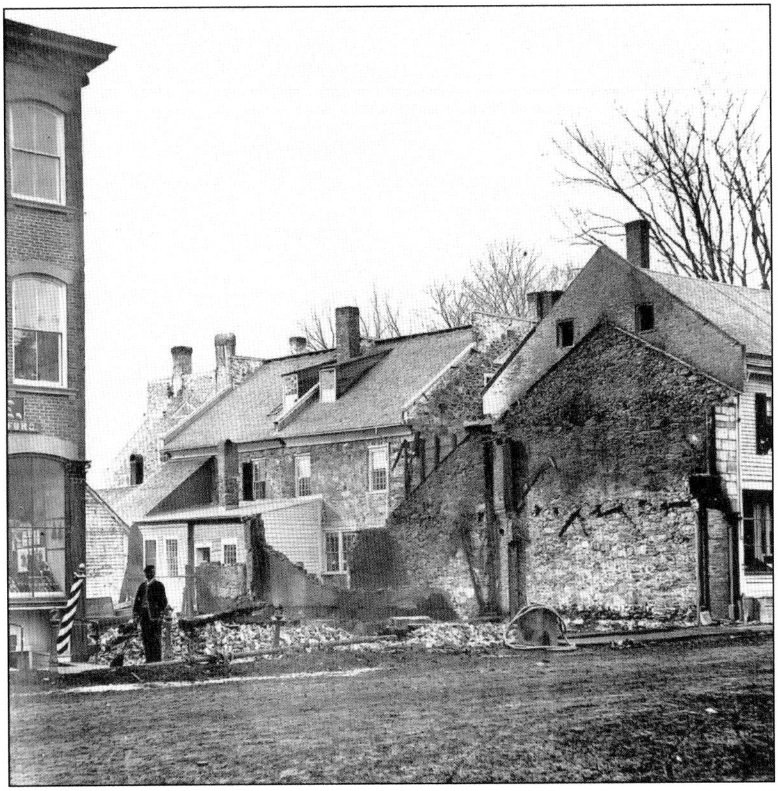

A fire in 1881 claimed the remaining section of the stone Edson Row block. With much effort, the fire was contained and did not spread to the wooden Churchill house to which the block was connected; however, the barber pole beside the Phoenix Block did wither from the heat of the fire. Quickly, a new brick replacement building was constructed that is still standing today.

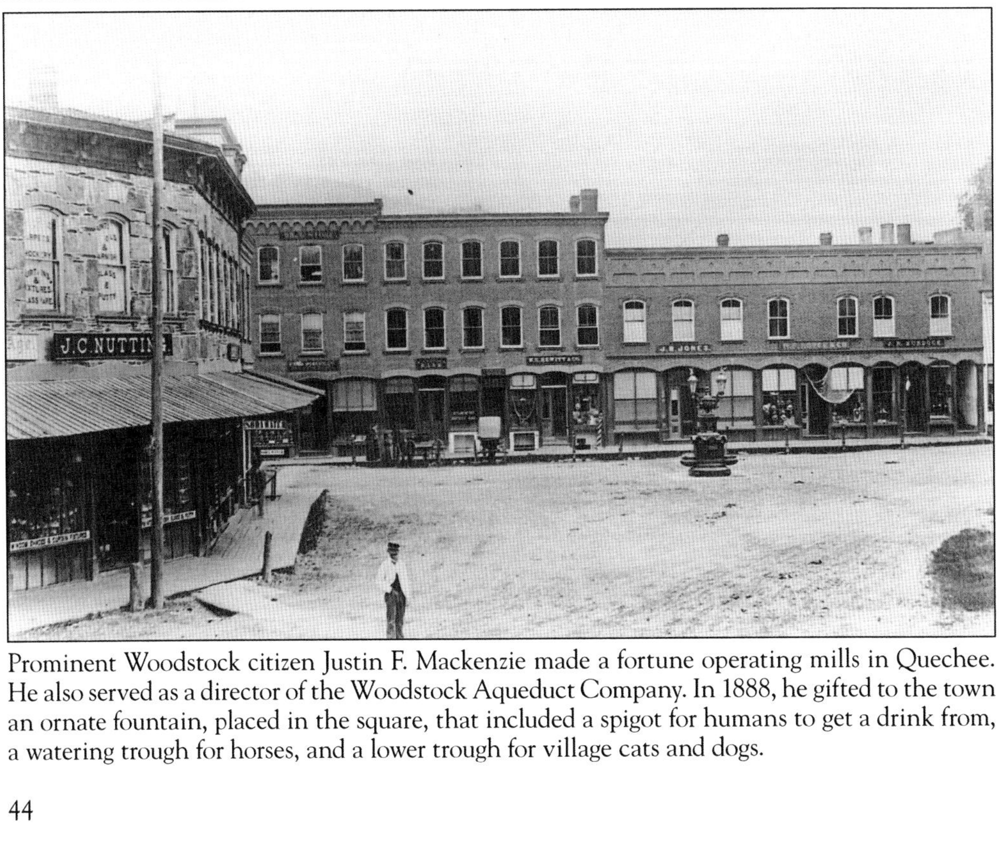

Prominent Woodstock citizen Justin F. Mackenzie made a fortune operating mills in Quechee. He also served as a director of the Woodstock Aqueduct Company. In 1888, he gifted to the town an ornate fountain, placed in the square, that included a spigot for humans to get a drink from, a watering trough for horses, and a lower trough for village cats and dogs.

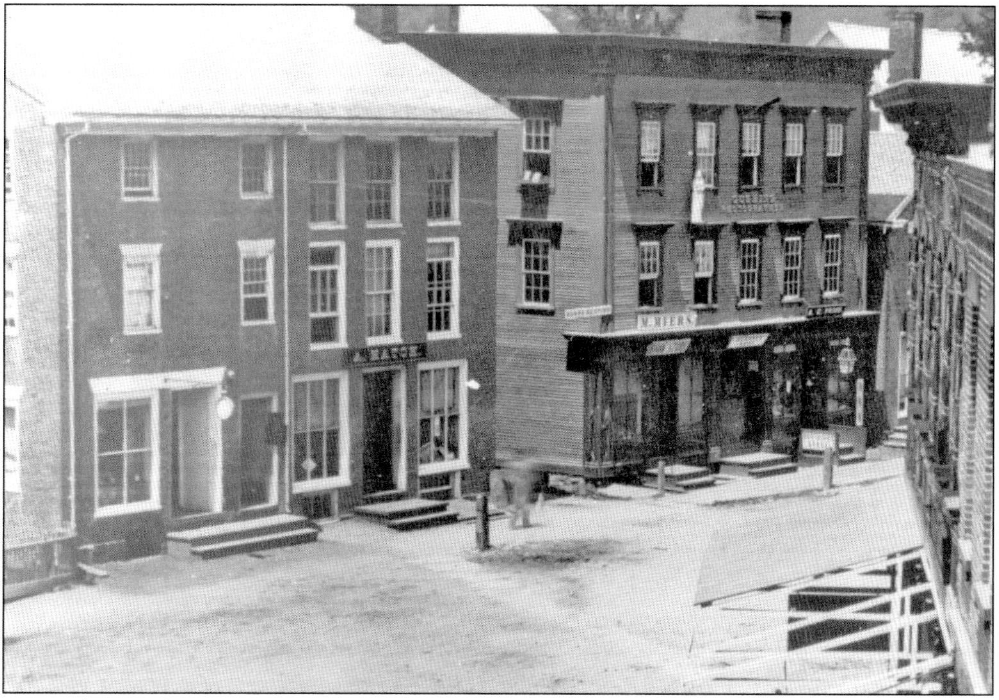

Pictured around 1875, the brick structure to the left appears as two buildings but is in fact one, constructed by attorney Titus Hutchinson and Sylvester Edson on speculation in 1810. A first-floor storefront to the right became Alvin Hatch's general store, and Hutchinson's law office was on the left. A central staircases accessed the upper floors, which were partially occupied by the Vermont State Bank. The Tracy Block is to the right.

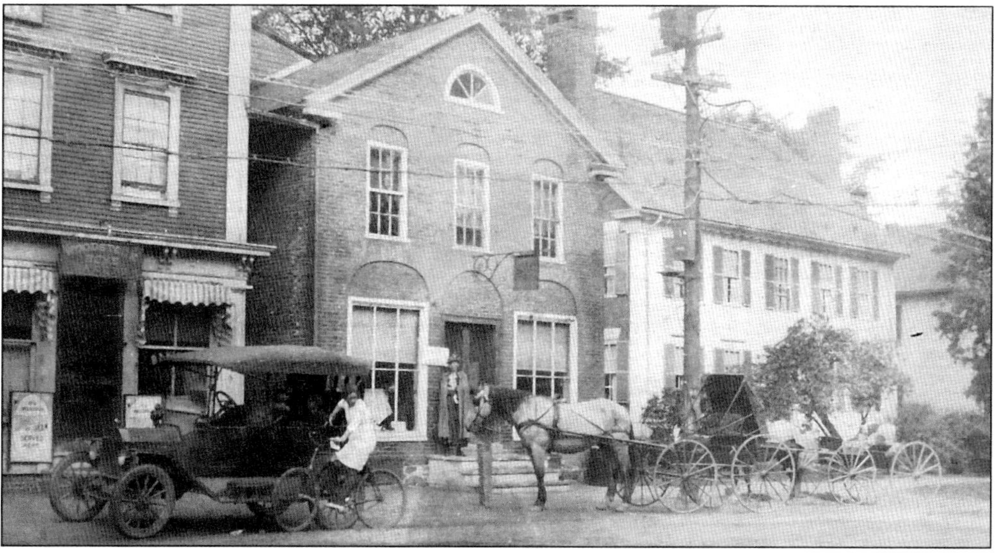

Charles Dana erected the brick building in 1820 that, for many years, was known as the New York Dry Goods Store before becoming the Elm Street Press in 1907. Shown parked out in front on Elm Street are the following three modes of transportation: a 1916 Ford Model T, a bicycle, and several horse-drawn buggies. The 1807 Dana House is visible behind the buggies. To the left is the Tracy Block.

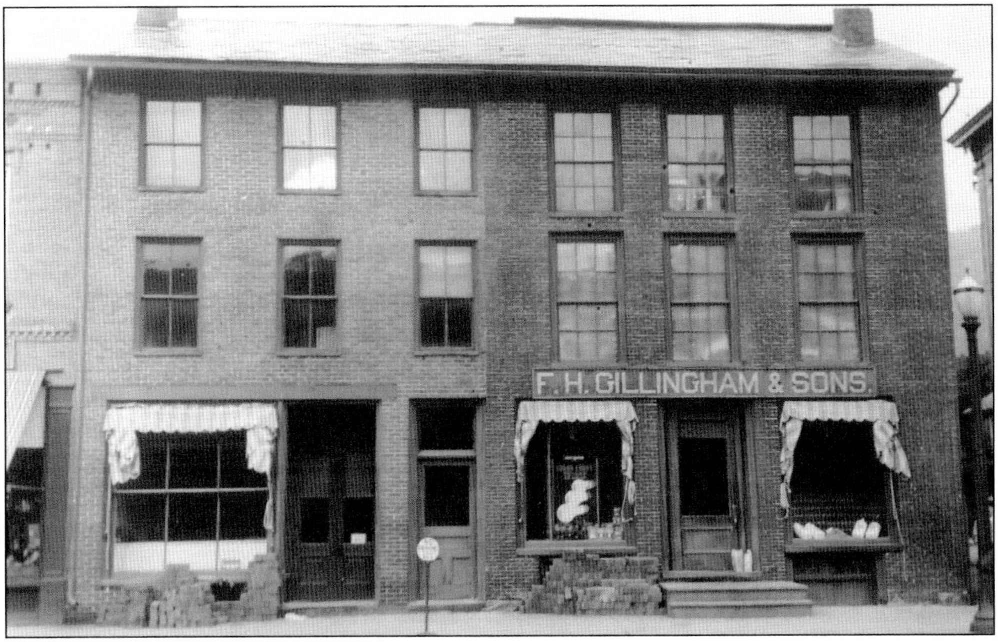

Frank Henry "F.H." Gillingham was still in high school when he started working in Alvin Hatch's general store. Soon thereafter, in 1884, Gillingham, with a partner, purchased the business. Two years later, Gillingham was on his own, and the store quickly became a phenomenal success. Gillingham was a very forward-thinking retailer, aggressively advertising his goods and utilizing the Woodstock Railway to bring in more and better products from afar.

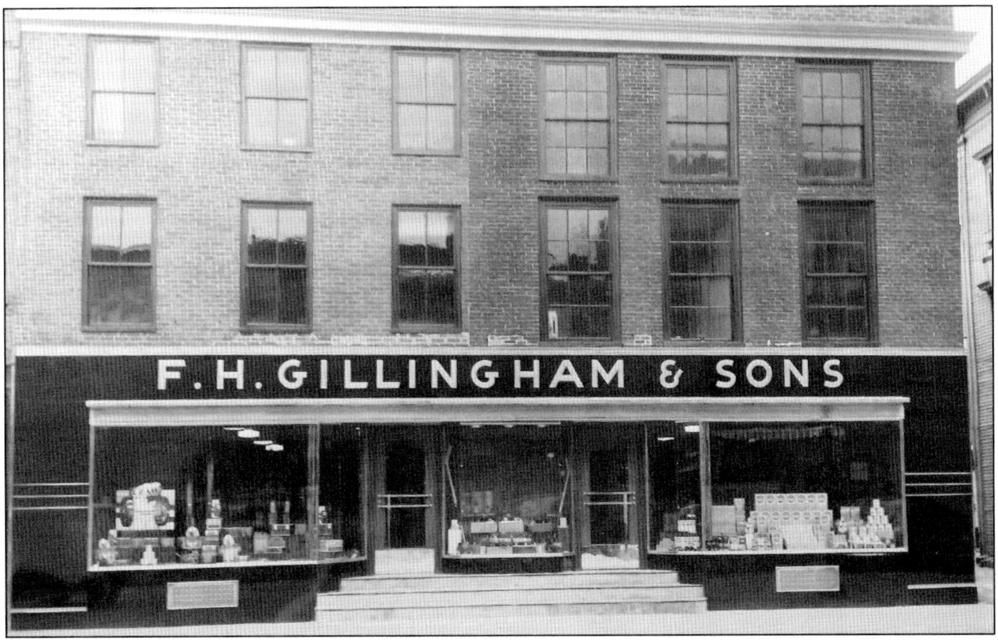

In 1938, Gillingham's was renovated to include a stylish Art Deco storefront and became a full self-serve grocery store. Although a fire on May 1, 1970, did extensive damage to the store, the business is now run by the fourth generation of the Gillingham-Billings family, and while in step with the present day, it proudly has on display the store's rich, unique, and colorful history.

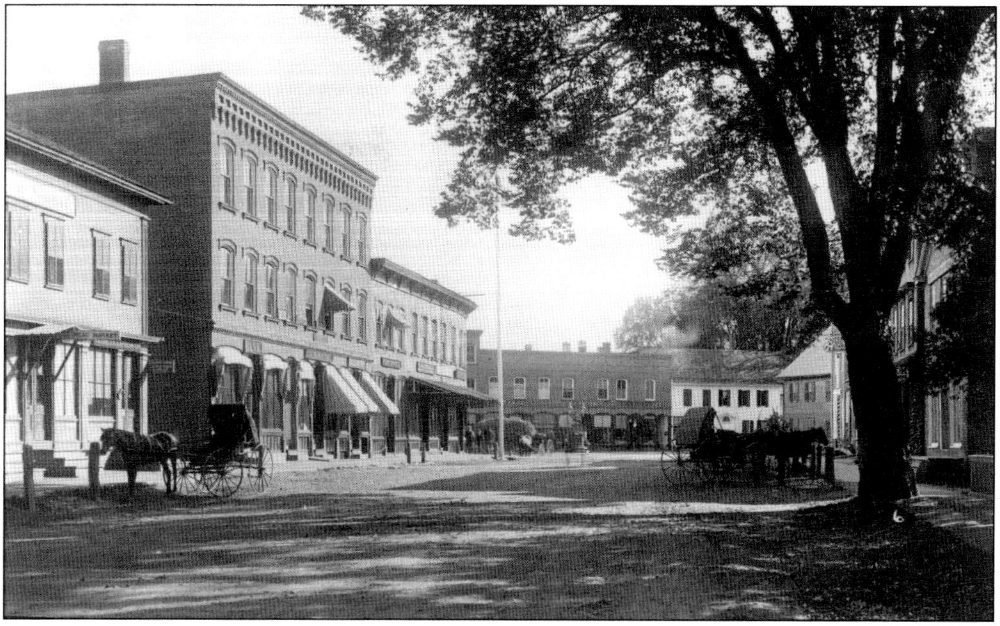

Taken with a view looking toward the square, this photograph shows Elm Street around 1890. The three-story brick block to the left was constructed after the 1867 hotel fire (see page 42). In the background is the 1793 Churchill house that was razed in 1901 and replaced by the Ottauquechee Savings Bank building. Clearly, the village was filling out and indeed looking prosperous as it entered the new century.

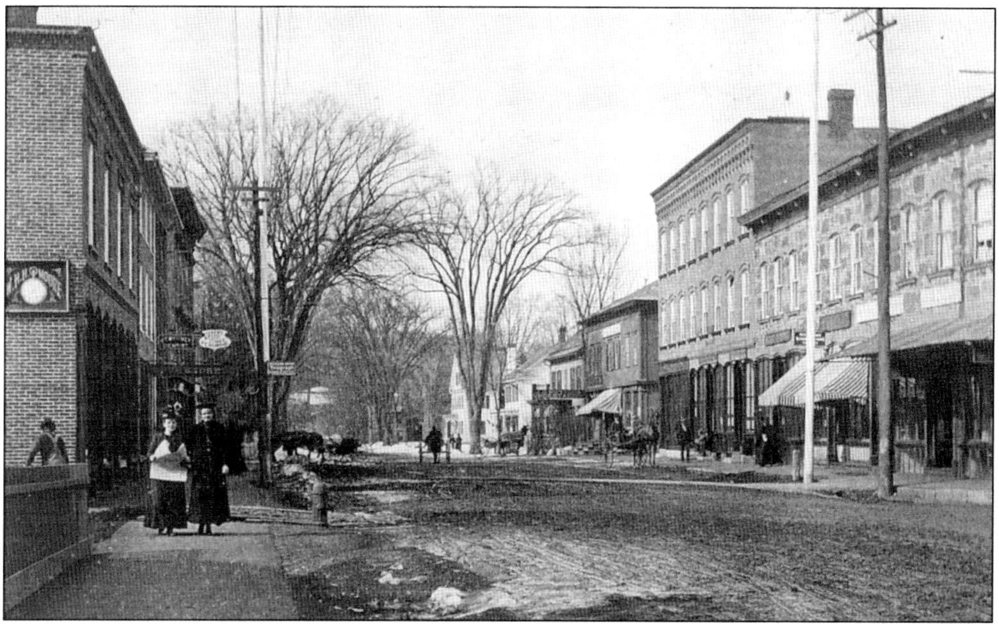

Looking away from the square, this view shows Elm Street around 1900. To the right is the stone Cabot Block. To the left are the Gilman Block (1894), Gillingham's, and the Tracy Block, which burned in 1972. The Western Union telegraph office was in the Tracy Block. Other than a few telephone and telegraph poles and lines, there is not yet any evidence of electrical power on the street.

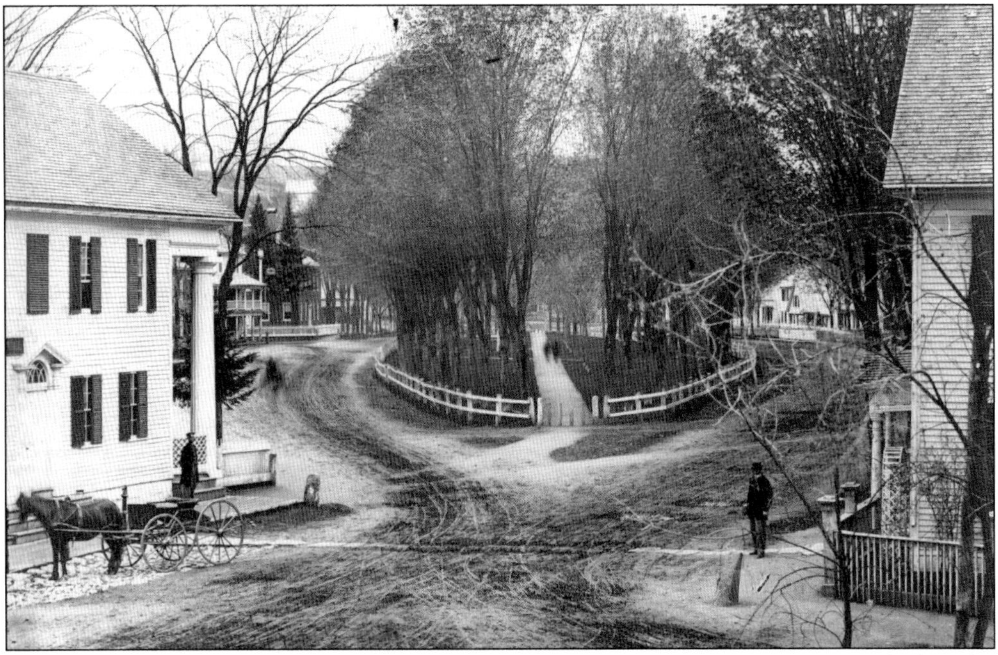

Although the Woodstock Green is the oldest part of the village, it was many years before the present green was laid out and trees planted around the perimeter in 1830. In 1878, at considerable cost, the iron fence replaced the granite posts' wooden rails, shown in this c. 1865 view. To the left is the 1793 Artemus Baker house. At the right is the 1798 Titus Hutchinson house.

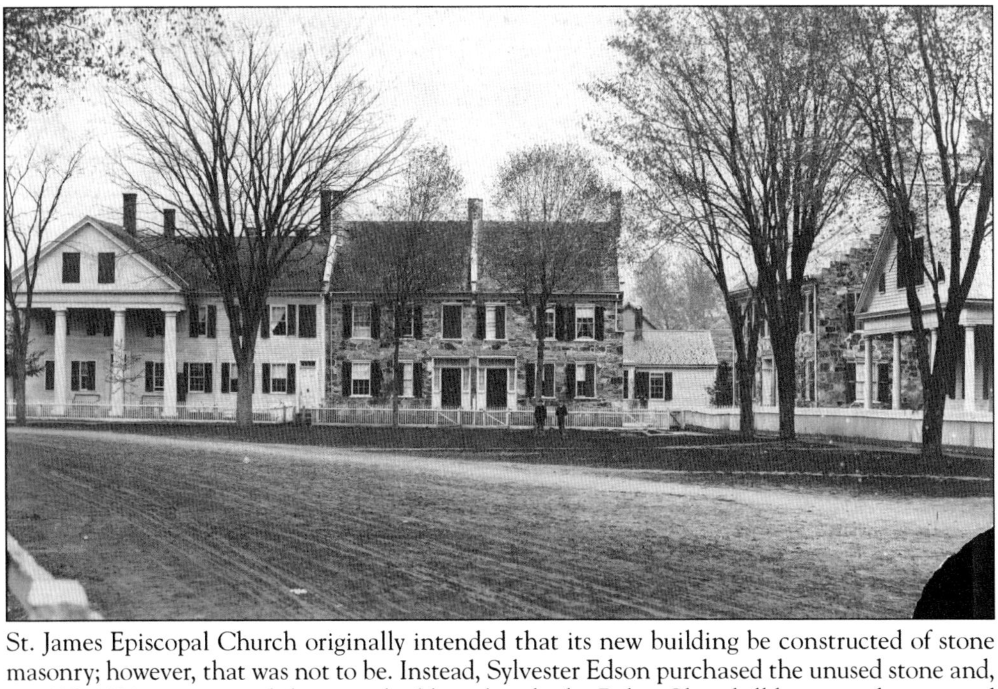

St. James Episcopal Church originally intended that its new building be constructed of stone masonry; however, that was not to be. Instead, Sylvester Edson purchased the unused stone and, in 1827–1828, constructed the stone buildings beside the Baker-Churchill house at the east end of the green. At far right is a Greek Revival–style Cape house erected in 1818 and razed in 1884 for the Norman Williams Public Library.

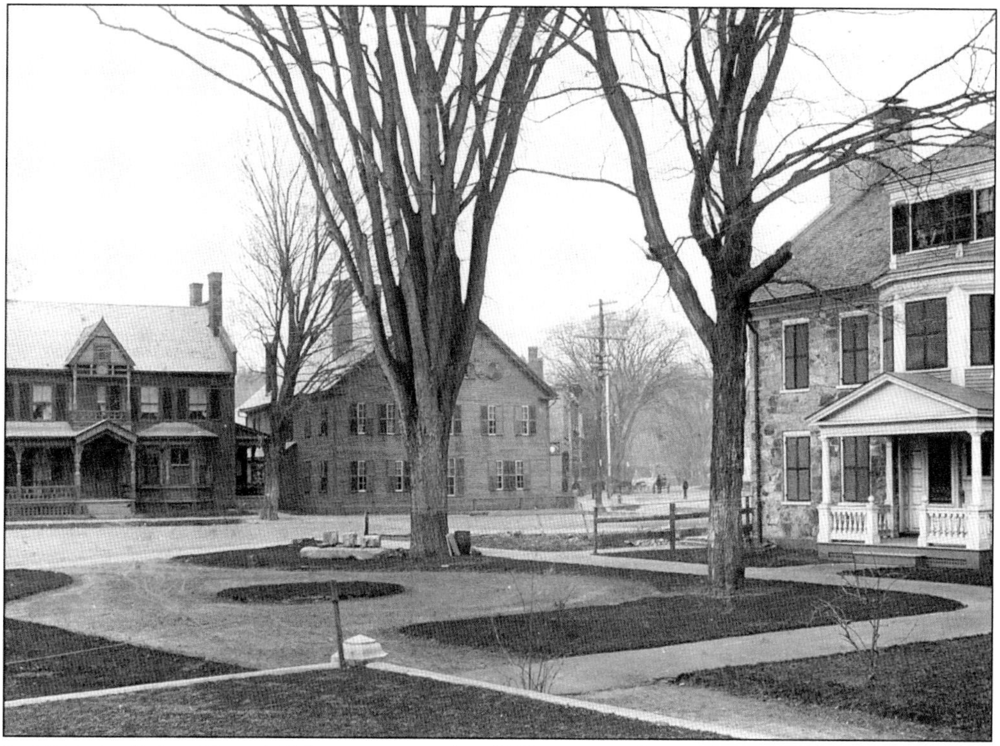

In 1901, the Baker-Churchill house, erected in 1793, was razed to make way for the construction of the new Ottauquechee Savings Bank building, and before construction of the new building began, this photograph was made. Across the street is the 1798 Hutchinson House, still standing at that location. Note the proliferation of Victorian-era porches and bay windows on the nearby older buildings.

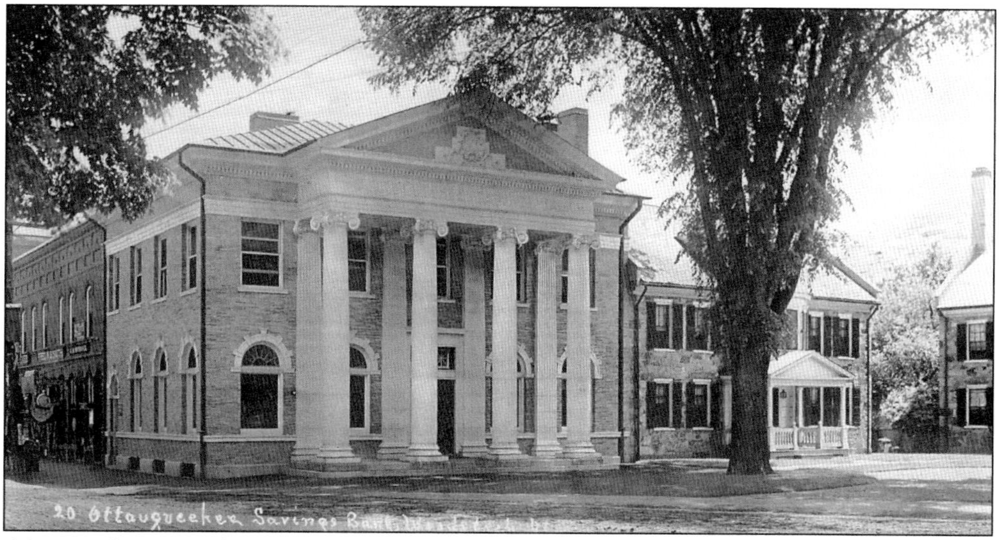

After purchasing and razing the old Baker-Churchill house in 1901, the Ottauquechee Savings Bank constructed its new building in the then very fashionable Neoclassical style, complete with yellow brick and stylish Corinthian columns. Upon completion, the new facility was said to be "one of the best arranged and lighted banks in the country."

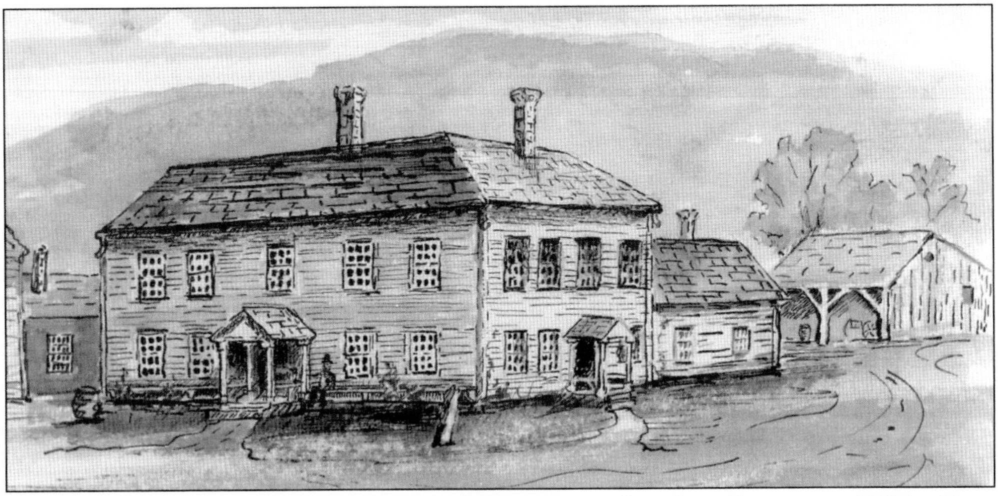

The first building of any permanence erected as a tavern within the village was in 1793 by Capt. Israel Richardson on the site of the present-day Woodstock Inn's front parking lot. With the first Windsor County Courthouse also facing the green adjacent to it, Richardson's Tavern (seen in this early sketch) quickly became a successful operation.

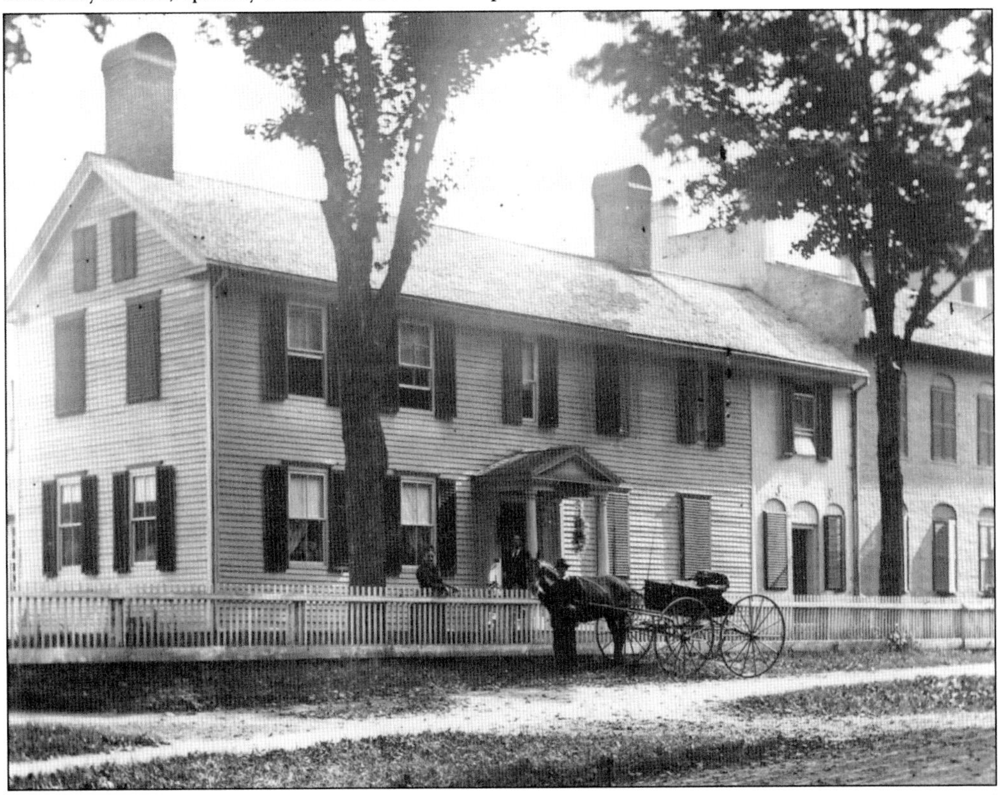

By about 1830, what had been Richardson's Tavern became known as the Eagle Hotel, and several additions had been made to the easterly side of the original building, both facing the green. The brick ell addition, complete with a reception hall, was constructed in 1822. Three years later, a lavish banquet was held in the hall for General Lafayette during his much-celebrated visit to Woodstock in 1825.

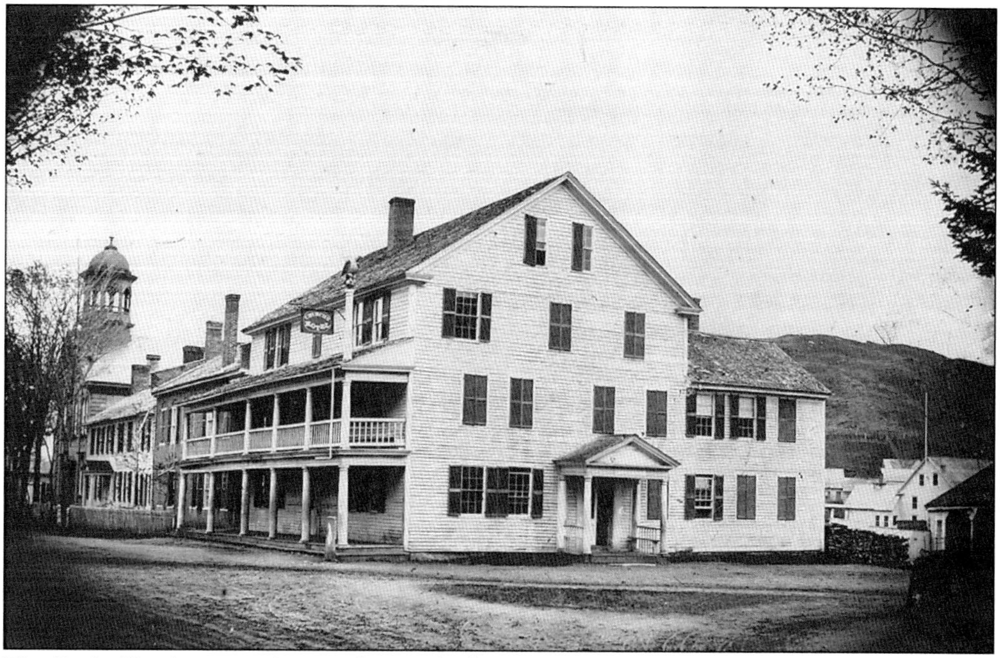

The Eagle Hotel, pictured around 1860, had gained not only a two-story front porch in 1830 but also a third floor in 1840. The wood ell burned in 1855 and was rebuilt. To the left beyond the main building are the brick and wooden annex additions, and in the far left is the Windsor County Courthouse, erected in 1854–1855 (see page 68). To the right is South Street.

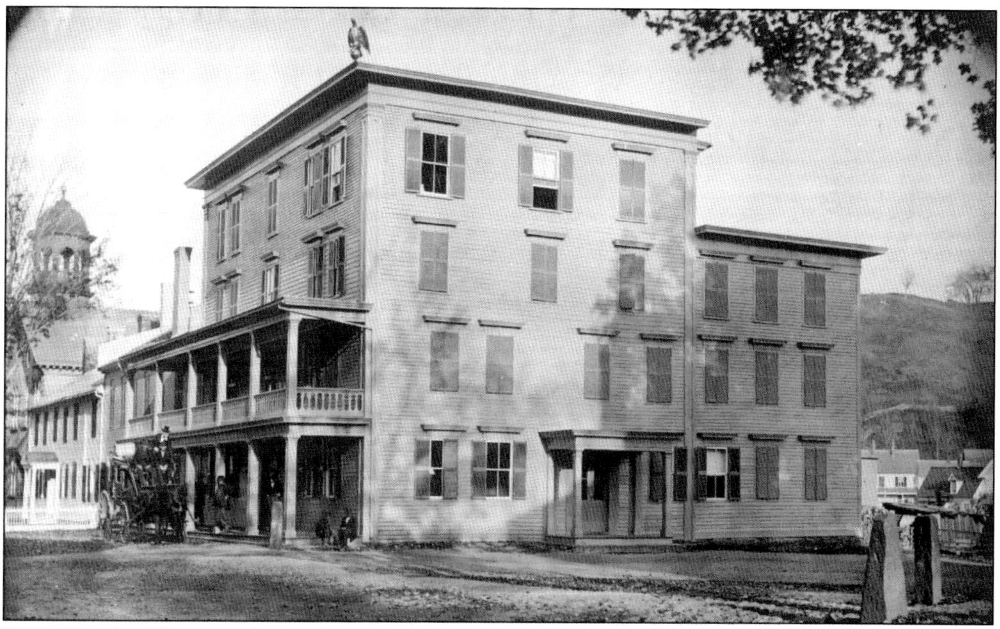

Immediately following the American Civil War in 1865 were the dawning years of Woodstock becoming a destination point for tourists. As a result, in 1867, the Eagle Hotel was modernized in the Italianate style and expanded to better accommodate that new trade. Earlier that same year, Barker's Hotel in the square had burned and was rebuilt as a commercial block and not as a hotel.

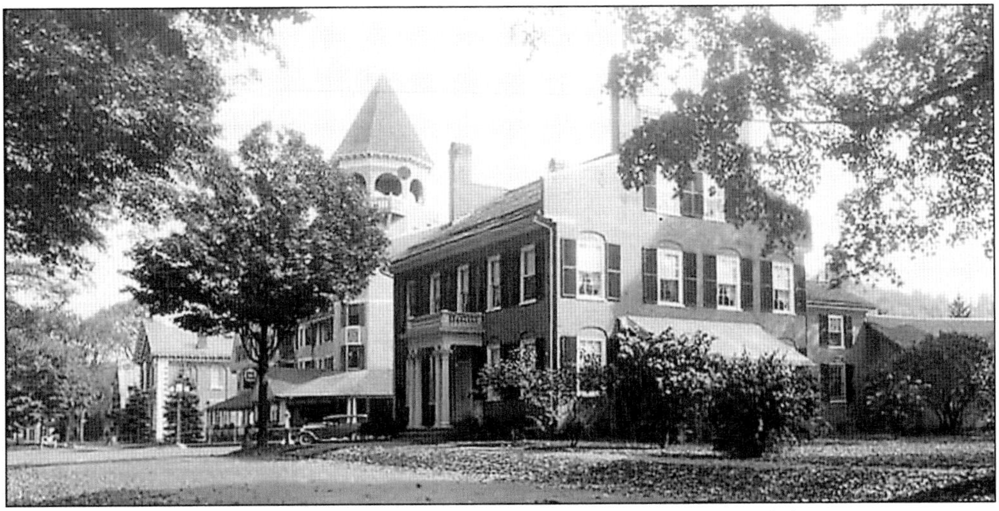

Woodstock has many fine examples of architecture, and perhaps one of the more prominent examples is this excellent Federal-style house, constructed in 1823 by Gen. Lyman Mower, whose wealth came from the wool picking and carding business. Situated on the site of Woodstock's first courthouse, and still majestically facing the southern side of the green, the general's house once boasted having the first bathtub in Woodstock.

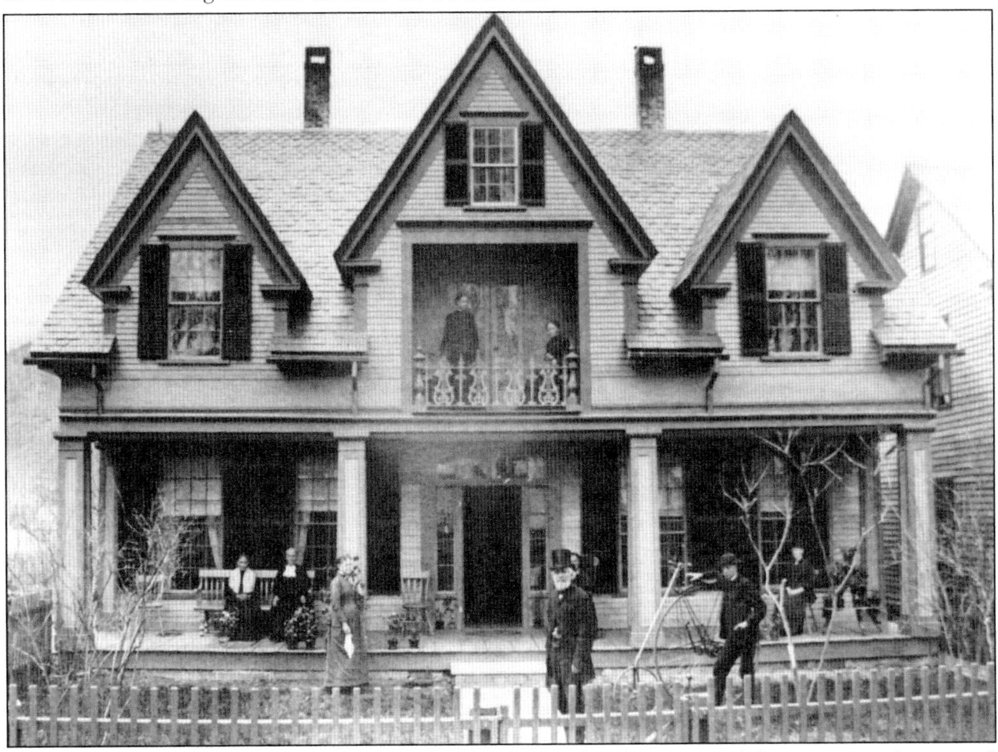

Woodstock is not only rich in buildings that represent the many eras of American architectural taste but also has buildings that can only be described as very eclectic examples of Vermont architecture. James H. Murdock's house on the north side of the green is such an example. It was started with some Greek Revival themes, and other mid-19th-century motives were then blended into this rather curious village home.

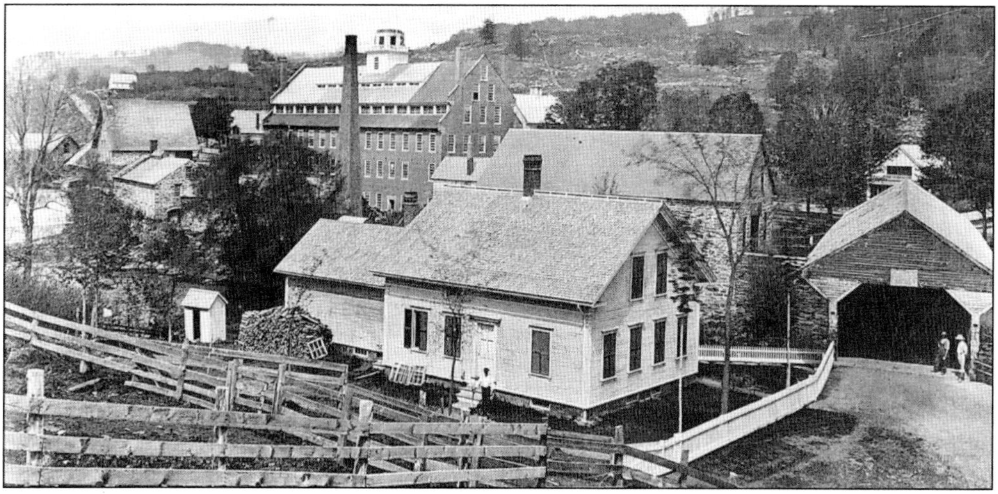

At the west end of the village, the first dam on the Ottauquechee River was constructed in 1790, and mill buildings appeared soon thereafter. The Woodstock Manufacturing Company built a large brick woolen mill in 1835. Over time, the site also included water-powered sawmills and gristmill equipment until permanently shut down in the early part of the 20th century. Today, the site is home to a theater and recreation center.

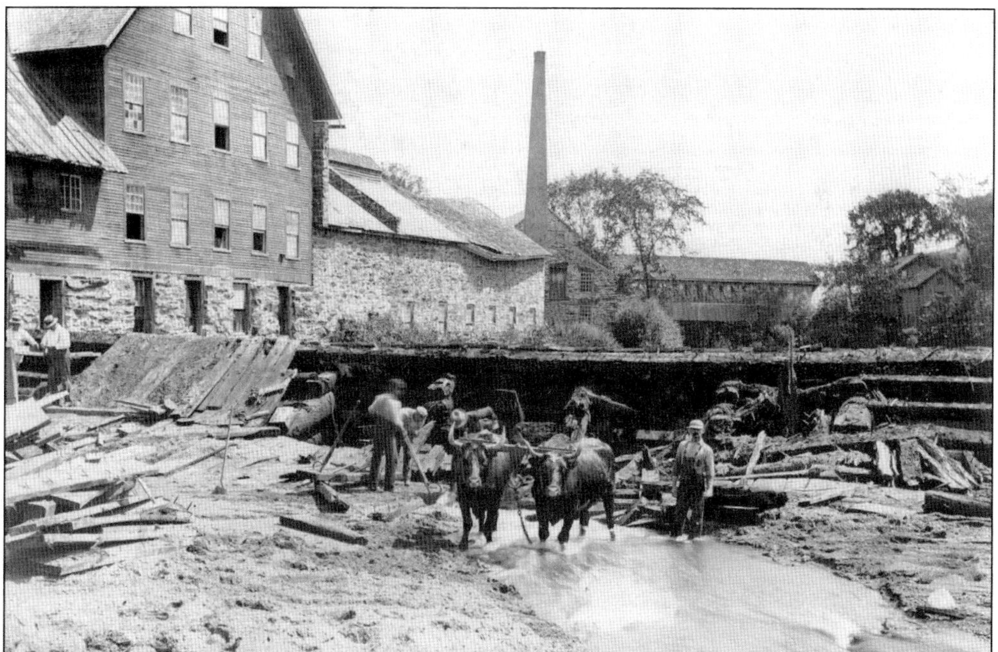

Prior to the use of concrete in dam construction in the 20th century, earlier dams constructed of wood cribbing and rock required almost constant maintenance and repair. Here, repair work is being completed after a freshet damaged the gristmill dam at the Woodstock Manufacturing Company mill site. In the background is the wooden covered bridge (see page 54).

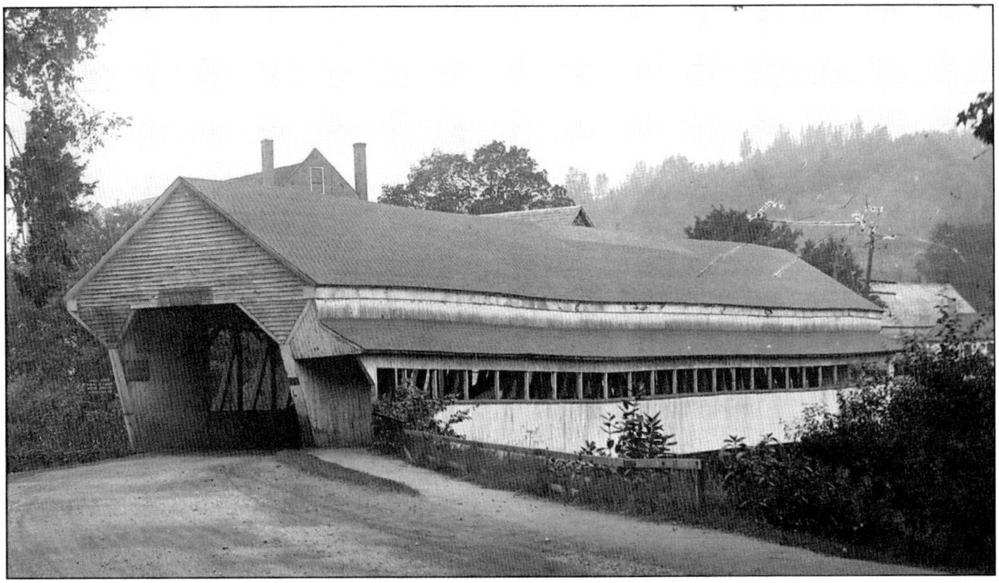

The first bridge across the Ottauquechee River at the west end of the village was erected in 1791 and cost $300—a controversial amount of money at that time for a bridge. By 1846, when this replacement bridge was erected, the cost had risen to $3,500. Regardless, the new wooden bridge served the traveling public well for 98 years until finally being replaced by a concrete structure in 1944.

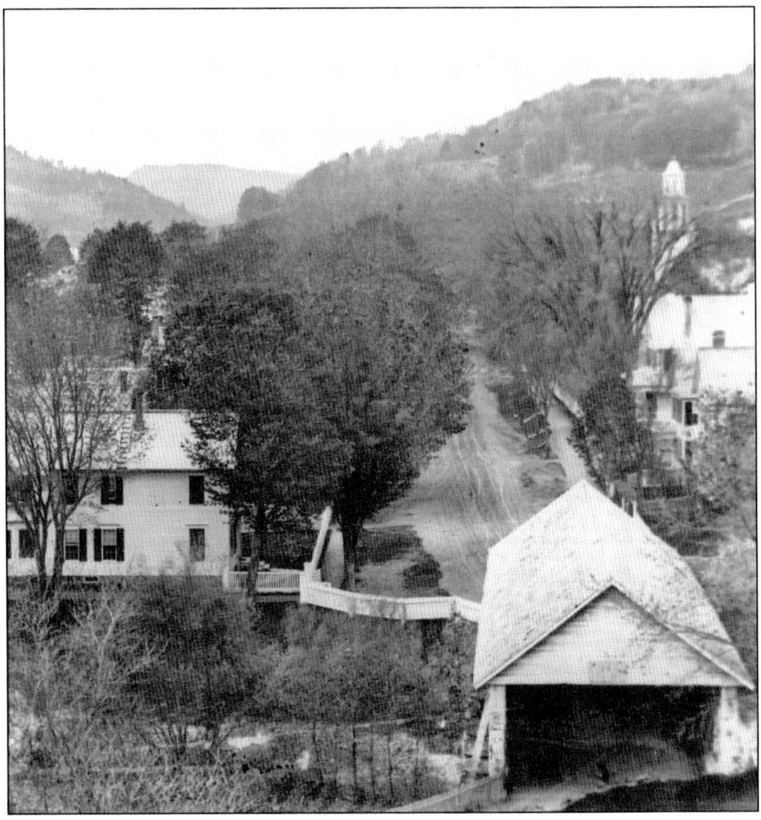

Between 1797 and 1870, there were at least seven bridges across the Ottauquechee River at Elm Street, which was also the Royalton and Woodstock Turnpike from 1801 to 1841. Three of those bridges were carried away by floodwaters, and the turnpike company rebuilt a total of six bridges at this site prior to its demise. This view of the last of those wooden bridges looks southerly toward the village.

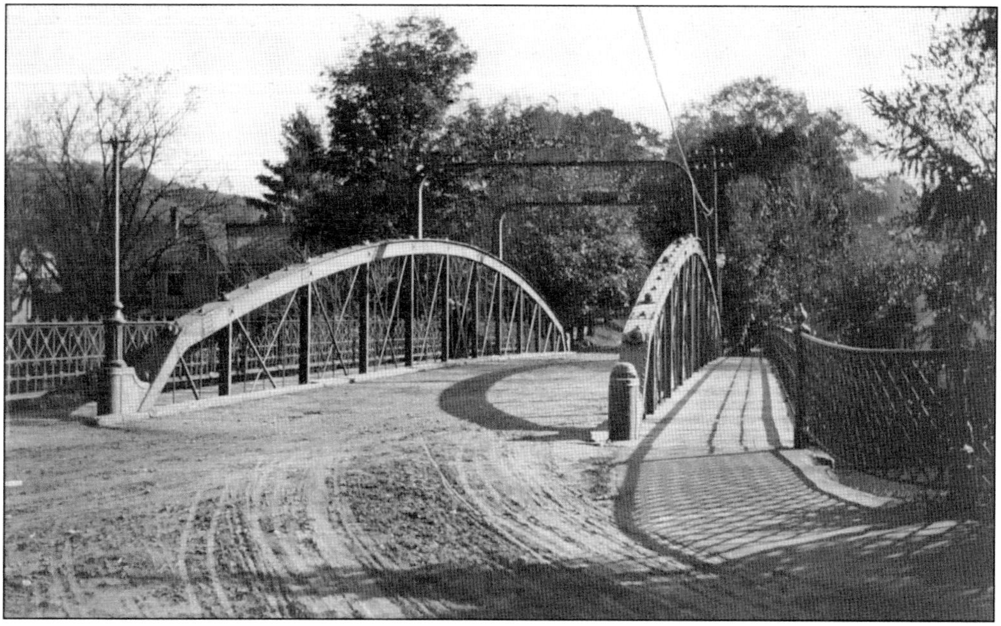

One of the most historically important early iron bridges in North America was erected at the Elm Street site in 1870 and is still in use to this day. Erected at an estimated cost of about $4,000 by the National Bridge and Iron Works of Boston, Massachusetts, the 110-foot-long structure was an early and noteworthy application of the evolving science of bridge engineering in the mid-18th century.

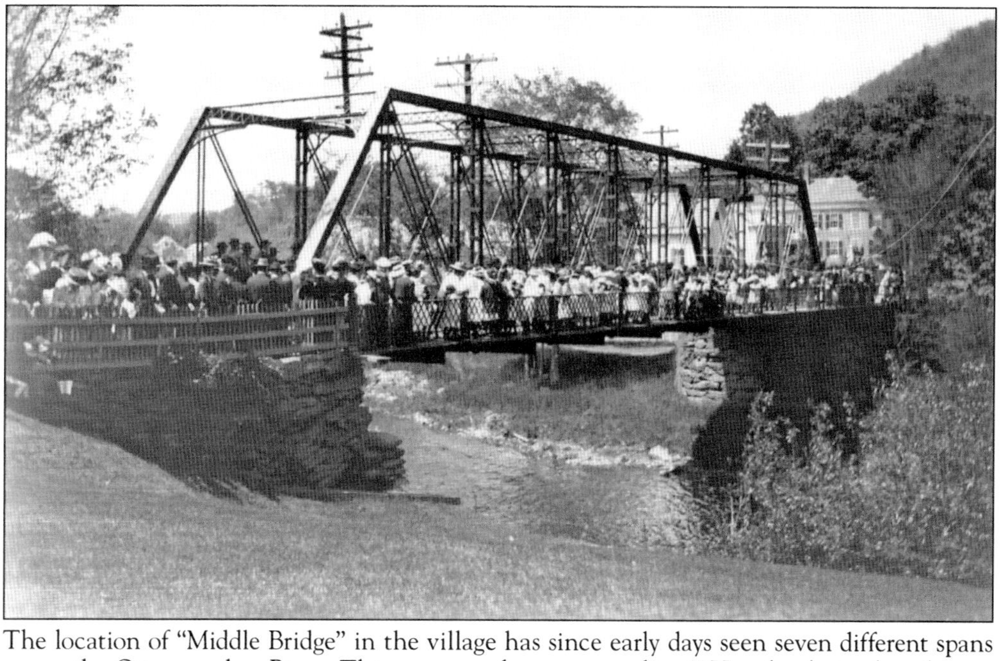

The location of "Middle Bridge" in the village has since early days seen seven different spans across the Ottauquechee River. This was a steel span erected in 1877—the design based upon railroad bridge engineering of the day. There was much grumbling by village wags when it was replaced in 1969 with a new wooden covered bridge that, despite catching fire on May 11, 1974, is still standing.

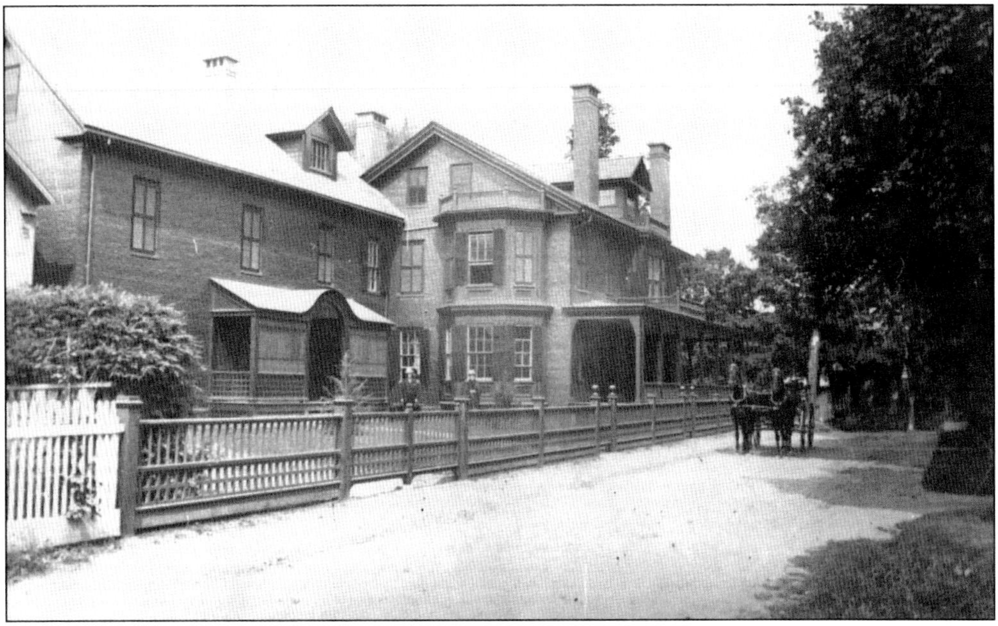

As previously noted, Woodstock has many fine examples of architecture and has witnessed the ever-present change of architectural fashion. The brick house constructed at 4 Bond Street by Amos Warren in 1808 is an excellent case in point. It was acquired by Franklin N. Billings in 1870, and four generations of Billingses have made changes reflective of the evolving time and place. Today, the residence is the home of Pauline Gillingham Billings.

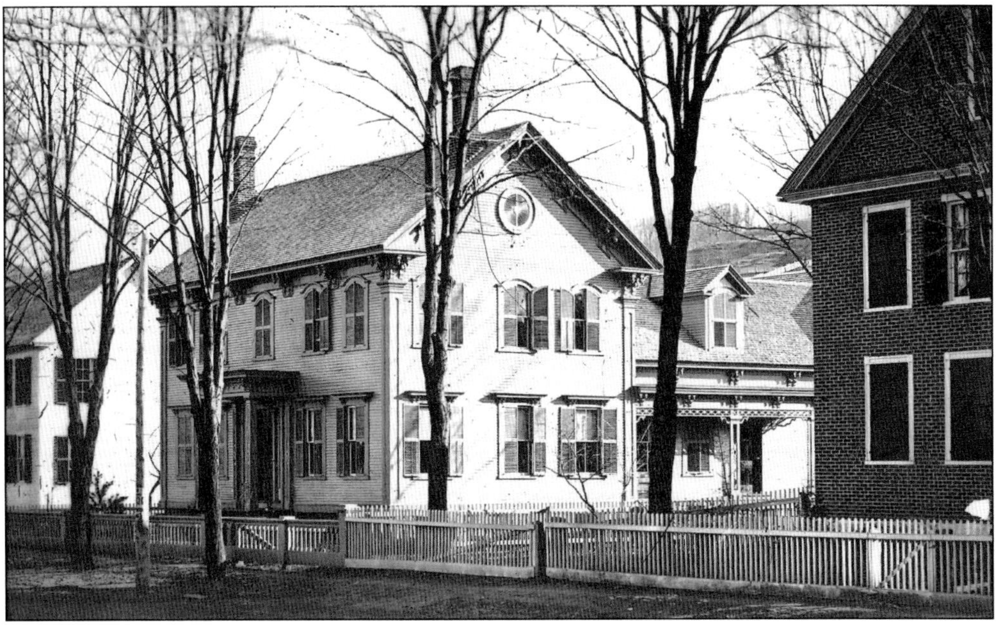

Oscar H. Freeman was a very successful Woodstock businessman operating a combination pharmacy and hardware store. Though a bachelor, he erected this large and excellent period house at 23 Pleasant Street in 1867. The interior of the house, noted for its elegant gaslights, utilized an older Georgian format; however, the exterior was richly detailed in decorative elements of the then fashionable Italianate style.

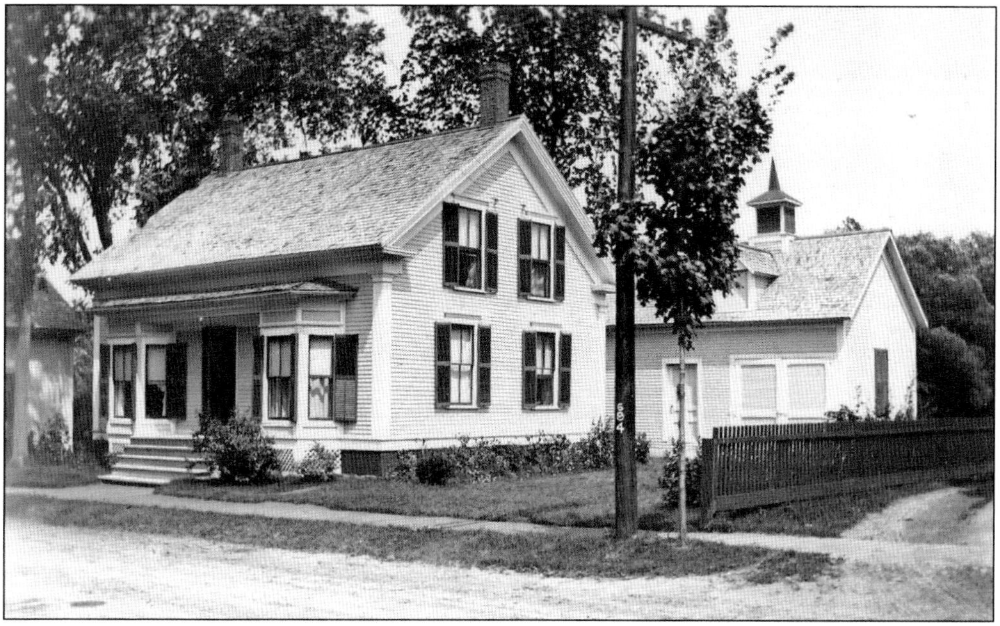

This modest home and attached stable building for the family horse and buggy are intriguing examples of village architecture. Originally an early-19th-century Greek Revival–style story-and-a-half Cape house, it features unique latter-century bay windows and covered front porch additions. The location of the two brick chimneys indicate that the home was heated with a series of wood-burning, and later coal-burning, stoves.

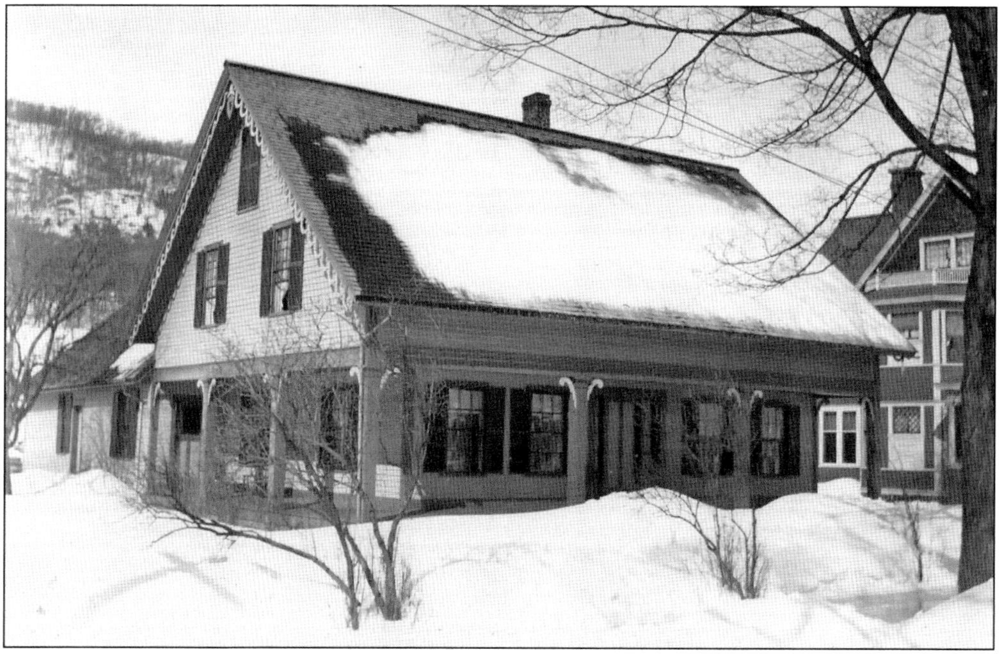

The mid-18th-century availability and proliferation of mechanized woodworking equipment allowed architects and carpenters alike greater and easier opportunities to economically embellish residential designs with architectural trim reflective of the era. This mid-1800s Woodstock Village home features highly decorative gable verge boards and ornately bracketed porch columns.

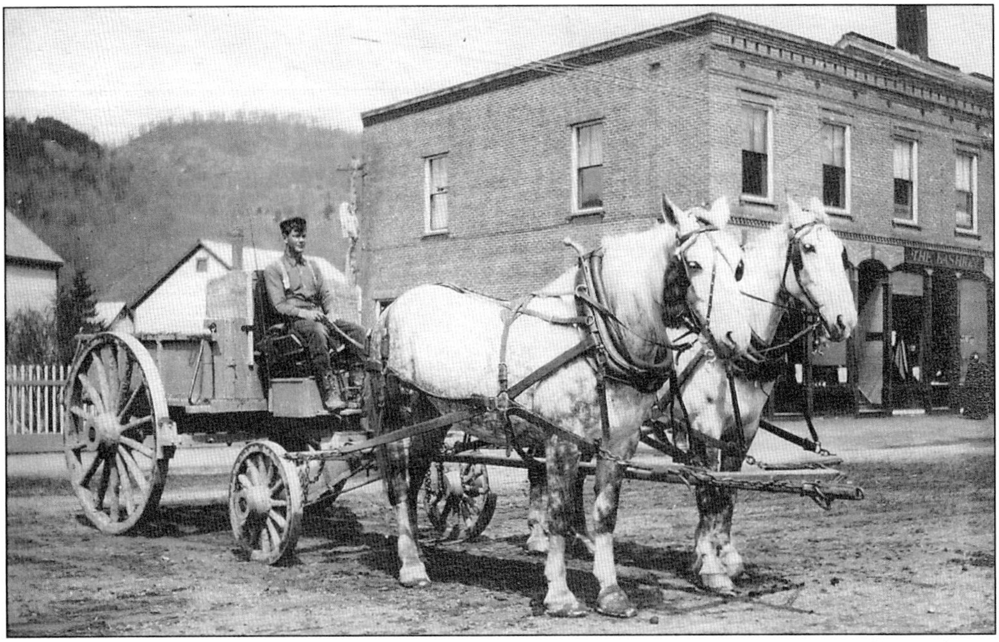

Until the popularity of trucks beginning in the 1920s, freight that was not moved by rail was typically hauled by wagons and teams of workhorses. Little is known about this teamster, his heavy-duty wagon, or powerful team, but the building in the background is the Gilman Block on Elm Street, constructed in 1894. Perhaps he had just made a freight delivery to Gillingham's from the railroad station.

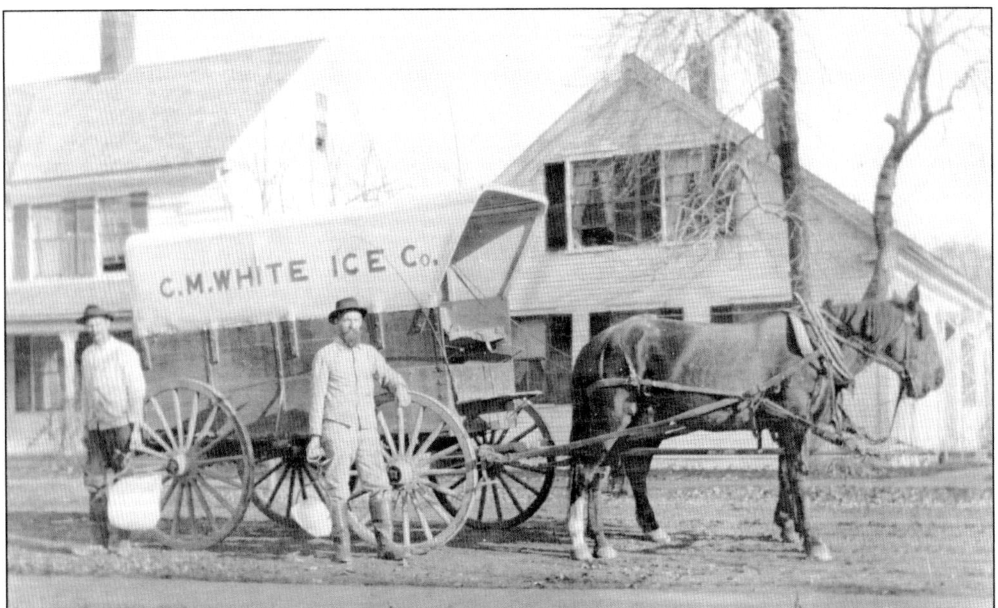

It was during the early 1920s that the first commercially available mechanized refrigerator units came on the market. Prior to then, and for a period of time thereafter, perishable food was kept cool in an icebox with chunks of ice. Here are employees of the C.M. White Ice Company delivering chunks of ice, harvested the winter before, to a Woodstock Village home.

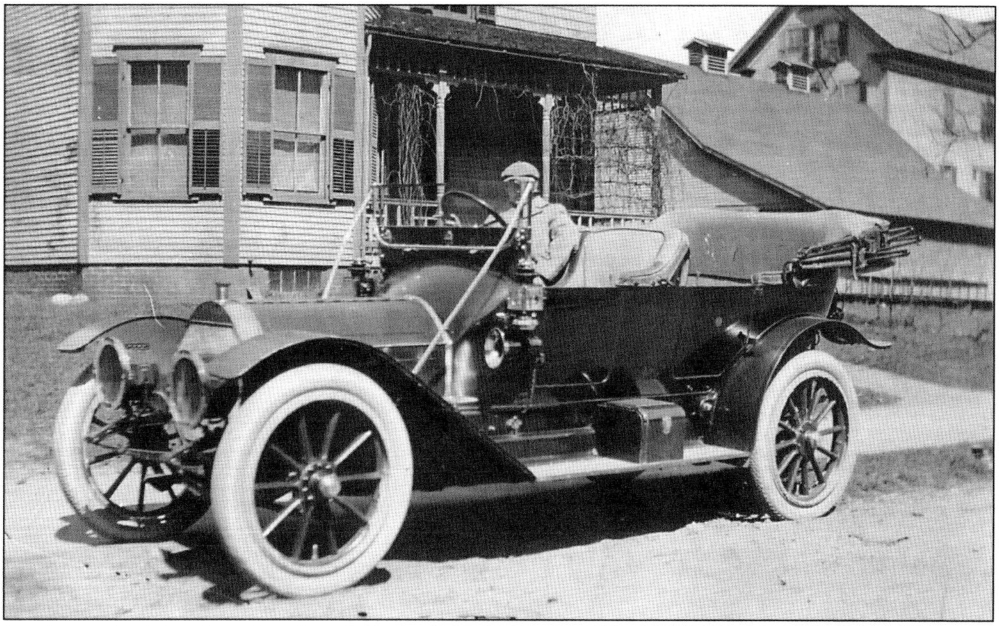

By the end of the first decade of the 20th century, America was in love with the automobile. And Woodstock, by then being an established resort community, undoubtedly saw some fine examples of the automaker's craft. This 1911 Pierce-Arrow, a car that cost in excess of $4,000 at a time when a Ford Model T could be had for only $780, was photographed in Woodstock Village at about that time.

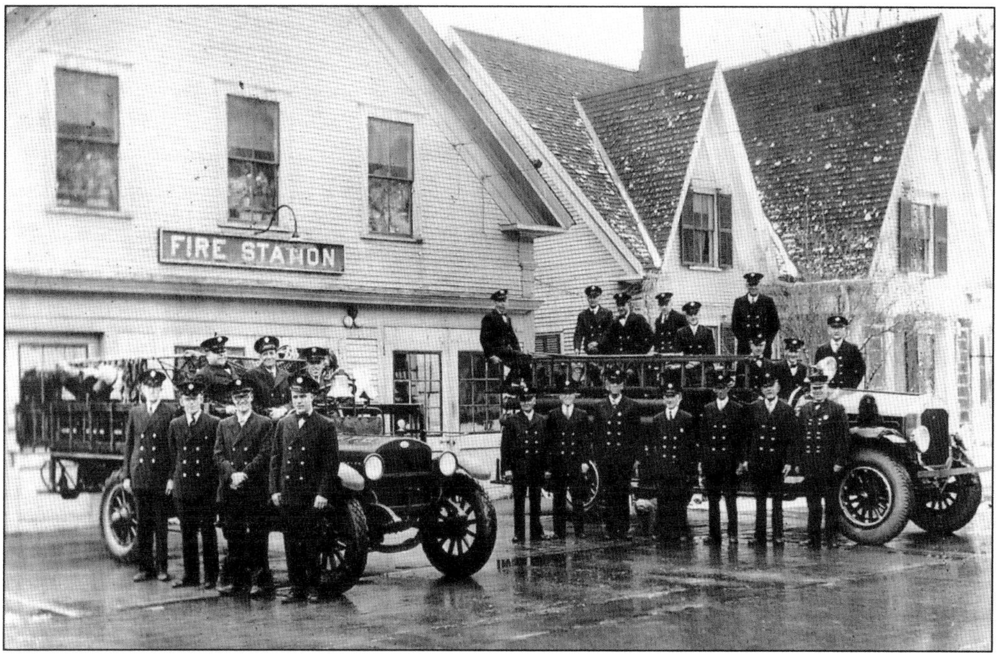

The mass production of trucks and automobiles in the 1920s also brought the availability of affordable motorized firefighting equipment. The Woodstock Fire Department is shown here with its REO Speed Wagon (left) and American LaFrance (right) fire trucks, both fine pieces of equipment in their day, in front of the fire station on Central Street, about 1928.

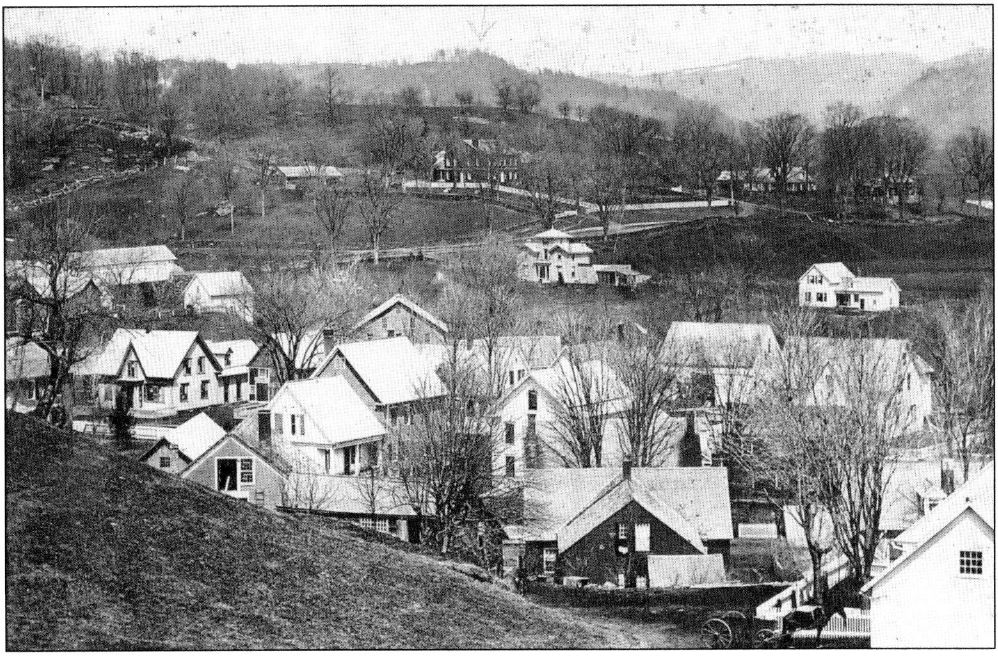

In 1806, Woodstock's first lawyer, Charles Marsh, constructed the impressive brick house shown in the upper center of this c. 1865 photograph. The house is facing toward the village and Elm Street. Marsh's son George Perkins Marsh was an accomplished man who, in 1864, wrote and had published *Man and Nature, Or, Physical Geography as Modified by Human Action*, one of the first very influential books concerning the natural environment.

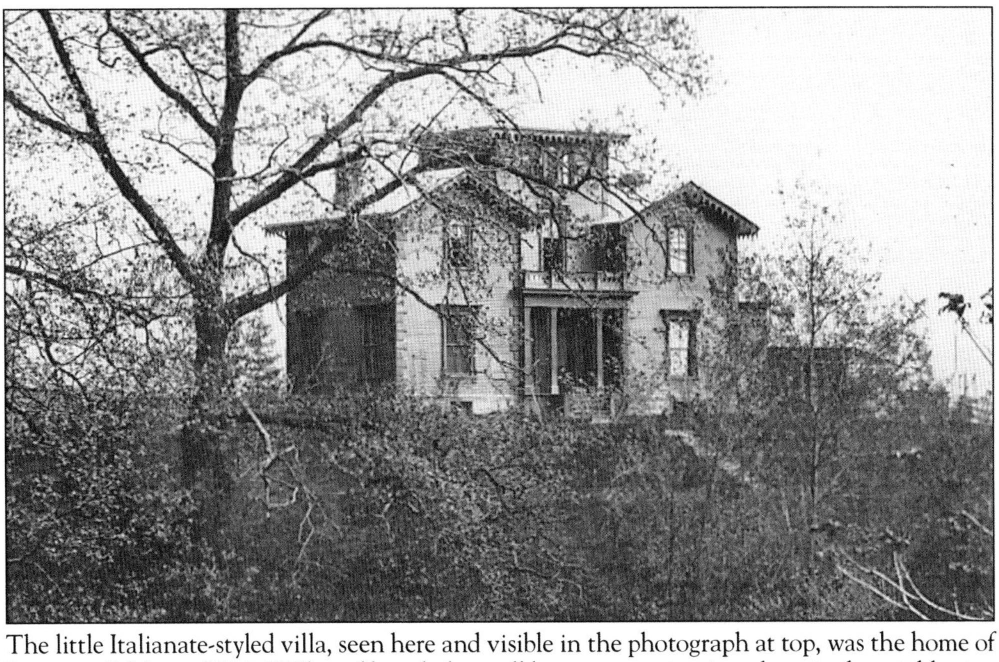

The little Italianate-styled villa, seen here and visible in the photograph at top, was the home of Benjamin F. Mason (1804–1871), a self-taught but well-known portrait painter born in the neighboring town of Pomfret. The architecturally engaging house, situated to look upon the Ottauquechee River, was erected in 1861 by Benjamin's brother Marshall, who was a fine regional carpenter.

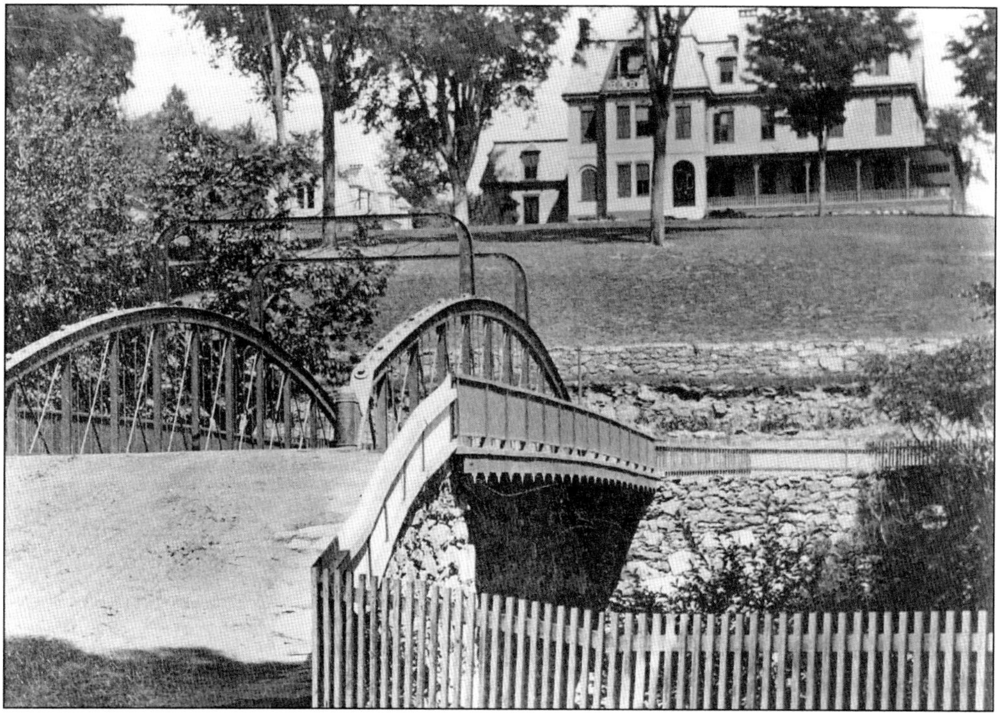

Frederick Billings (1823–1890), born in Royalton but raised in Woodstock, made his fortune in California practicing law and investing in western railroads. He returned to Woodstock and, in 1869, purchased the 270-acre Marsh estate. Soon thereafter, very substantial additions to and a remodeling of the old house were completed in the fashionable Second Empire, or French, style. In the foreground is the historic iron Elm Street Bridge.

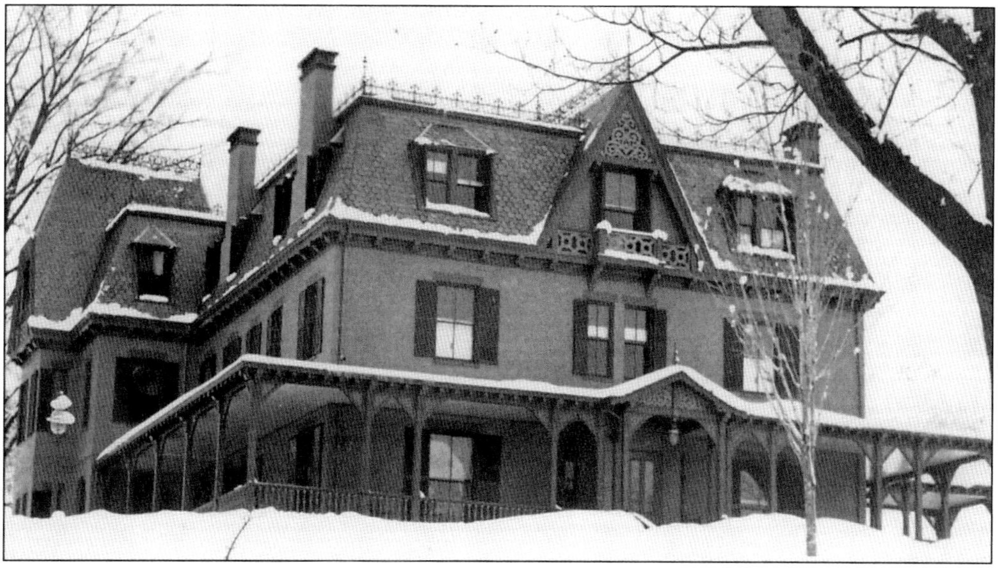

A close-up view of the Marsh-Billings house clearly shows the finely detailed remodeled and expanded home of Frederick Billings and his family. By this time, little of the original Marsh brick house constructed in 1806 remained recognizable. Undoubtedly, by the standards of the 1870s, this was as fine a residence as there then existed in the state of Vermont.

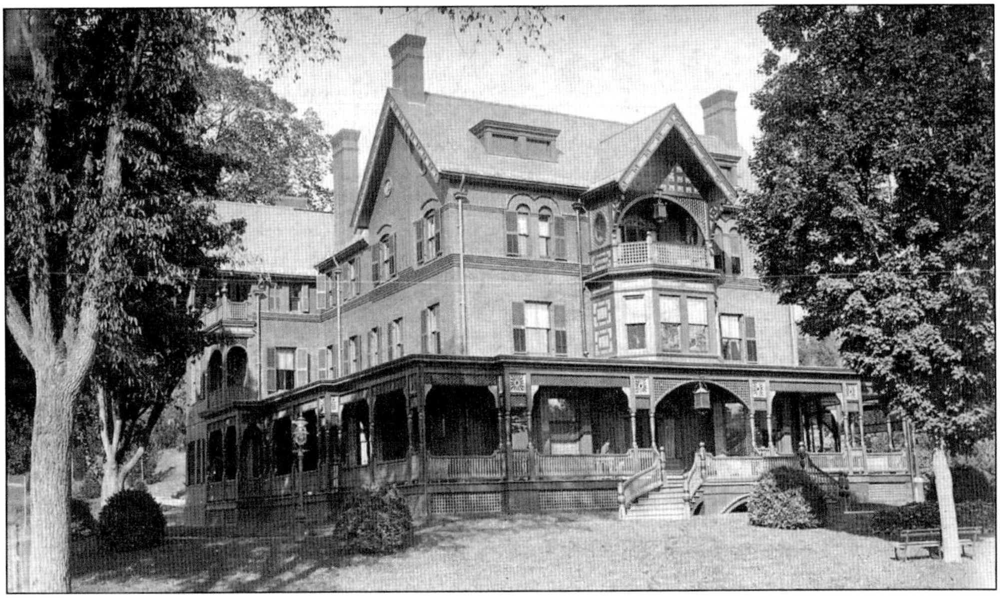

Even in retirement, Frederick Billing's wealth continued to grow, as did his home on the hill in Woodstock. In 1887, the house was again remodeled and expanded by New York architect Henry Hudson Holley, but this time, it was done in the so-called Queen Anne style of architecture. And by this time, the estate included extensive greenhouses and miles of beautifully landscaped carriage roads on Mount Tom.

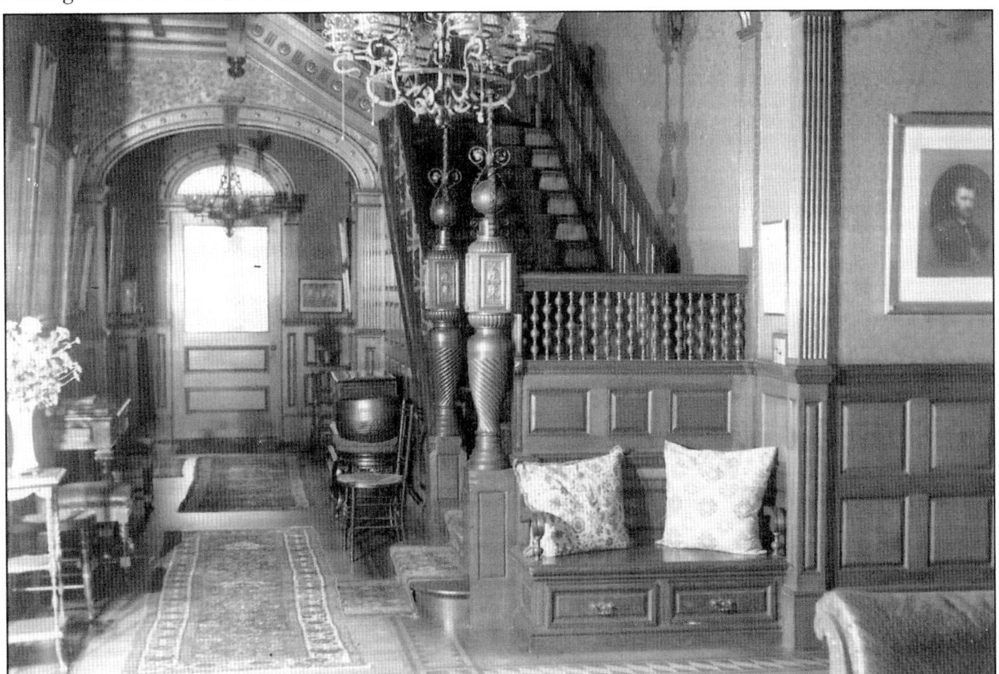

Here is how the front entry of the remodeled main house looked after its second remodeling in 1887 by Frederick Billings. By this time, Billings was in poor health. However, many family members and live-in help were in residence to oversee the extensive house and grounds, which also included a large farm across the road.

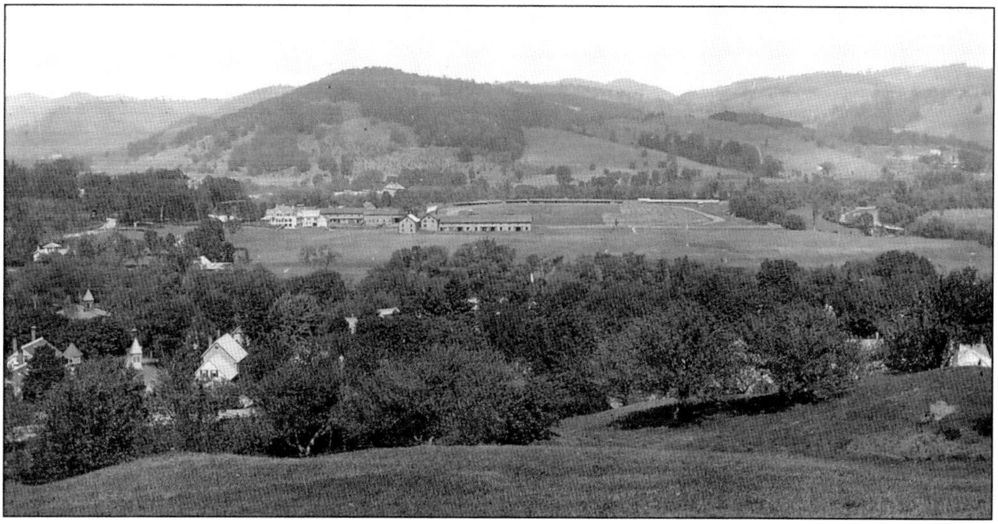

When Frederick Billings acquired the 270-acre Marsh estate in 1869 for $27,500, it included the farm and meadowlands spread out along the Ottauquechee River. Not included were adjacent lands of the Windsor County Agricultural Society (1846–1932), much to Billings continued frustration. This c. 1900 view looking north shows the Billings farm complex, and behind it are the fairground's buildings and racetrack.

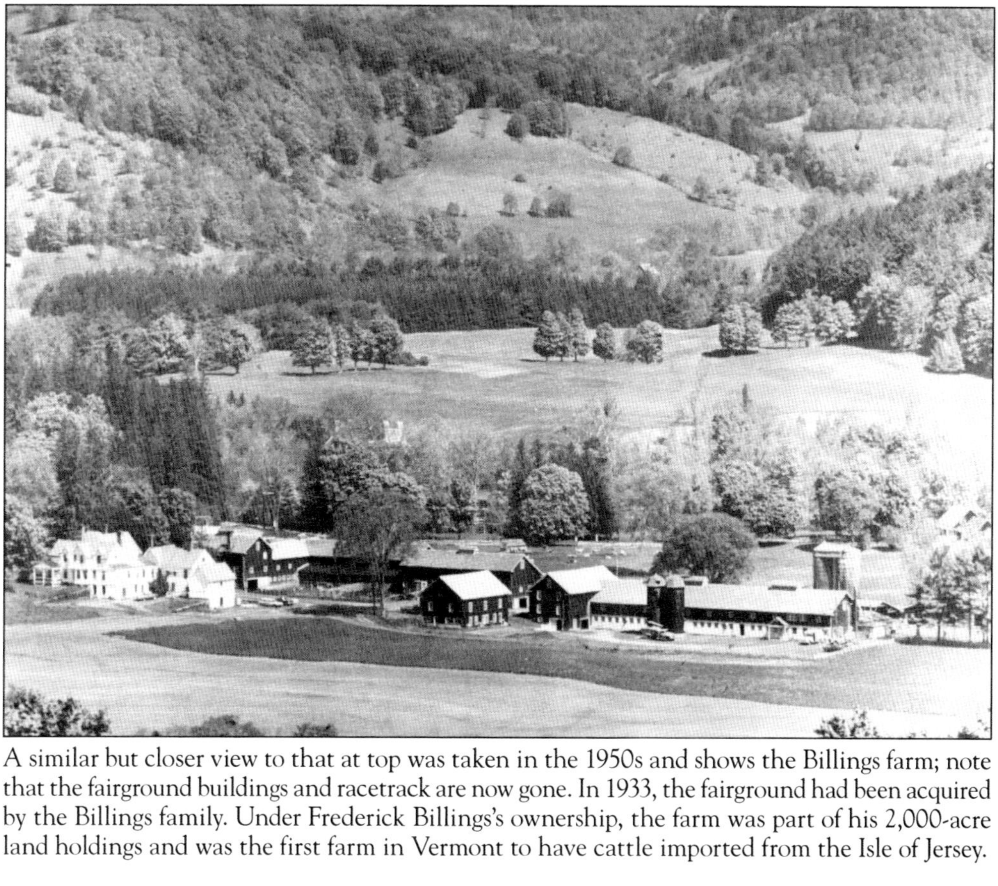

A similar but closer view to that at top was taken in the 1950s and shows the Billings farm; note that the fairground buildings and racetrack are now gone. In 1933, the fairground had been acquired by the Billings family. Under Frederick Billings's ownership, the farm was part of his 2,000-acre land holdings and was the first farm in Vermont to have cattle imported from the Isle of Jersey.

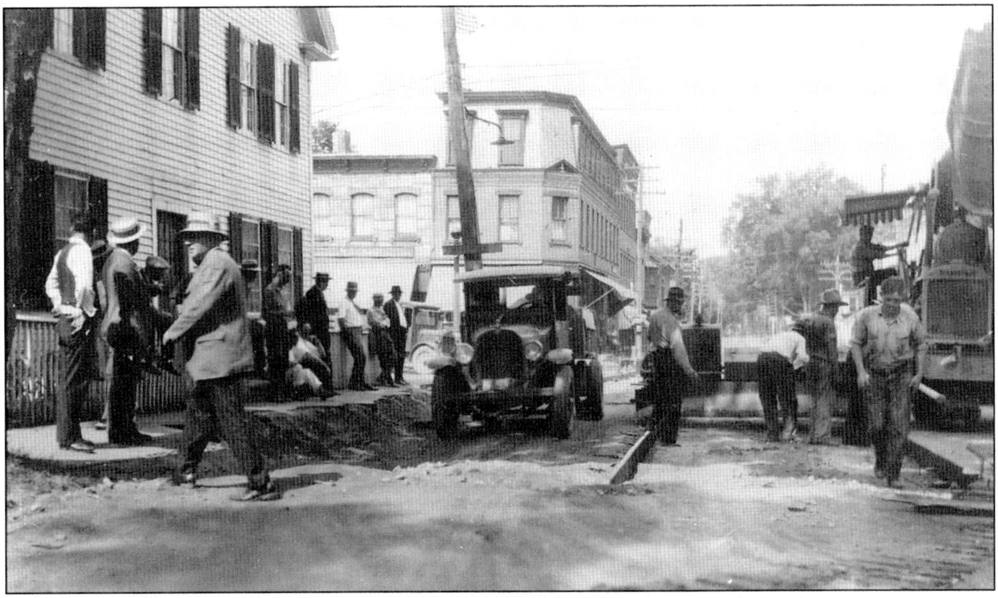

The first year that the federal government handed out money to the states for highway improvements was 1916, and in 1926, an integrated nationwide highway system was authorized. This created US Route 4, a 253-mile-long highway that passed through Woodstock as it crossed Vermont. As a result, additional money for improvements became available. Here, in the late 1920s, Central Street at the square is being paved.

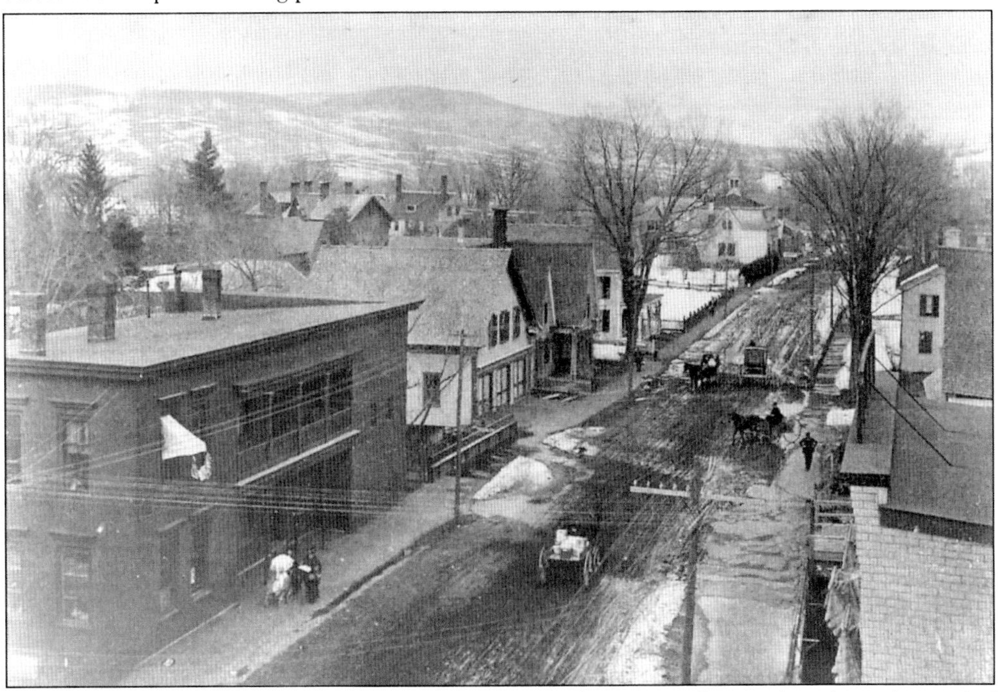

This turn-of-the-20th-century view looks down Central Street and was taken from the roof of the three-story Phoenix Block. To the far left is the Windsor County jailhouse, constructed in 1868. Beside it is the village's first firehouse, rebuilt as such in 1883. The jail, now the site of the post office, was razed in 1937.

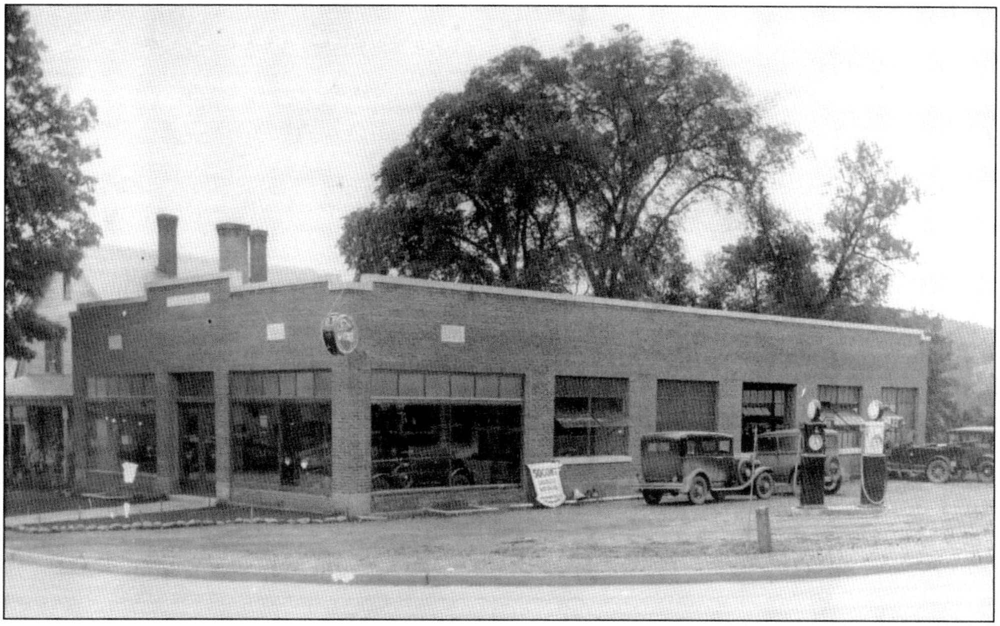

In 1922, when Ford automobile dealer F.A. Richmond, Inc., went into business, almost 60 percent of the cars on the nation's roads were Ford Model Ts, and being a Ford dealer was profitable indeed. In 1930, Richmond built this handsome new facility east of the village. The building has since been carefully repurposed and preserved and is today the convenience store Maplefields.

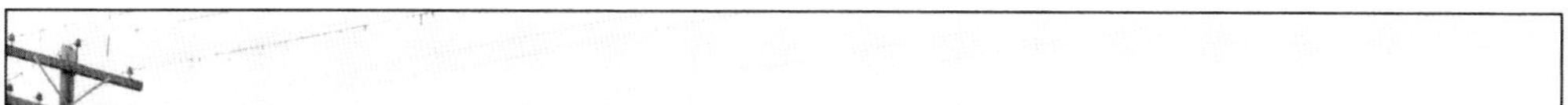

Emmett Racy and Gordon Colton opened their new Chevrolet dealership in 1952 in a building that is today the Woodstock police and fire station, shown here in 1955. In August 1957, Kenneth B. Gerrish and his son Kurt D. Gerrish purchased the premises, and until moving to Lebanon, New Hampshire, in March 1988, their business was known as Gerrish Motors—a successful multi-marque auto dealership.

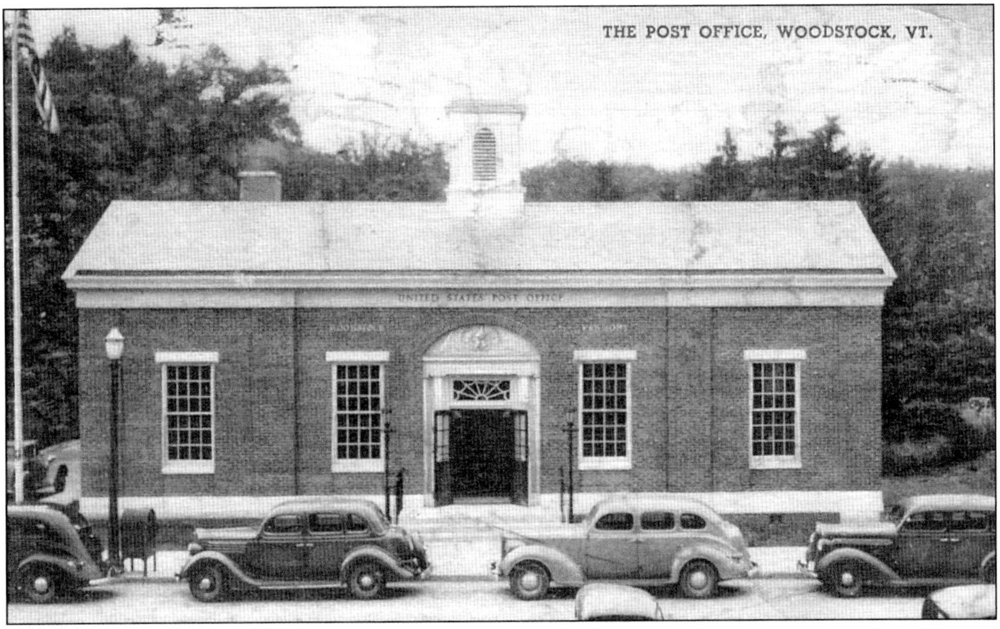

After a new county jail facility was constructed in 1937 east of the village, the old jailhouse was razed and a new post office building was constructed on the site. It was erected as part of a New Deal–era federal government project. In its lobby, it has a mural, *Cycle of Development of Woodstock*, that was painted by noted artist Bernadine Custer (1900–1991). The building was officially opened January 2, 1942.

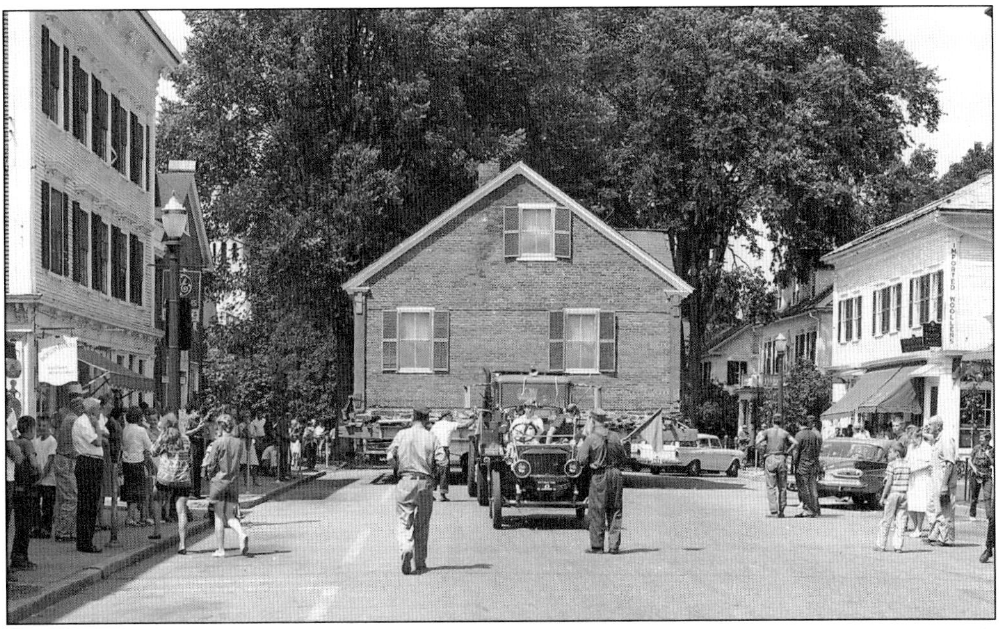

The construction of a new modern supermarket in 1961 threatened the existence of a small brick Cape-style house built in 1826. Therefore, on July 25, 1961, the house was moved from 37 Pleasant Street to a new site on the southerly side of the green, where the Methodist church had formerly stood. Paul Bourdon is leading the house-moving parade through the village in his antique Stanley Steamer.

Four

Courts, Churches, Schools, and Libraries

By 1786, the boundaries and towns that make up Windsor County had been agreed upon. That same year, the Vermont General Assembly appointed Woodstock as the shire town of the county and directed that a jail and courthouse be constructed accordingly. Both a jail and a separate courthouse came to be constructed by 1788. Thus, Woodstock became the center of county government and saw the arrival of the earliest judges and lawyers in town. As much as 15 years earlier, Woodstock had held its first town meeting whereby local town government was established.

As early as 1776, the towns of Hartford, Pomfret, and Woodstock agreed to equally share the first preacher in the area, a Congregational minister, and by 1781, Woodstock had organized its own Congregational church and erected a meetinghouse made of logs. At about this same time, other denominations began to gather in Woodstock, first Baptists, then Universalists, and by the end of the 18th century, Methodists and others followed.

At the 1779 annual Woodstock town meeting, it was voted to divide the town into five school districts for the benefit of schooling. Eventually, the town would be divided into 18 school districts in all. At the 1782 town meeting, it was voted for the first time to tax land to raise revenue to construct school buildings. Also in 1782, it was voted to erect the first schoolhouse near the center of town. Over the many following decades, individual schoolhouses were opened and typically staffed with single teachers handling multiple grades and ages of youngsters.

The first two men to enter in and occupy the lands that became Woodstock were reputed to have been great readers—although they probably did not bring books with them at that time. With Woodstock being chosen as a county shire town, and in turn becoming a place for learned men such as lawyers and judges, it stands to reason that books and small personal libraries soon followed. The first public library opened in South Woodstock on January 26, 1797.

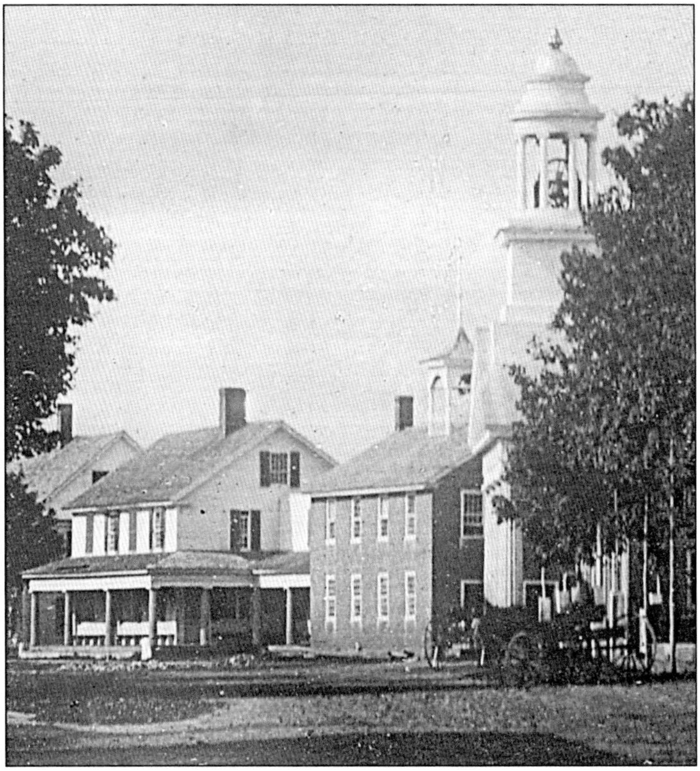

Taken prior to 1854, this image, with a view looking toward the green from the square, is believed to be the earliest known photograph of Woodstock. To the right is the white belfry of the Windsor County Courthouse, erected in 1797 on the north side of the green—the second such courthouse structure. It was remodeled in 1836 and burned down on July 4, 1854. Beside it is the brick village schoolhouse constructed in 1812.

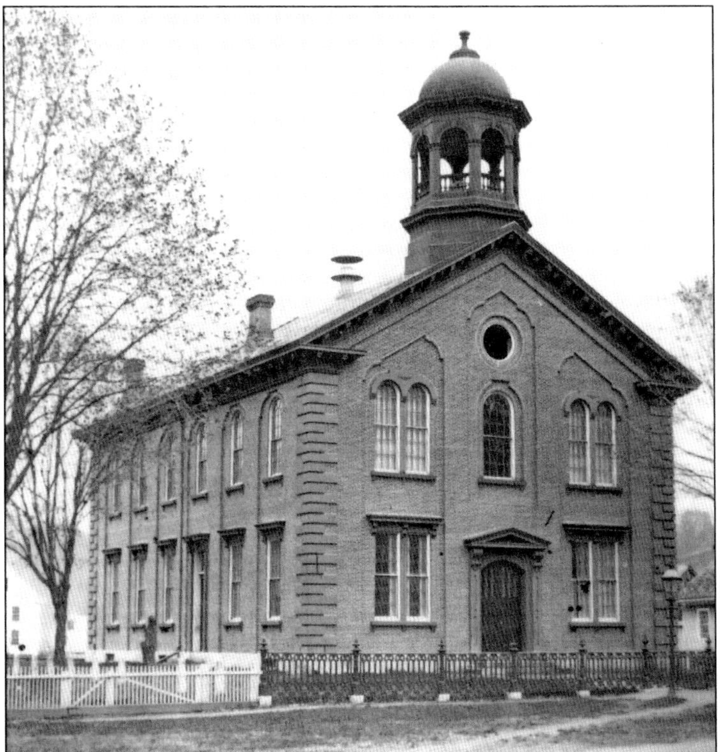

Following the destruction of the county courthouse in 1854, the county set about purchasing land on the south side of the green and, that same year, constructed this impressive new facility. Designed in the then very fashionable Italianate style, the new courthouse cost an equally impressive amount of $14,000 upon completion in 1855. The building still stands beside the Woodstock Inn.

For many years, Woodstock used the county courthouse as a town hall, but in 1899, it constructed its own facility. Designed by architect Arthur H. Smith of Rutland in a Neocolonial style, with an opera house on the second floor, the impressive new building was constructed by John F. Germain, also of Rutland, and cost $20,000. The 400-person capacity opera house had both a stage and a balcony.

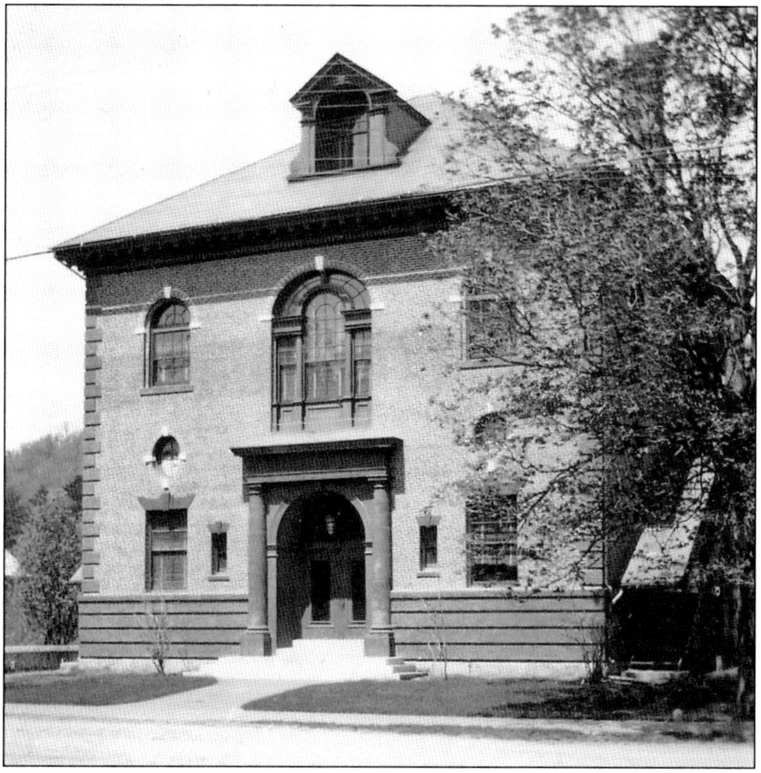

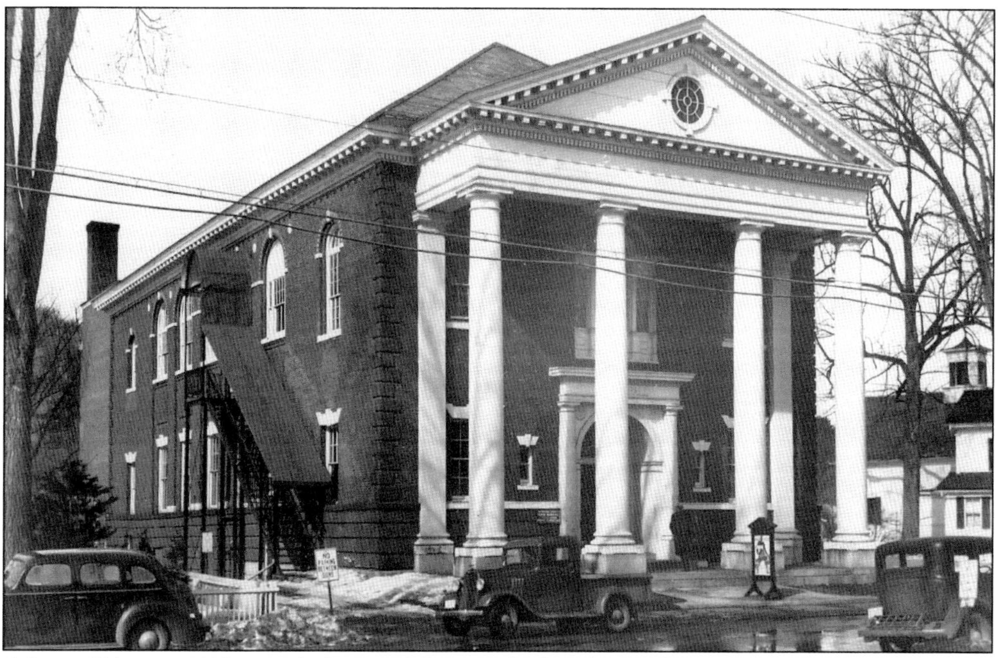

A fire in February 1927 severely damaged the town hall and opera house. After much heated debate, it was decided to rebuild the structure in a more favorable Colonial Revival style of architecture, at a cost of $50,000. Adding a large tower to the building was briefly considered. The building was reopened with a gala on July 17, 1928.

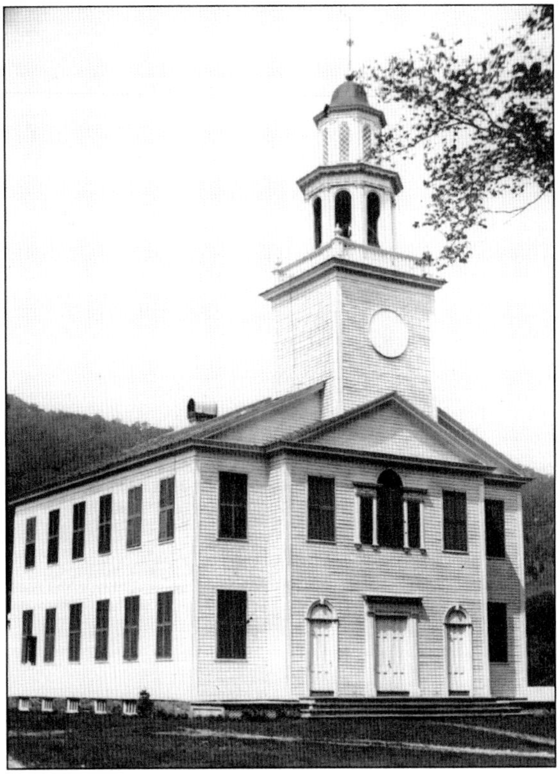

By the early 1780s, Woodstock had organized its first Congregational church; however, this finely designed meetinghouse was not completed until 1808. Situated on land given by Charles Marsh on the west side of Elm Street, the heavy timber frame was raised by Nathaniel Smith, the builder, on July 4, 1806. For years, the building was called the "White Meetinghouse," or simply as "Old White."

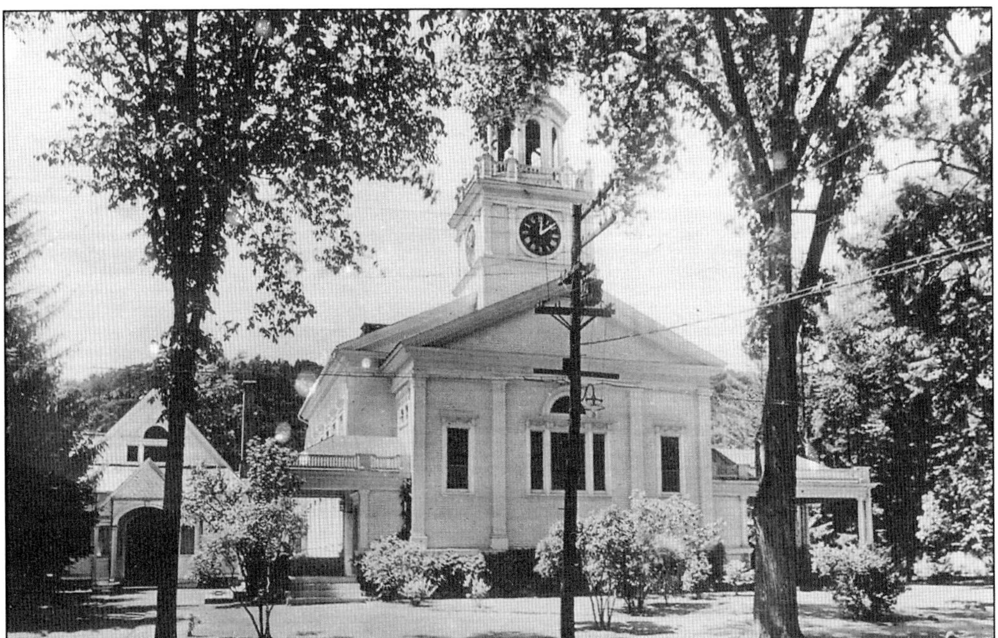

A chapel designed by noted New York architect Henry Hudson Holly was added to the south side of the church in 1880. Nine years later, the austere classic lines of the original meetinghouse were transformed because of the generosity of parishioner Frederick Billings, whose mansion was at the head of Elm Street and looked down upon the church to the south.

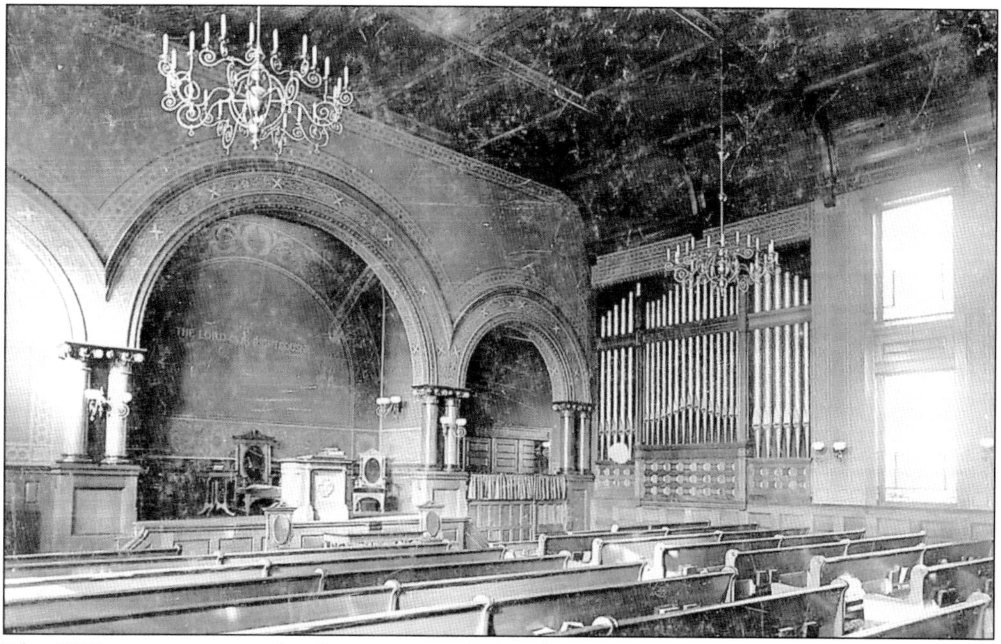

The 1889 renovations to the Congregational church were not limited to just the exterior. The interior was completely remodeled in the heavy Romanesque Revival style that was then popular for church architecture and other public buildings. This was one of Frederick Billings's last generous gifts, and he carefully supervised the work before passing away in September the following year at age 67.

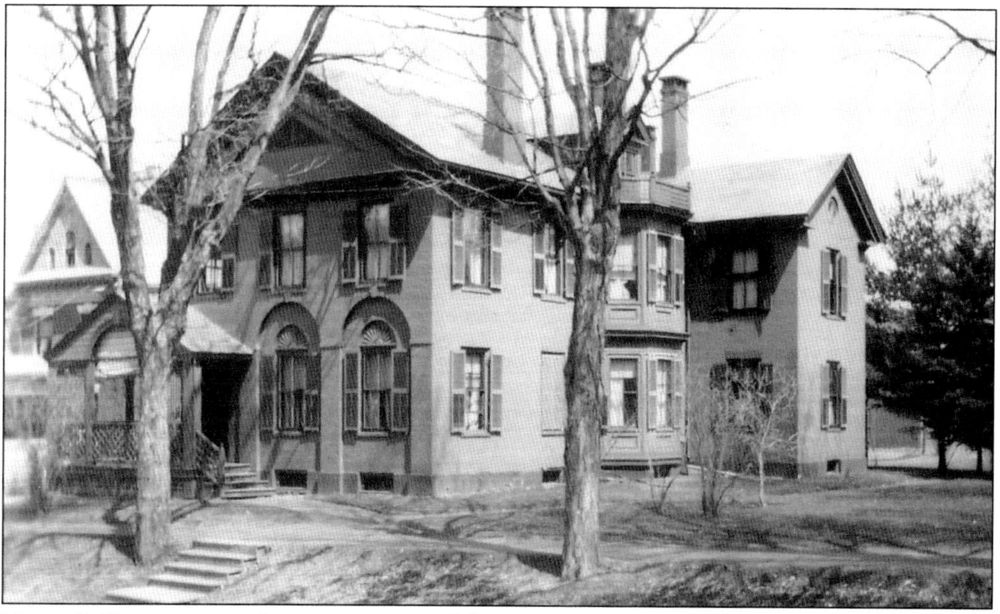

Henry B. Dana oversaw the construction of the parsonage at the Congregational church; it was finished and occupied in November 1829 and still stands and is used as such at 41 Elm Street. In 1882, Frederick Billings gifted the church $15,000 that was spent on renovating the house, barns, and grounds. Note the Victorian-era embellishments in this c. 1890 view of the former Federal-period house.

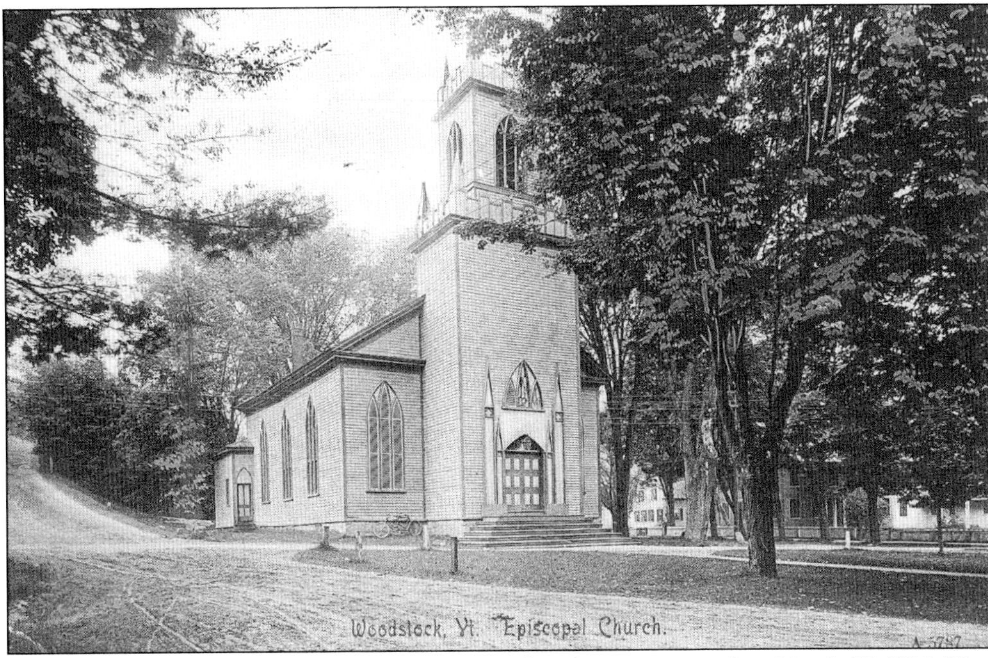

The parish of St. James Episcopal Church in Woodstock was organized on March 27, 1826. That October, church leaders proposed the "building of a Church 46 by 62 feet: The walls to be made of stone, 25 feet high" at the west end of the green. Costs dictated that wood construction be used, and the building was completed for church services on Christmas Eve, December 24, 1827.

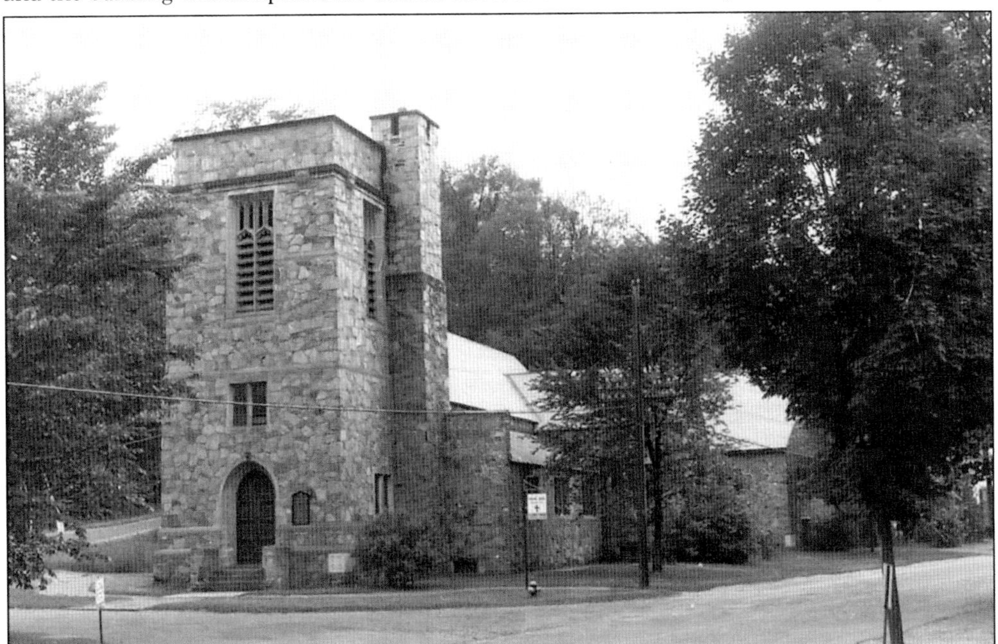

Eighty years later, in 1907, St. James Episcopal Church finally had the stone building that it originally desired. The old wood-frame building was razed, and during 1907–1908, a new stone Gothic Revival–style building took its place, complete with a parish house wing that the old facility never had. The massive stone tower was set to majestically face the green.

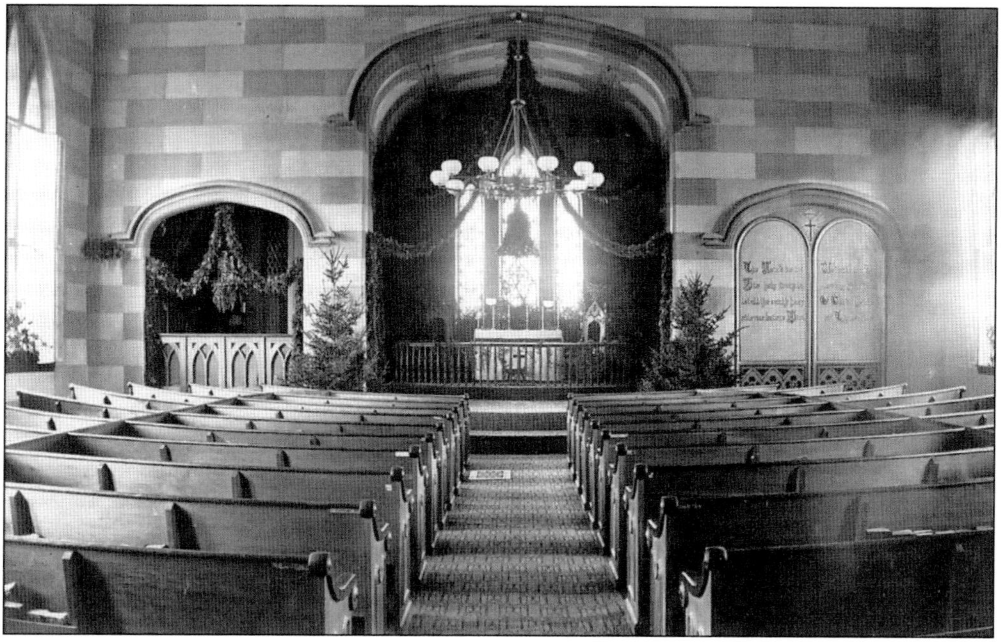

The new St. James Episcopal Church was designed by the noted Boston, Massachusetts, architectural firm of Cram, Goodhue & Ferguson, a leader in the Arts and Crafts movement in architecture then popular in New England and beyond. This building is certainly a masterpiece of both that firm and the period.

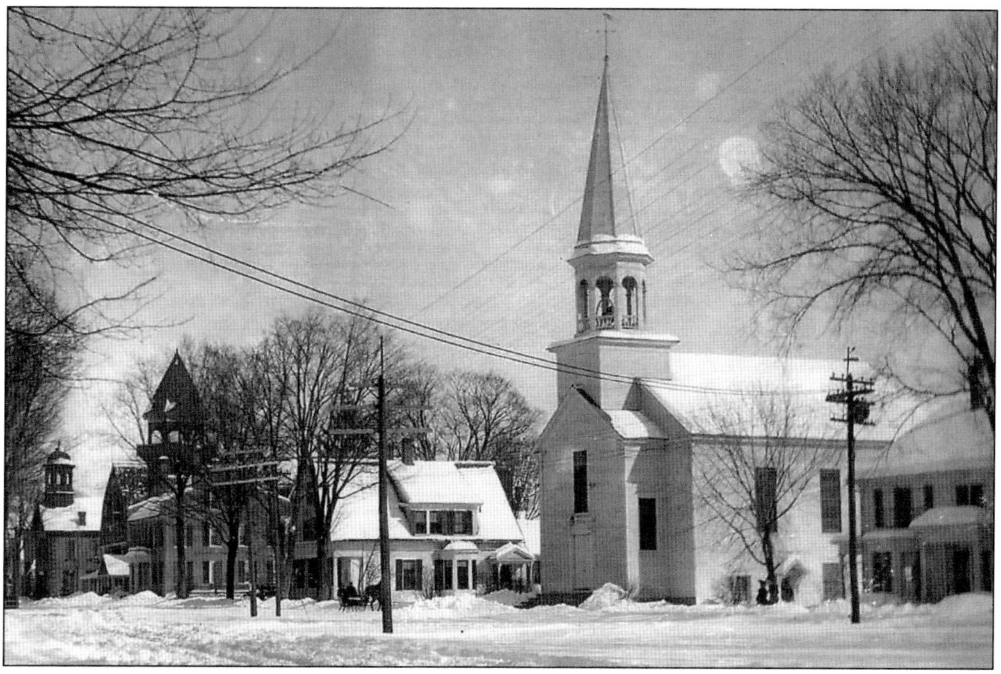

Methodism was brought to Woodstock as early as 1797, and in 1807, the first Methodist church building was erected outside the village area. In 1836, members of the church erected this building, which was extensively renovated in 1865, on the south side of the green. Last used as a Methodist church in 1936, the building then became a movie theater until it was razed in 1961.

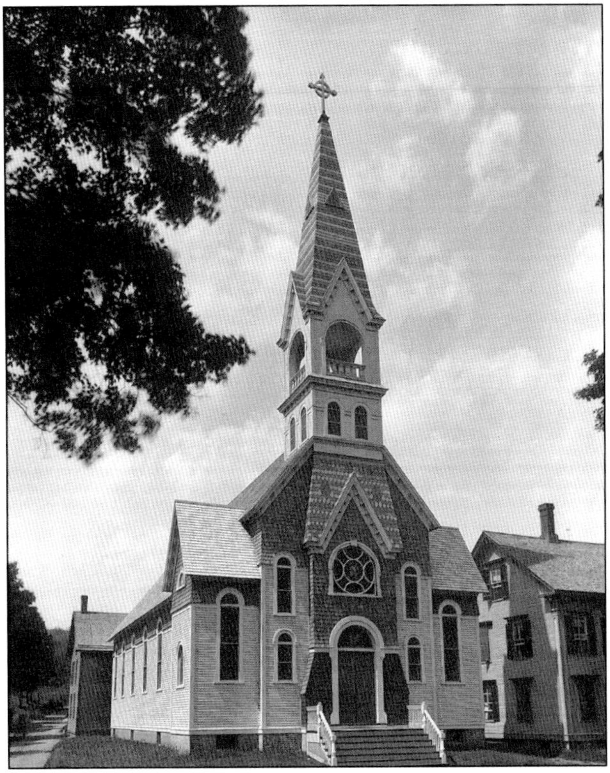

Our Lady of the Snow Roman Catholic Church erected its first building on South Street in 1899. Designed by George Guernsey of Montpelier, who had been the general contractor for the Norman Williams Public Library in 1885, the new building cost $8,000 and was dedicated and placed into service on October 18, 1899. The wood-frame building was highly decorated with varying patterns of shingles and eclectic architectural features.

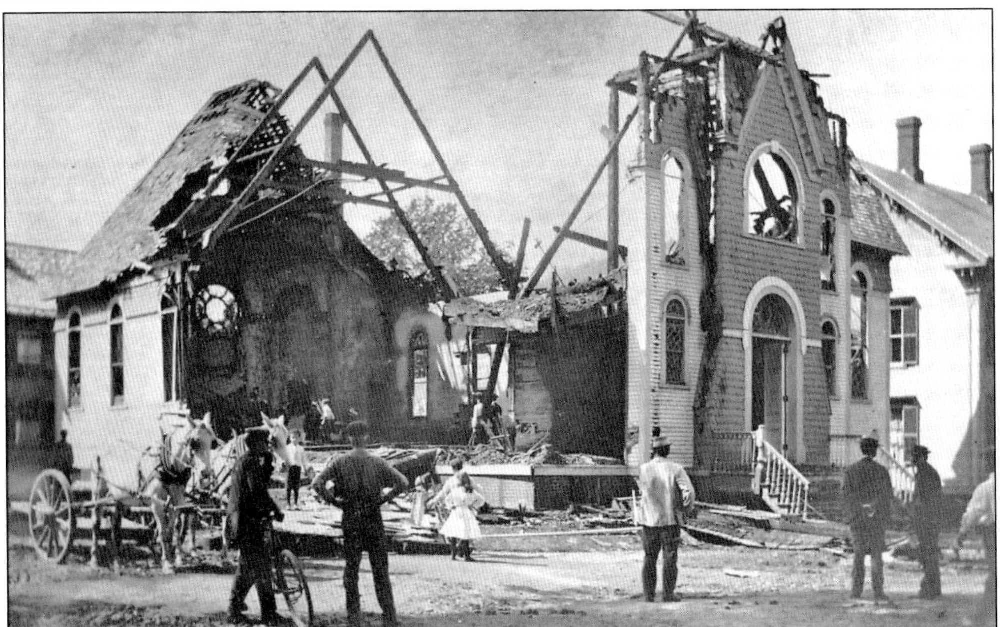

Fifteen minutes after evening confirmation on September 1, 1903, the four-year-old building was aflame with devastating consequences. Quickly consumed by fire, the spire and bell collapsed, and the building was a total loss. The Woodstock Village Fire Department tried to save what it could. Seen here, parishioners and a team of horses are looking over the ruins the following day.

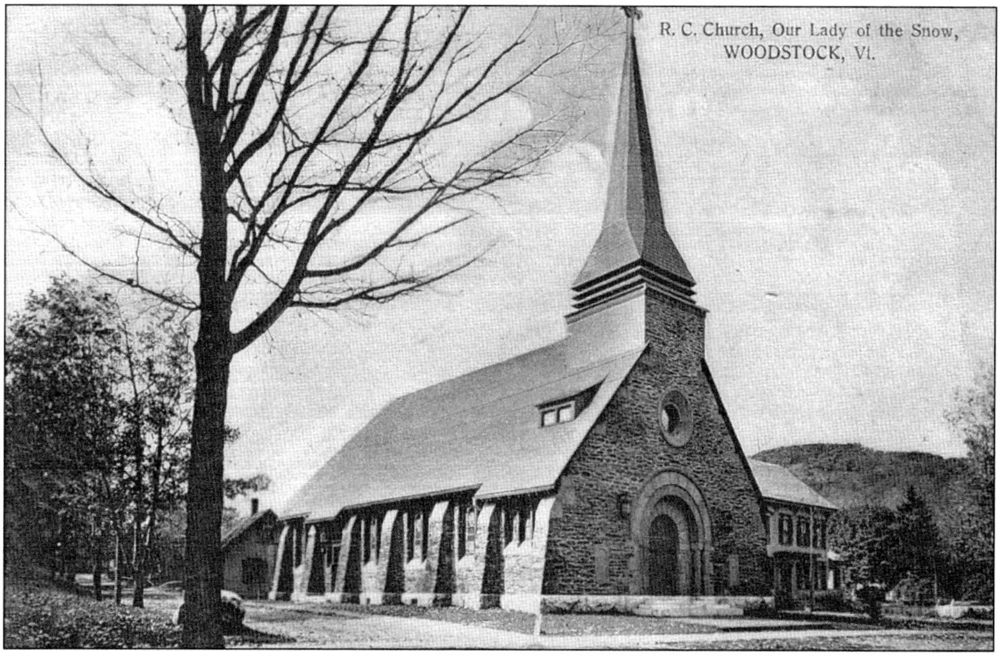

The parishioners of Our Lady of the Snow regrouped, and on the site of the destroyed building, they constructed this superbly designed new stone facility. Construction began during the last week of May 1904, and the first church service was held in the new building on Christmas Eve of that same year.

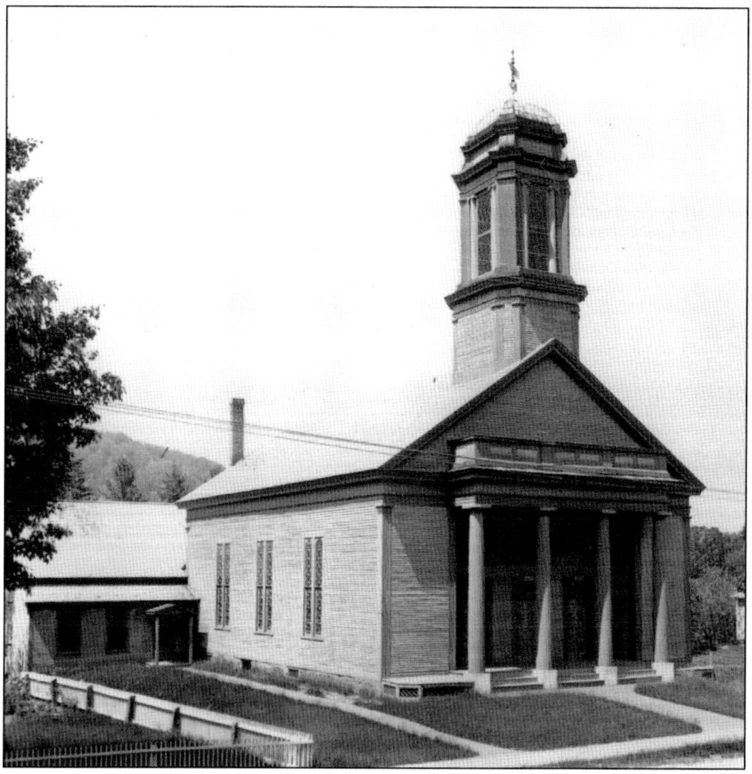

Having broken away from the Congregational Church, a Universalist Society was established in Woodstock by about 1786. For almost the next 50 years, the society experienced many up and downs until 1834, when new leadership formed the North Universalist Chapel Society. The following year, the newly formed society erected this handsome facility, which still stands on Church Street, and dedicated it in November 1835.

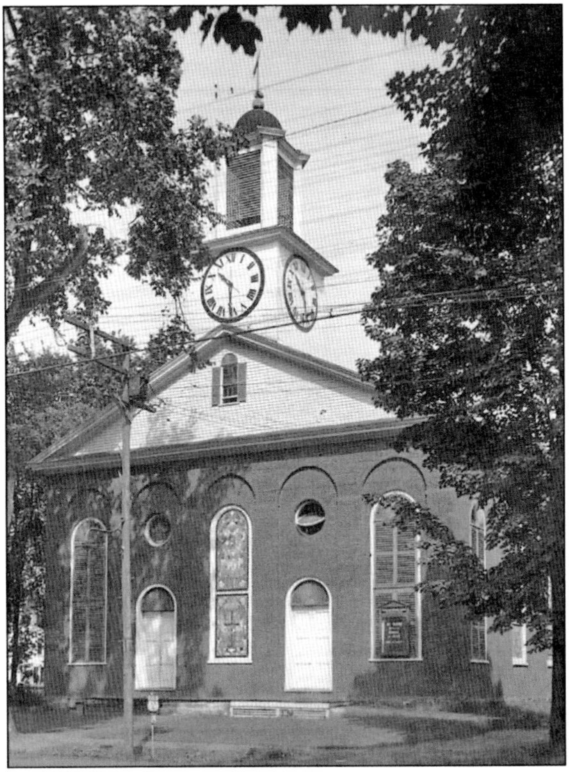

The earliest notice in town of the first Christian Society church was in 1806, about the time of the breakup of the Baptist church. The church had no permanent home until 1825, when land was purchased on Pleasant Street. The following year, the magnificent brick building pictured here was constructed. The "meetinghouse for the Christian Society" was dedicated in January 1837 and is a Masonic temple today.

What is often referred to as South Chapel was originally constructed as a facility for the so-called South Parish of Universalists, who had organized in South Woodstock. Erected in 1839, this impressively designed Greek Revival–style meetinghouse was restored by the Community Church in 1957. Marshall Mason designed the facade, belfry, and interior gallery. Today, the building is part of the South Woodstock Village Historic District.

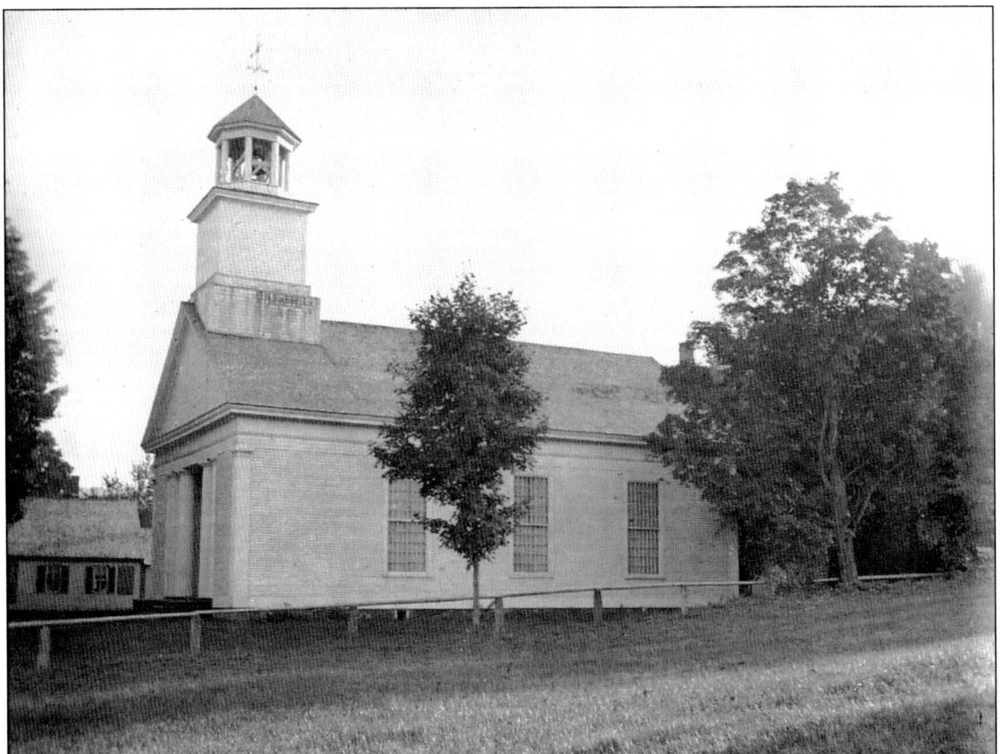

The Green Mountain Liberal Institute, located in South Woodstock, was organized in 1848 by a group of Universalist ministers and laymen, with a strong curriculum that included the arts, astronomy, and the classics. In 1848, this fine and architecturally important example of an academy building was erected and served as such until closed in 1898. Today, the building is beautifully preserved and open to the public during summer months.

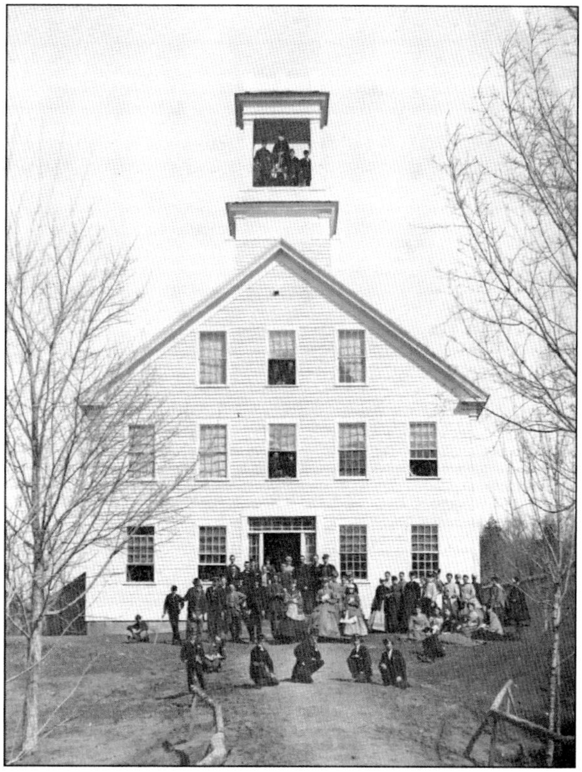

This interesting village schoolhouse building located in South Woodstock was erected in 1906. The building is considered a good period example of the so-called Queen Anne style of architecture interpreted vernacularly. Elements of clapboards, shingles, round-headed louvers, brackets, and a tower are all part of the overall building design, as illustrated in this c. 1910 view.

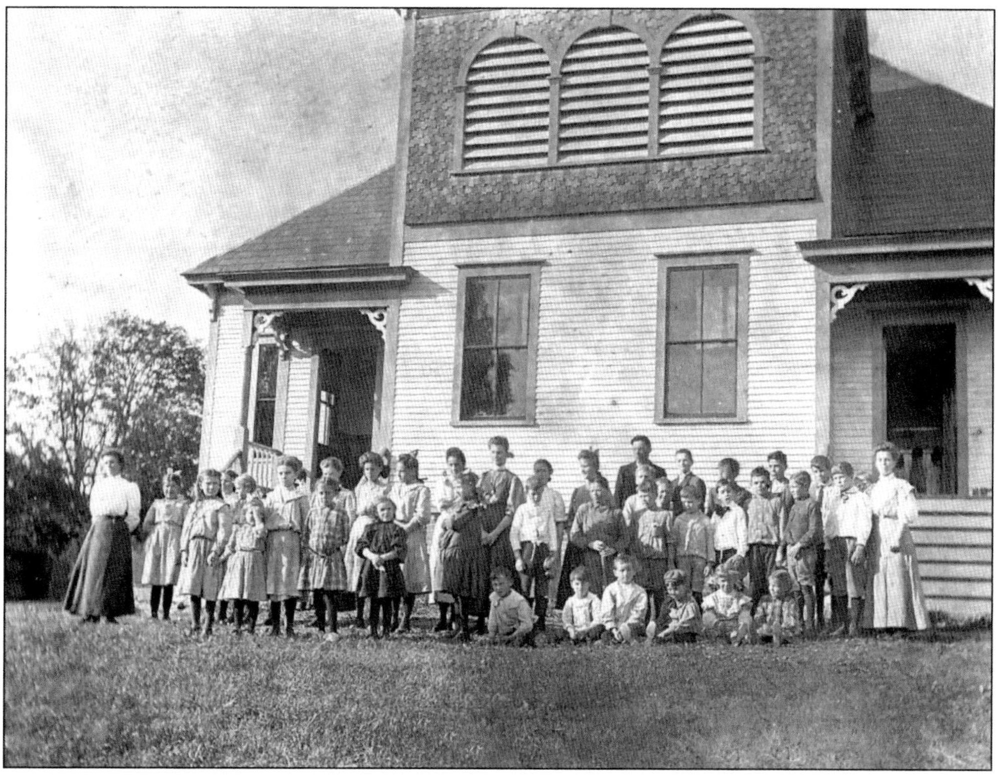

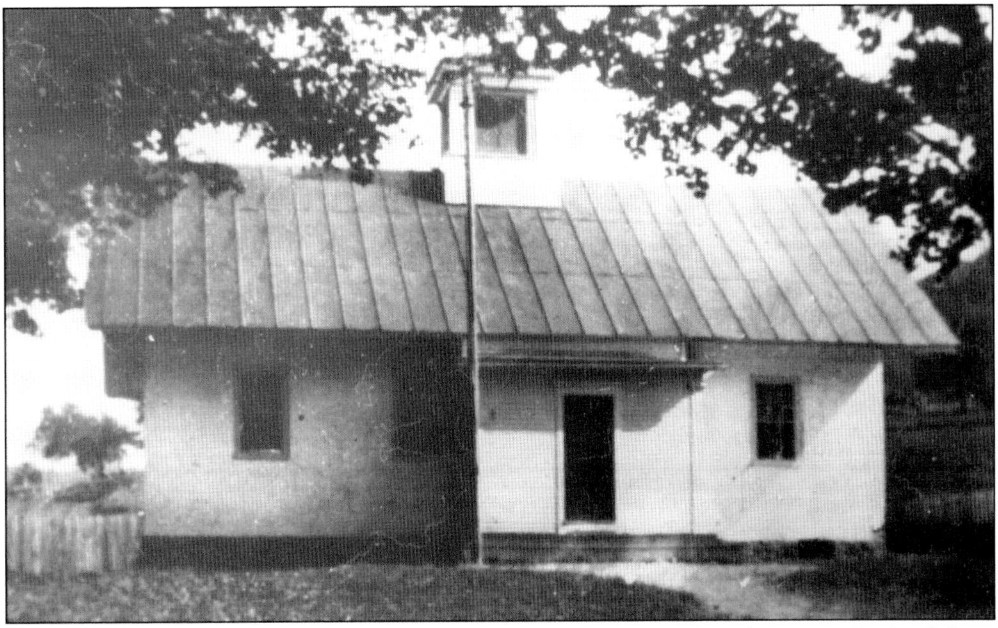

The greatest number of school districts at any one time in Woodstock was 18. Each of these districts once had its own schoolhouse—some were just one room and some had two or more rooms. Similarly, some of these schoolhouses were of wood construction, and some, like the one shown here in District No. 7 in Taftsville, were of brick construction, painted white, with two rooms inside.

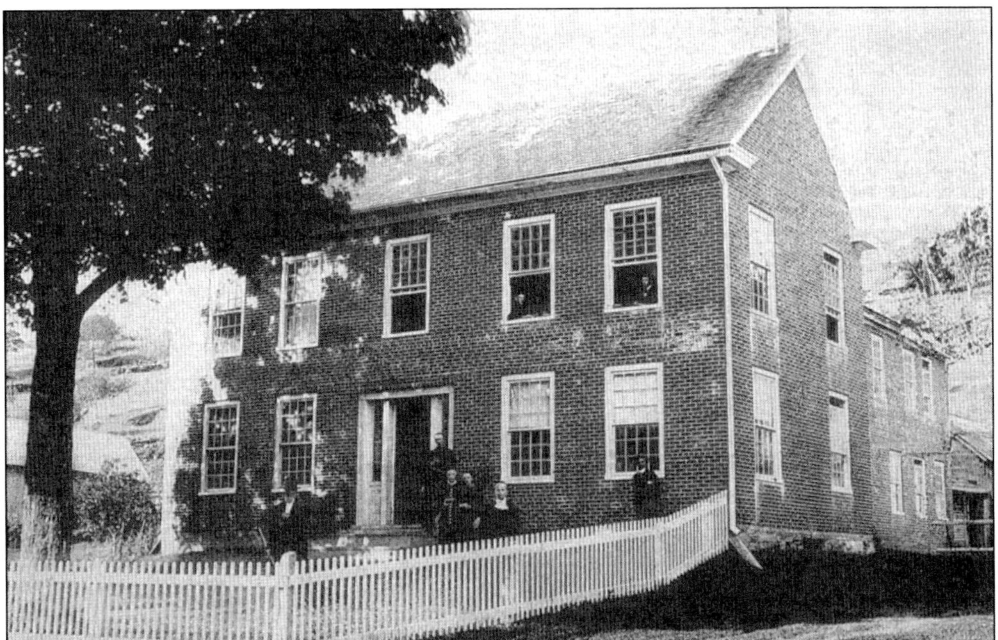

One of the very unique aspects of Woodstock during the 19th century was the number of private schools located within the town. Henry Swan Dana's 1889 history of Woodstock details at least 11 such institutions, and there were others, all offering high-quality education to locals and youth from away. This is one of those such schools; however, the author is not sure which one.

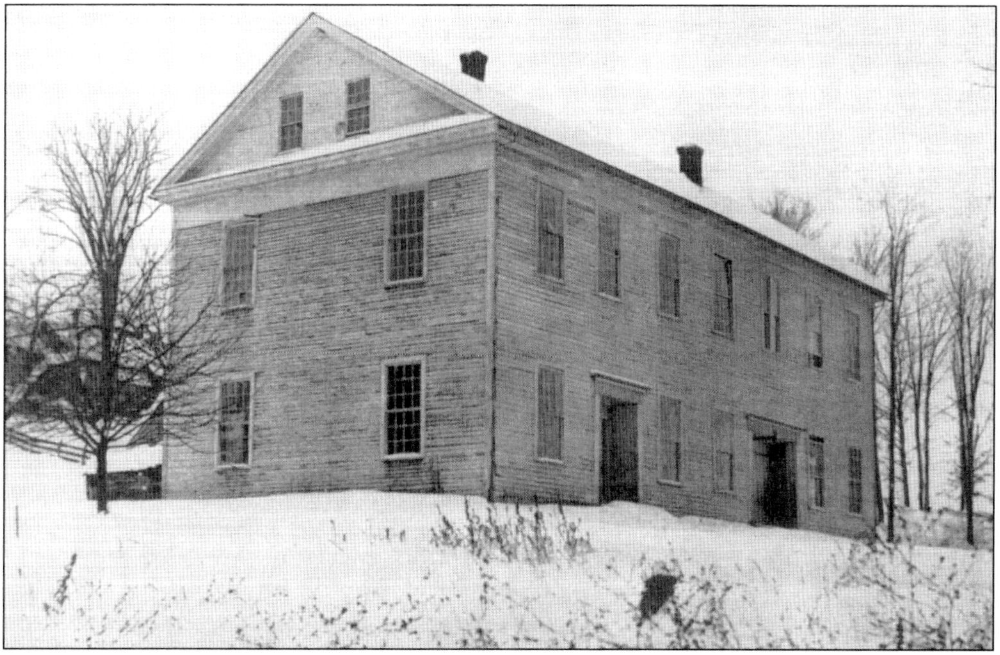

An act of the state legislature in 1827 created the Clinical School of Medicine and the Vermont Medical College in Woodstock. This spacious seven-room building was completed in 1839, and the college, with some amount of difficulty, operated here until 1856. By 1862, the property located on College Hill at the edge of the village had been sold, and about 1913, the building was razed.

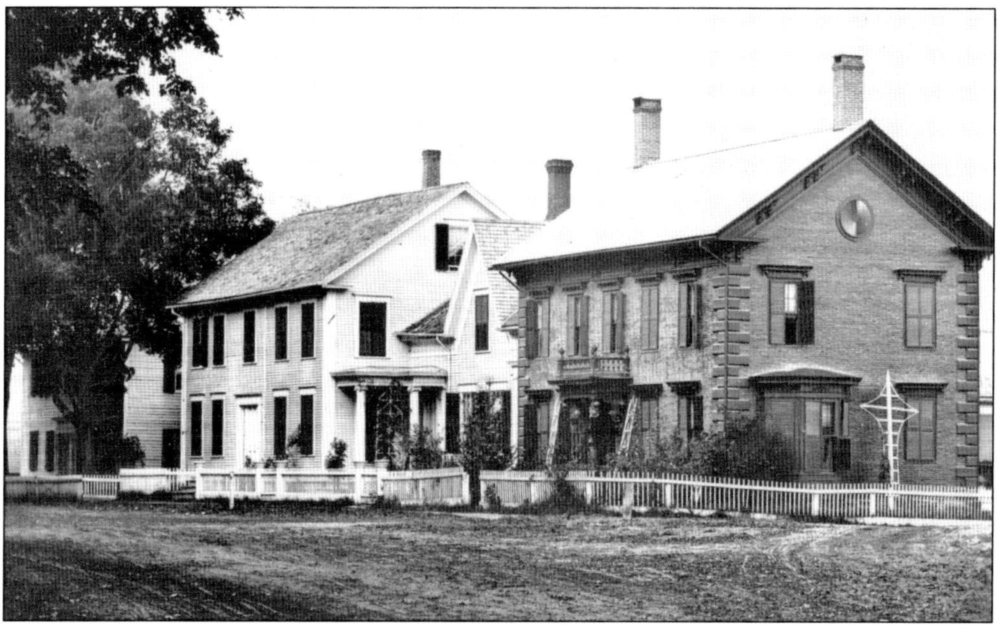

The brick building to the right of this late-19th-century image was originally constructed at a cost of $1,210.79 in 1812 as a simple unadorned schoolhouse, facing the north side of the green. After no longer serving as a school, the building was fully made over with Italianate decorative elements. The building still stands facing the green at the corner of Mountain Avenue and North Park Street.

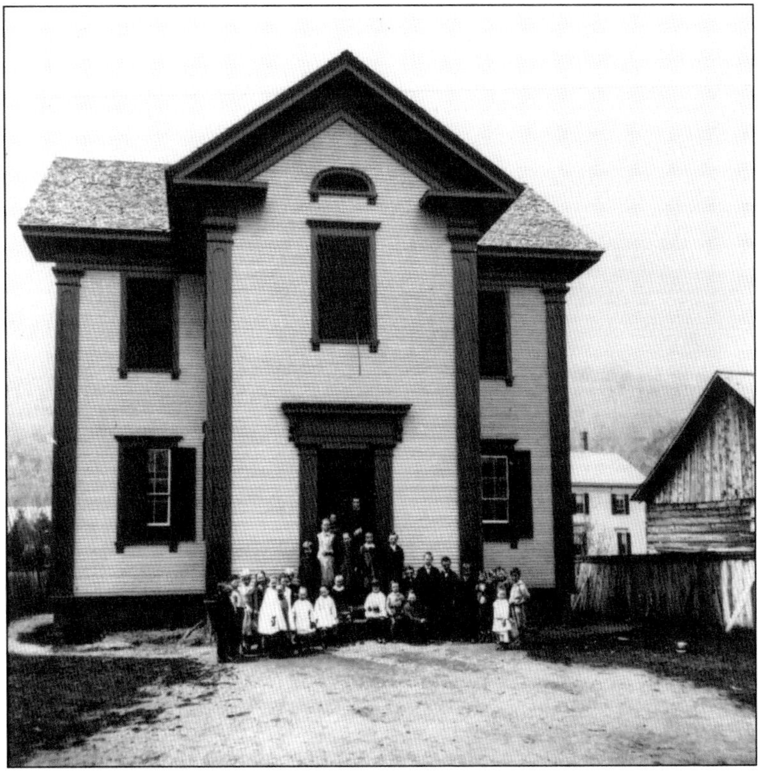

Throughout the 19th century, as both the overall town and village areas of Woodstock became more densely settled, the number of individual school districts with their own schoolhouses continued to grow. Within the Woodstock Village area, increasing growth continued to put pressure on the public school system, and that, in turn, caused this building, the River Street District School, to be erected in 1867. The building was last used about 1903.

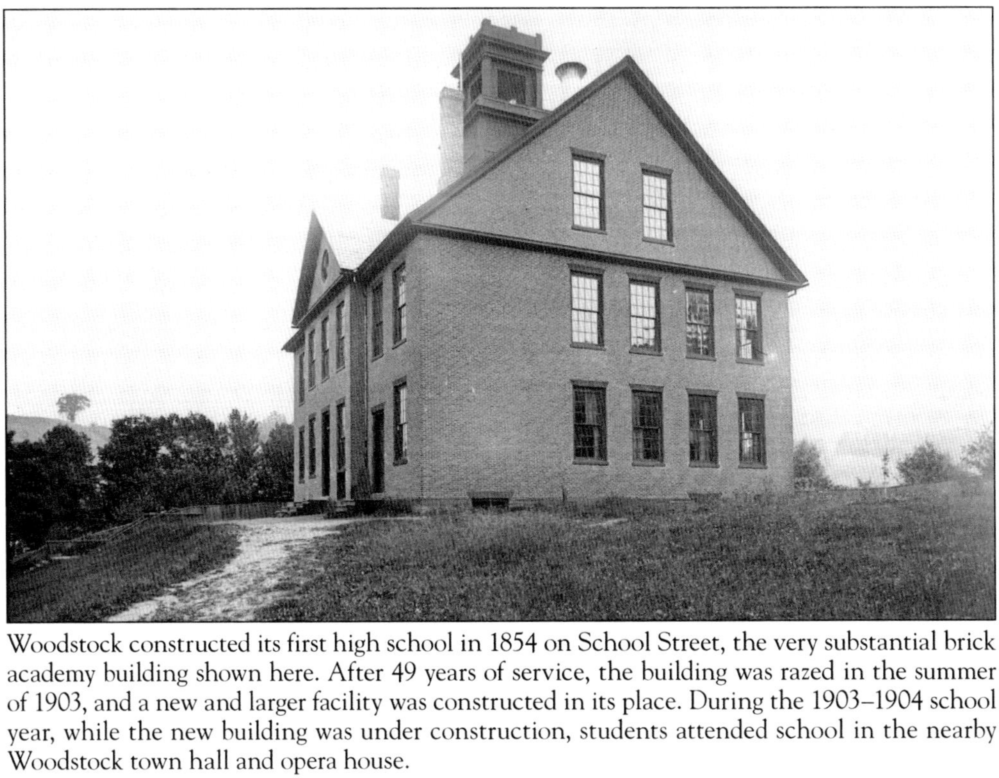

Woodstock constructed its first high school in 1854 on School Street, the very substantial brick academy building shown here. After 49 years of service, the building was razed in the summer of 1903, and a new and larger facility was constructed in its place. During the 1903–1904 school year, while the new building was under construction, students attended school in the nearby Woodstock town hall and opera house.

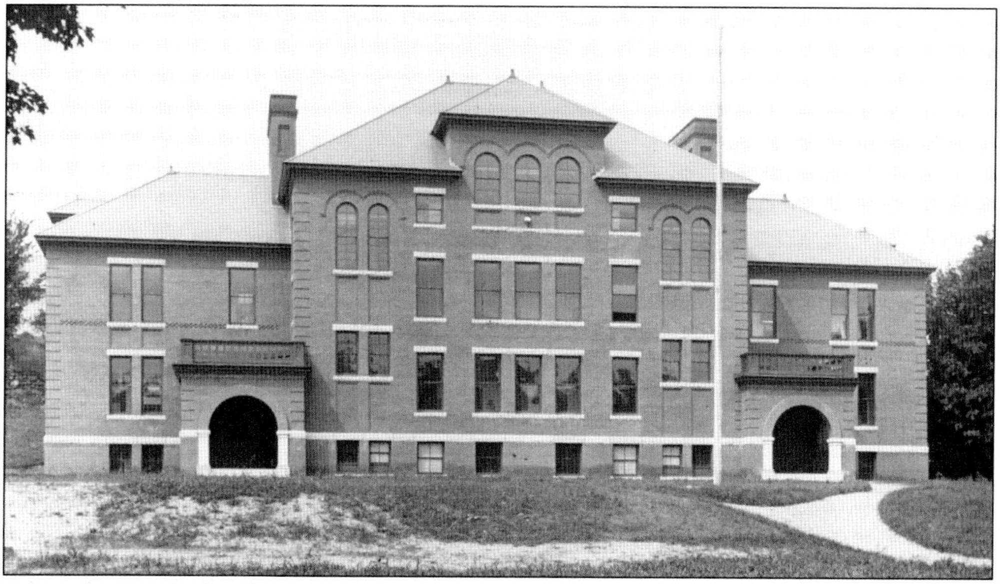

When the new high school opened in 1905, it also, for a time, served the needs of the grade school. A state-of-the-art facility in its day, the new building cost $35,000—a very substantial sum of money at that time. By the mid-1970s, this building too would be razed and replaced by the present elementary school facility now on the site.

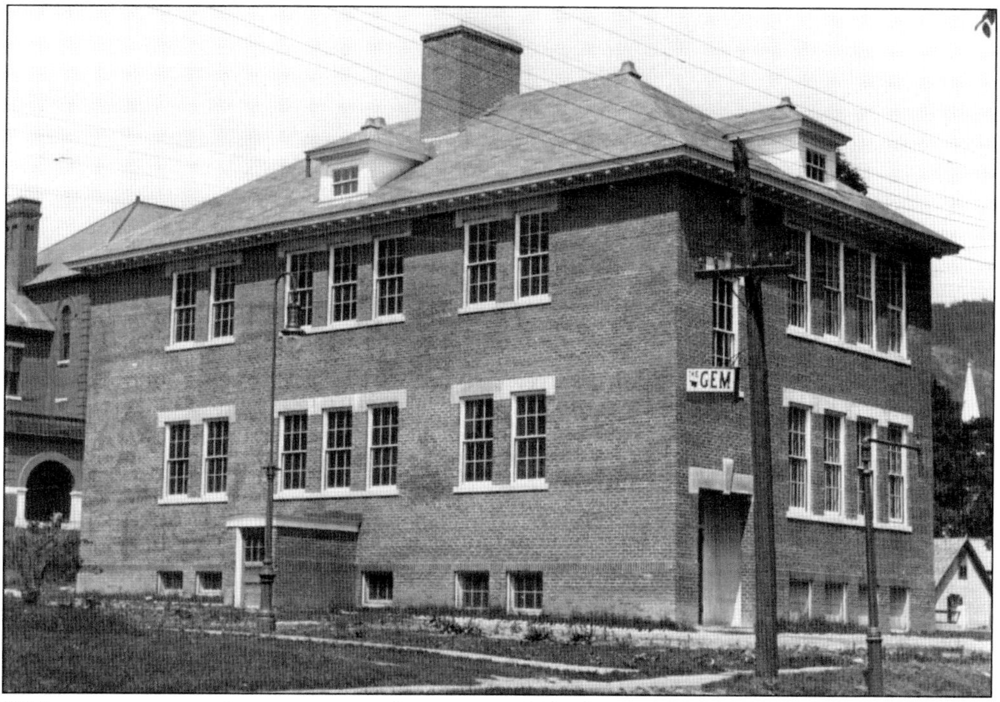

With some amount of controversy at the time, in 1913, this new elementary school building was constructed in front of the 1905 facility located on School Street. By this time, a newer Colonial Revival style of architecture and public taste had replaced the former Romanesque-inspired design of the school building constructed a decade earlier. The older building is somewhat visible in the background.

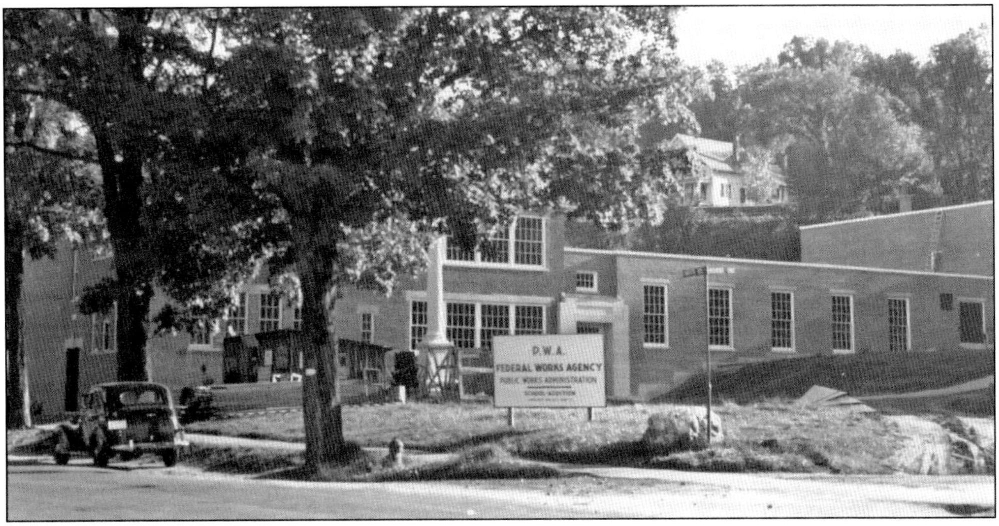

The Federal Emergency Administration of Public Works was formed by the Roosevelt Administration in 1933 to help combat the devastating effects of the Great Depression. By 1935, the name was changed to the Public Works Administration. Until the agency closed in 1944, over $6 billion was spent nationwide on construction projects, including this $55,000 addition connecting Woodstock's two school buildings. This work was completed in 1939.

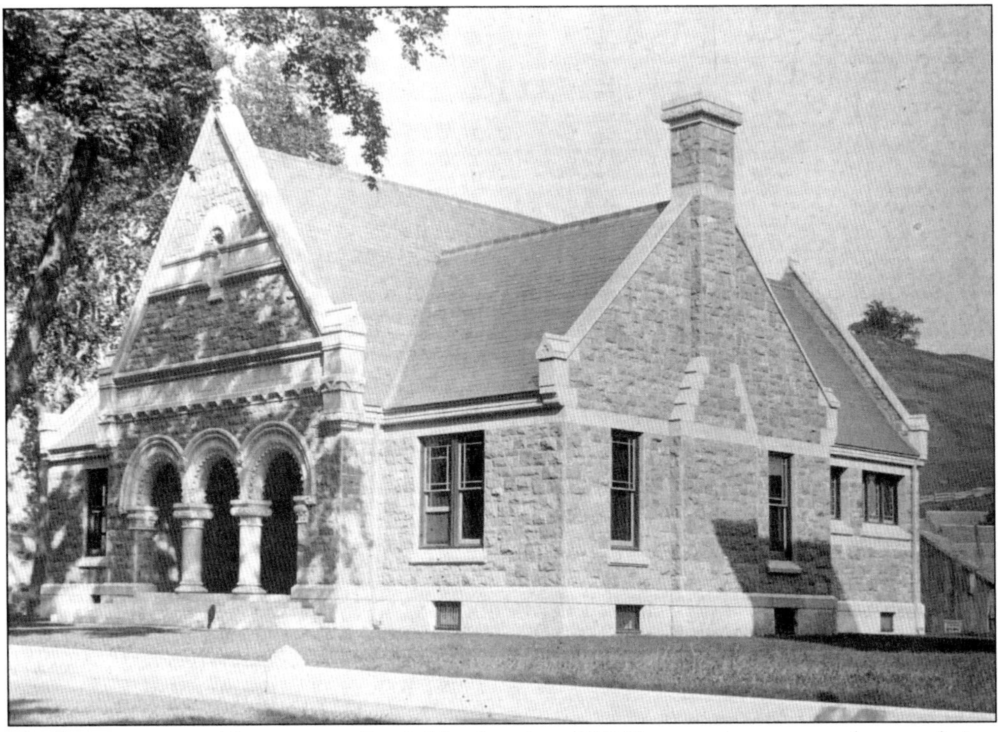

The first attempt at a library was in South Woodstock in 1797. However, it was upon the completion of the Norman Williams Public Library in 1885 that the town had its first really permanent facility. Designed in the Norman Romanesque style by Wilson Brothers & Company Architects of Philadelphia, the building was the gift of Dr. Edward H. Williams in the name of his parents Norman and Mary Williams.

Five

The Woodstock Railway

The 1840s saw a national epidemic of "railroad fever" break out across the land, and it touched communities large and small—Woodstock included. By 1851, railroads had been constructed across New England, including into the upper Connecticut River valley, and as far west as the Great Lakes. For the first time, Boston and New York were a relatively easy distance away, and the Upper Midwest was not far beyond.

In 1847, a railroad study was published that caught the attention of folks in Woodstock. The ambitious plan was the Atlantic & Pacific Railway, a transcontinental railroad that would connect Portland, Maine, with "points west," passing through Woodstock. Although the coming of the American Civil War largely halted railroad development in the region, business and civic leaders in the towns of Woodstock and Bridgewater, as well as in the nearby manufacturing hamlets of Quechee and Dewey's Mills, kept alive the idea of at least building a railroad from White River Junction to serve those communities, with hopes, at some point in time, to build west over the Green Mountains into Rutland and beyond.

On October 30, 1863, the Vermont General Assembly issued a charter incorporating the Woodstock Railroad Company. The directors and investors were, for the most part, local business and civic leaders. By January 1868, the proposed route for the first 13 miles of new rail line had been decided upon, at an estimated cost of $16,000 per mile. The directors had so far raised $226,300, with $30,000 pledged by the Town of Woodstock alone. That winter, competitive bids were received, and come spring, construction of the new road began.

The continued funding necessary to complete the work proved to be a struggle, and it would not be until September 1875 that the line was finished as far as Woodstock. The Woodstock Railway, as it was called, never built west beyond Woodstock. However, for the next 58 years, the road provided excellent service and greatly facilitated the town to transition into the resort community that it soon became.

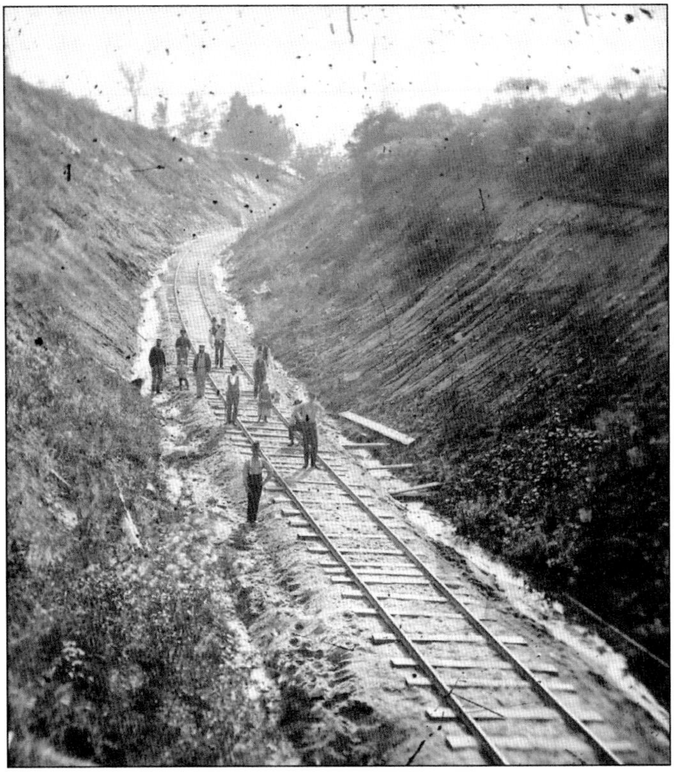

Although the necessary funds to construct the entire 13.88-mile-long railroad were lacking, in April 1868, a contract was signed and work began at Sallies Hill in Hartford, where a great cut had to be made. By May, 500 men, working with only hand shovels and paid $1.75 a day, were attacking the hill from both sides. For the next year, work continued grading other sections of the line until funding temporarily dried up.

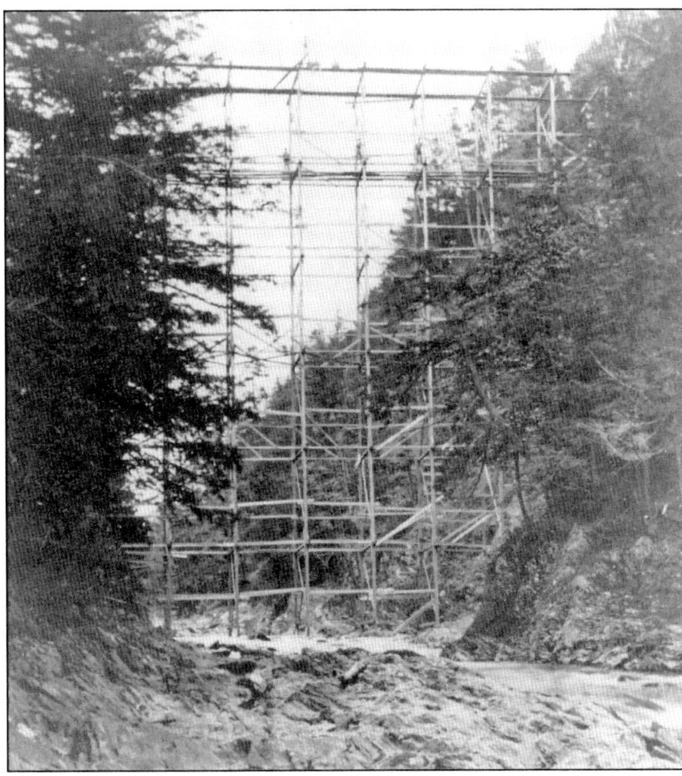

The most difficult challenge was crossing Quechee Gulf with a bridge that would be 163 feet above the water level. In July 1875, bridge builder R.E. Peabody of Groton, Vermont, erected temporary staging 135 feet high upon which the new wooden bridge would be assembled. Two stone abutments had been constructed into the sides of the great gorge.

By late July 1875, rails were in place from White River Junction to the eastern rim of the gorge, allowing work trains to transport prefabricated, numbered wood and iron components of the new bridge. This view shows the top of the temporary scaffolding leveled and ready to receive bridge workers, who, a piece at a time, connected the parts into a completed bridge.

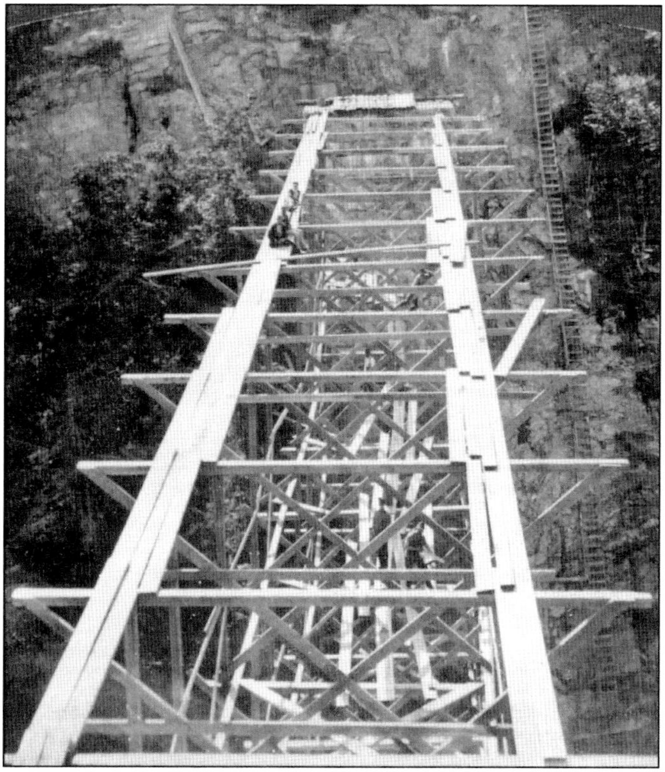

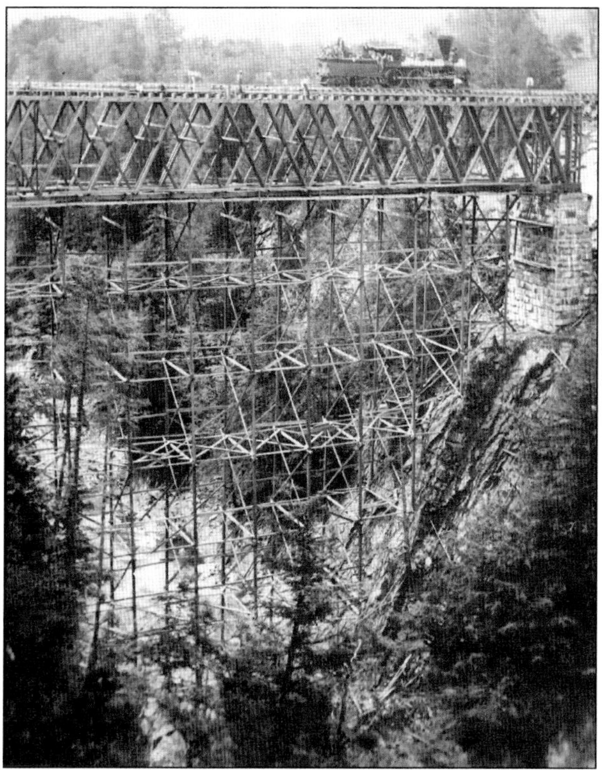

On August 12, 1875, in hushed fascination, hundreds of observers watched as the already historic work locomotive *Winooski* crept cautiously across the new bridge, a Howe truss design of wooden horizontal and diagonal timbers with vertical iron rods. The bridge deflected no more than a quarter of an inch under the weight of the 23-ton steam locomotive and tender.

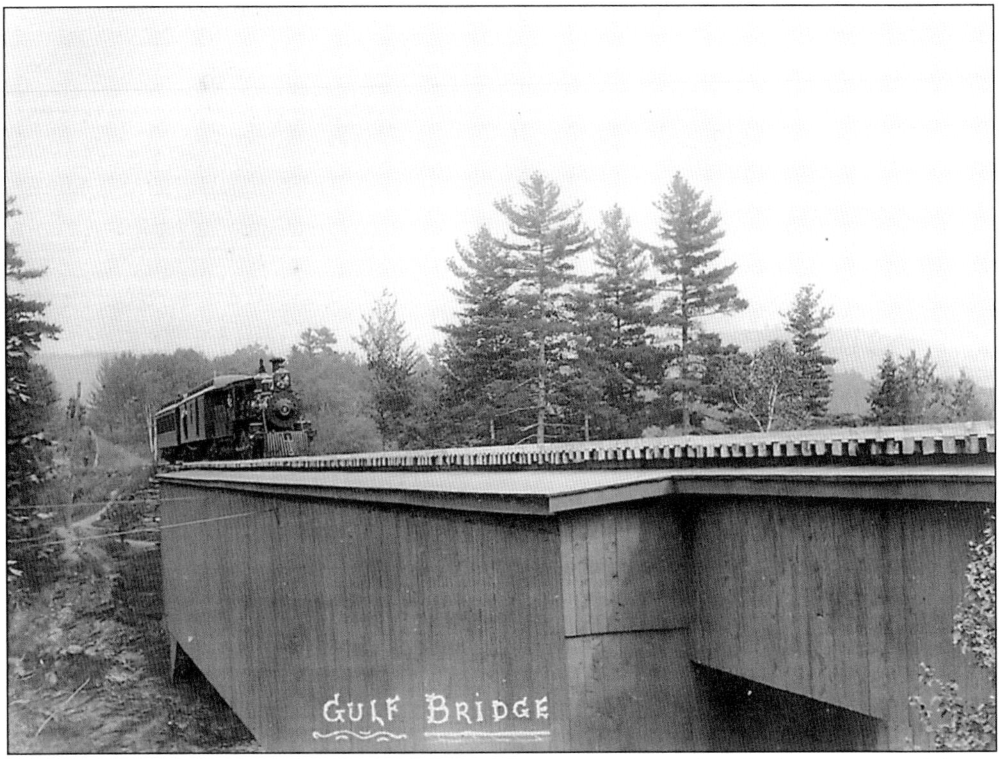

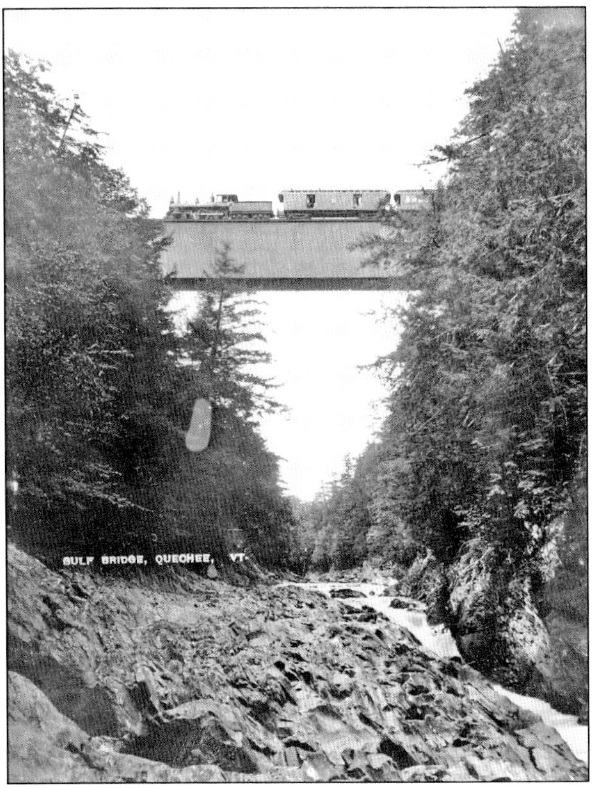

Soon after the historic test of the Gulf Bridge, vertical boarding was installed to protect the structure from weather-related damage, and the temporary scaffolding was removed from the gorge below. The 163-foot-high bridge spanned 280 feet and cost in excess of $20,000. By mid-September 1875, rails had finally reached Woodstock Village.

For many years, four times a day and twice on Sundays, this was a familiar sight, as regularly scheduled trains connecting Woodstock with White River Junction made their way across what became one of the most famous bridge structures in the state of Vermont. The trip each way took between 35 and 45 minutes, depending on the stops, traveling at about 30 miles an hour.

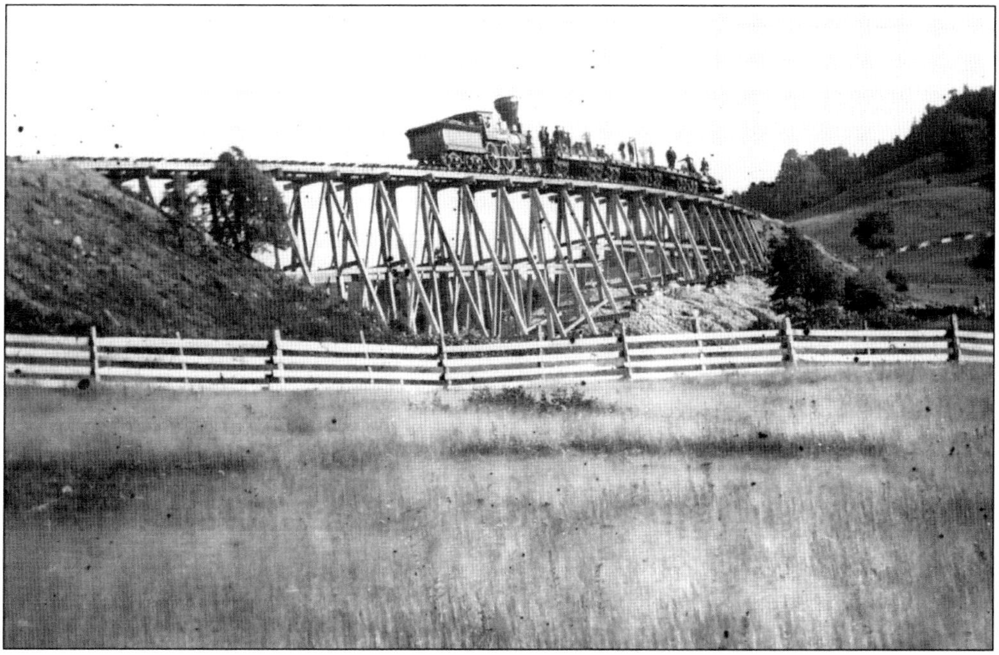

When constructing early railroads, it was not unusual to erect temporary wooden trestles across low ground to get the line in operation, and then to later come back and permanently fill in around them—burying the trestle. Here is the work locomotive *Winooski* with a trestle filling train just west of where present-day US Route 4 and Interstate 89 cross.

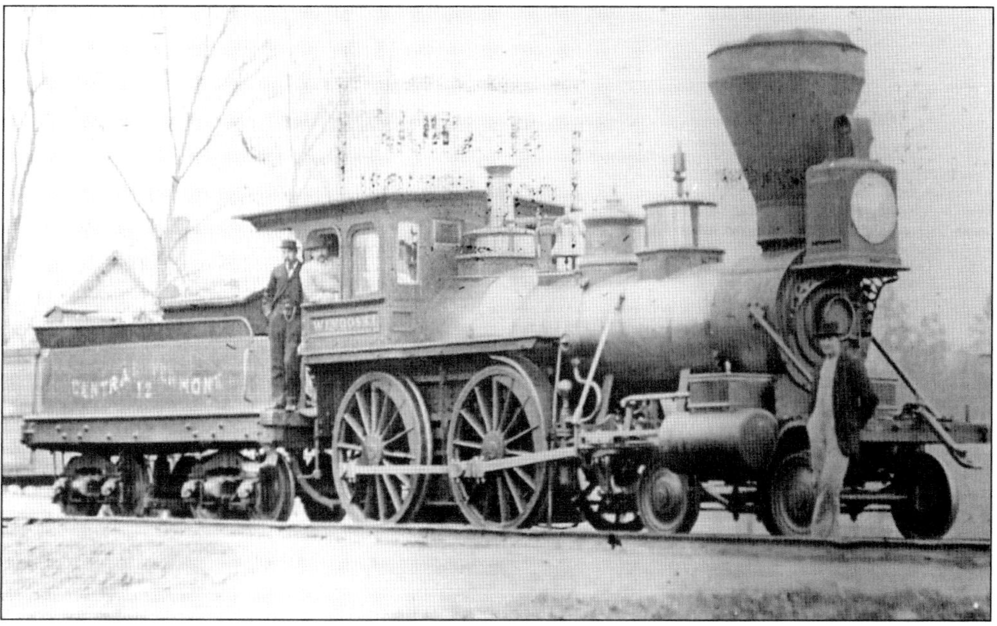

The *Winooski*, built by Hinkley & Drury of Boston in 1848 and on loan from the Vermont Central Railroad, helped build the Woodstock Railway and pulled the first train into Woodstock Village on September 29, 1875. The historic locomotive had on June 26, 1848, pulled the first train in Vermont from White River Junction to Bethel. In 1880, the VCRR scrapped the locomotive, shown here in old age,.

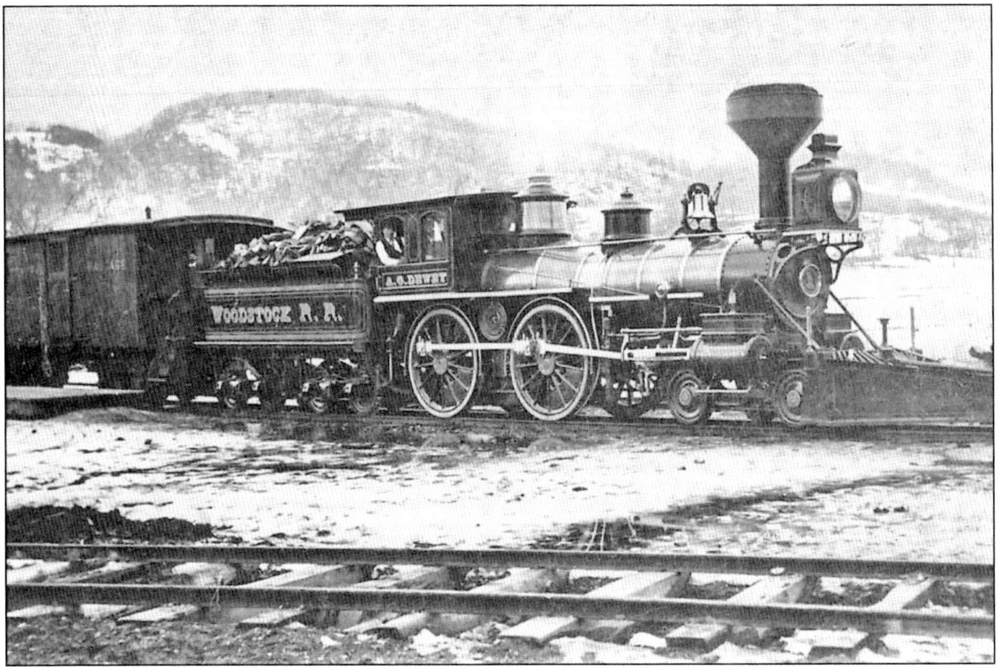

The first locomotive owned by the Woodstock Railway was the A.G. *Dewey*, named for the company president. Built in 1875 by the Manchester Locomotive Works of Manchester, New Hampshire, the 30-ton *Dewey* was a fine locomotive but too heavy and not suitable for the Woodstock Railway. Therefore, in February 1882, it was traded to the Connecticut & Passumpsic Rivers Railroad, and by 1894, it had been scrapped.

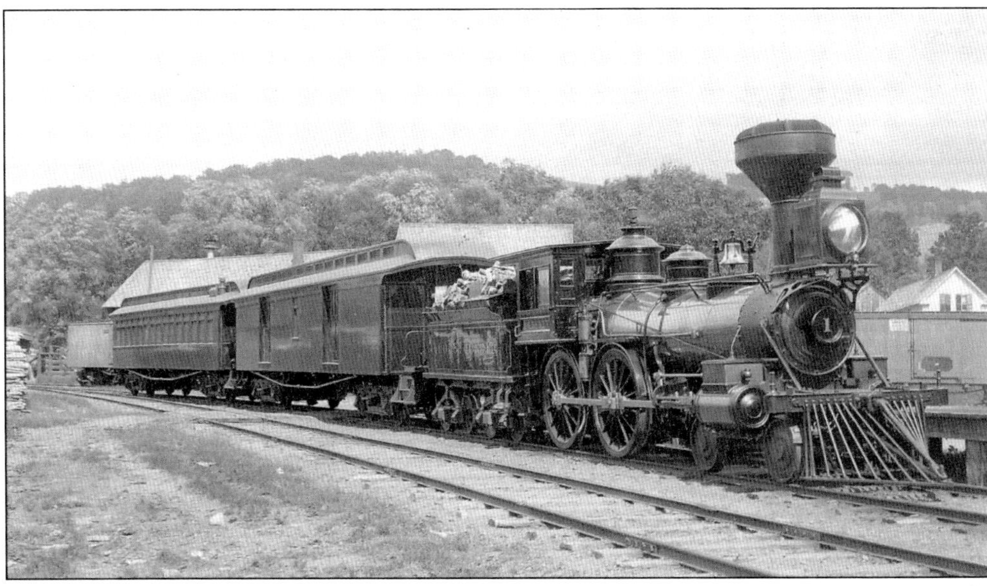

The second locomotive was also named the A. G. *Dewey*. Built in 1872 for the C&PRR, the wood-burning, 26-ton *Dewey* served the Woodstock Railway long and well, and was regarded by all with great affection. Reboilered and converted to burn coal in 1899, the locomotive was finally sold to a new owner in 1918 and eventually scrapped in 1934.

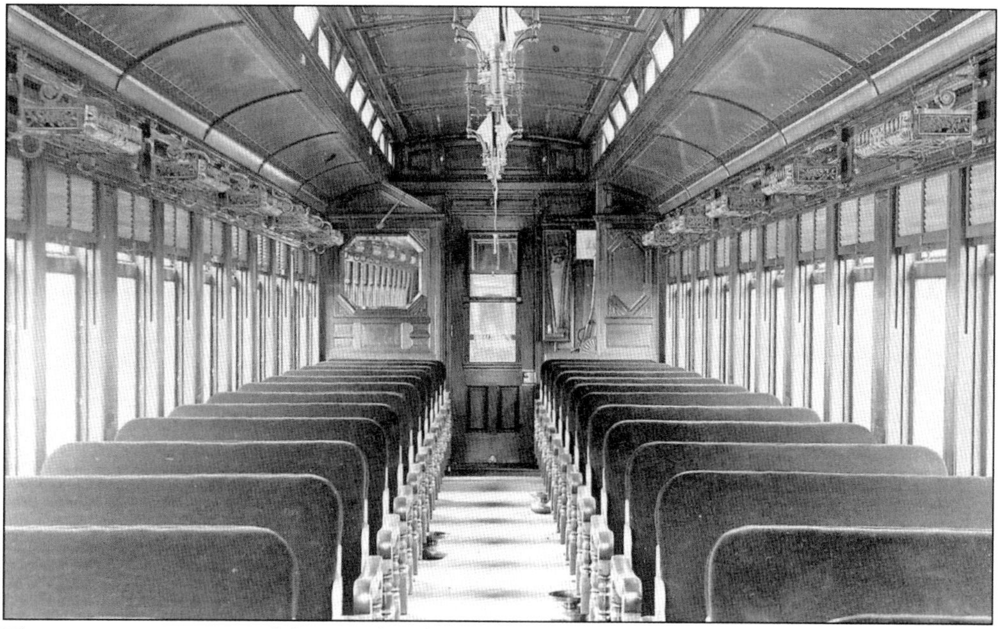

This is an interior view of the *Woodstock*, a combination passenger and baggage car purchased new by the Woodstock Railway in 1876. It was a fine piece of railroad equipment, and this rare photographic view clearly shows the period velvet-covered seats, kerosene-burning chandeliers, and brass package racks above ornate glass windows. The *Woodstock* was always part of each daily train between Woodstock Village and White River Junction.

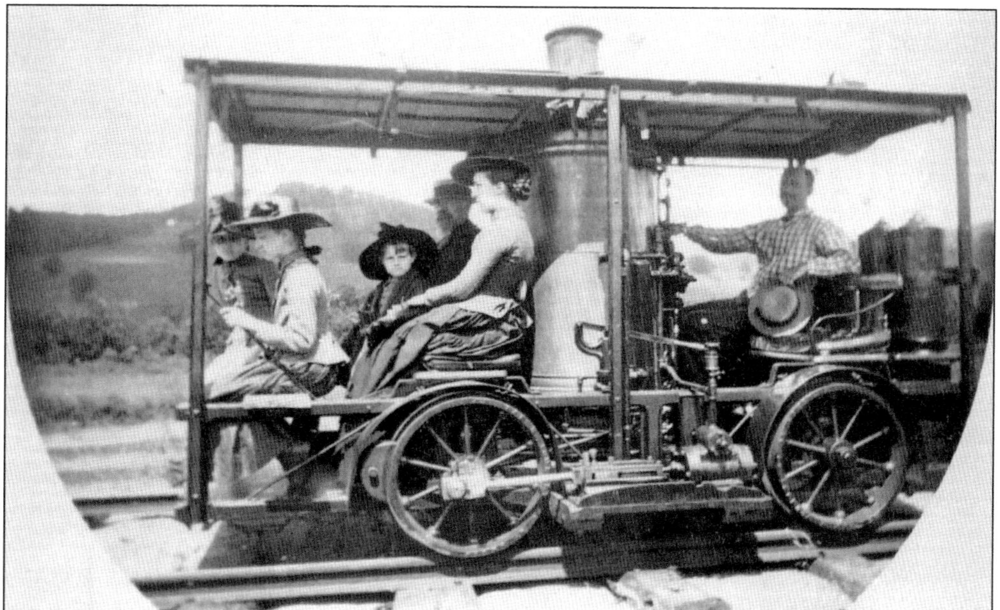

Albert Galatin Dewey was the first president of the Woodstock Railway and owned large woolen mills at the head of Quechee Gorge. In 1878, Dewey had constructed this individual steam-powered car named the *Gerty Buck*. For years, Dewey family, visitors, and VIPs used the car to travel between Woodstock and White River Junction. Today, the *Gerty Buck* is on display at the Shelburne Museum in Shelburne, Vermont.

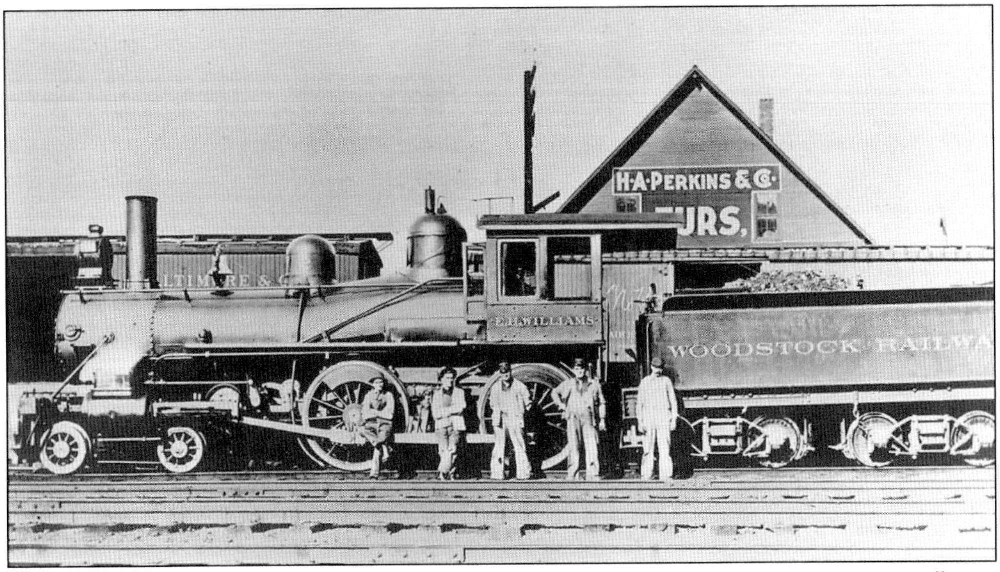

As traffic increased on the Woodstock Railway, a second locomotive, named the *E.H. Williams*, was purchased in 1892. Edward H. Williams was a Woodstock native who had done well as part of the famed Baldwin Locomotive works of Philadelphia, Pennsylvania, the builder of the *Williams*, seen here in White River Junction around 1900. Often plagued with boiler problems, this 40-ton locomotive was not successful and was gone by 1930.

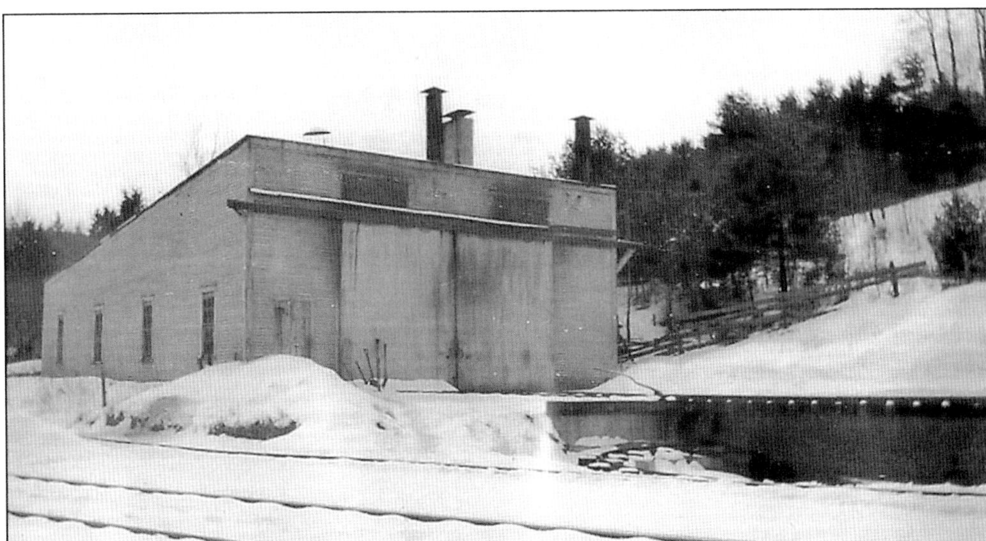

The purchase of the *E.H. Williams* necessitated the construction of a two-stall enginehouse costing $1,000, a turntable, and a coaling facility at the White River Junction end of the line. Located at about the present-day intersection of US Routes 4 and 5, the enginehouse and turntable are shown here shortly before being demolished in 1935.

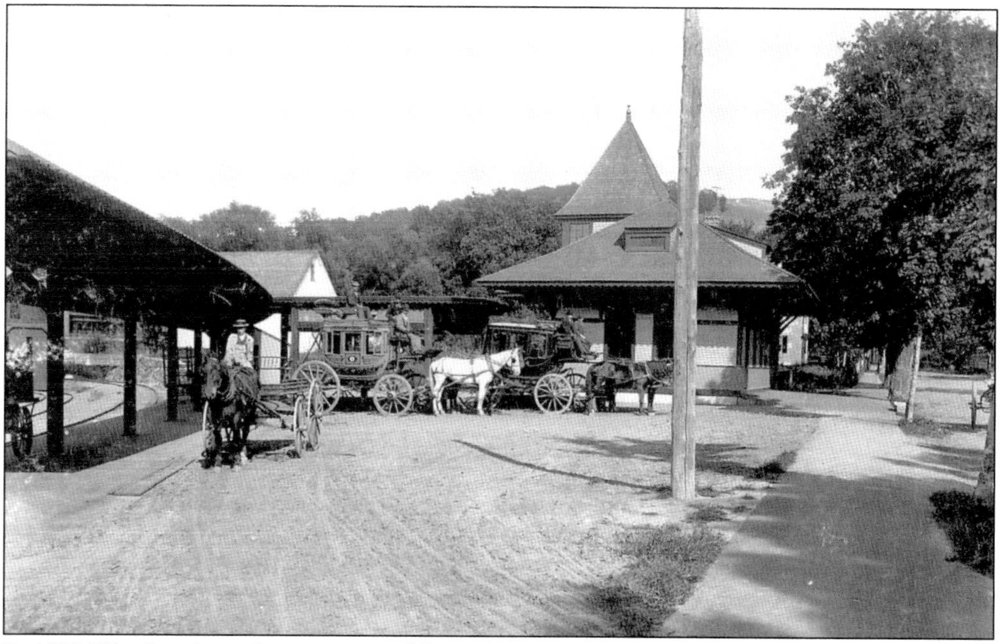

By 1892, Woodstock was becoming a well-known recreation destination point, and a new passenger station was erected to better serve the increasing volume of traffic to and from the village. It is train time about 1900, and the stagecoach from the Woodstock Inn and a delivery wagon from F.H. Gillingham's store, both located in the village, are awaiting the afternoon train.

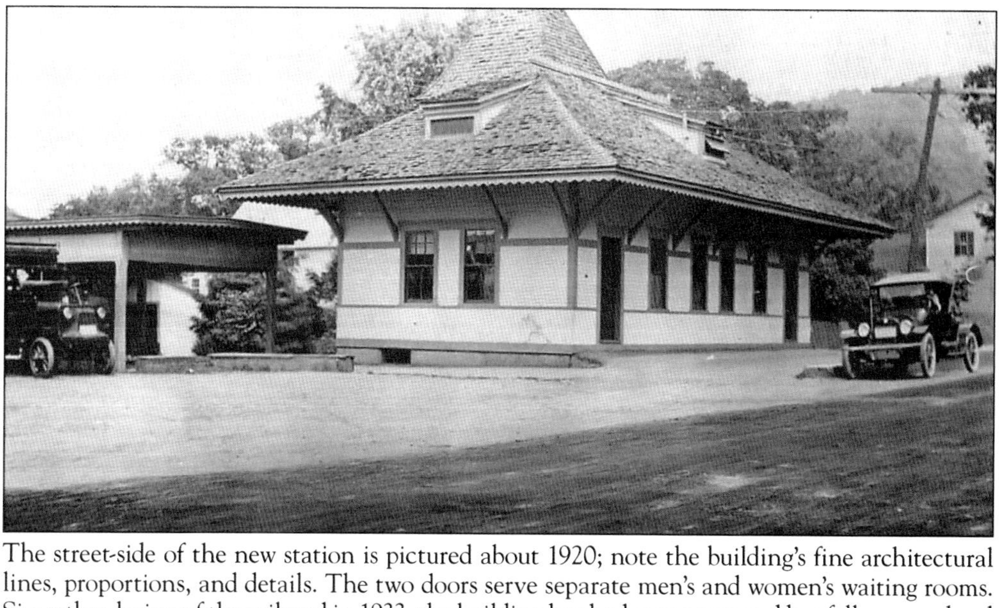

The street-side of the new station is pictured about 1920; note the building's fine architectural lines, proportions, and details. The two doors serve separate men's and women's waiting rooms. Since the closing of the railroad in 1933, the building has had many uses and has fallen upon hard times. Now, in 2016, the long-abused building is being revitalized, giving it a new lease on life.

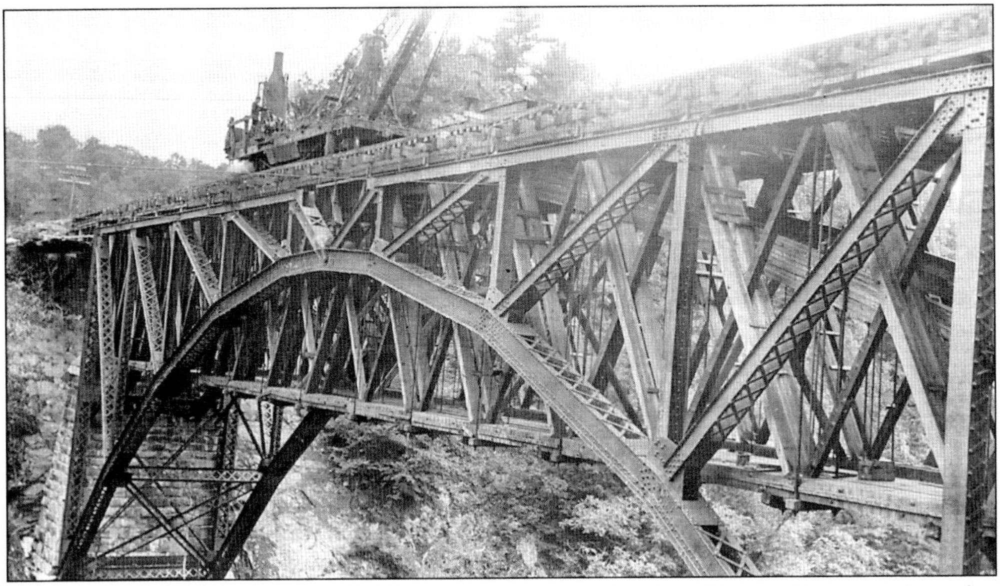

The 1875 bridge across Quechee Gulf had been stiffened with the addition of laminated wooden arches in 1906, but with increasingly heavier trains, that was not enough. During the summer of 1911, the American Bridge Company erected a new iron bridge around the existing wooden structure, all the while keeping the railroad in operation. This view shows the last piece of new supporting steel about to be set into place.

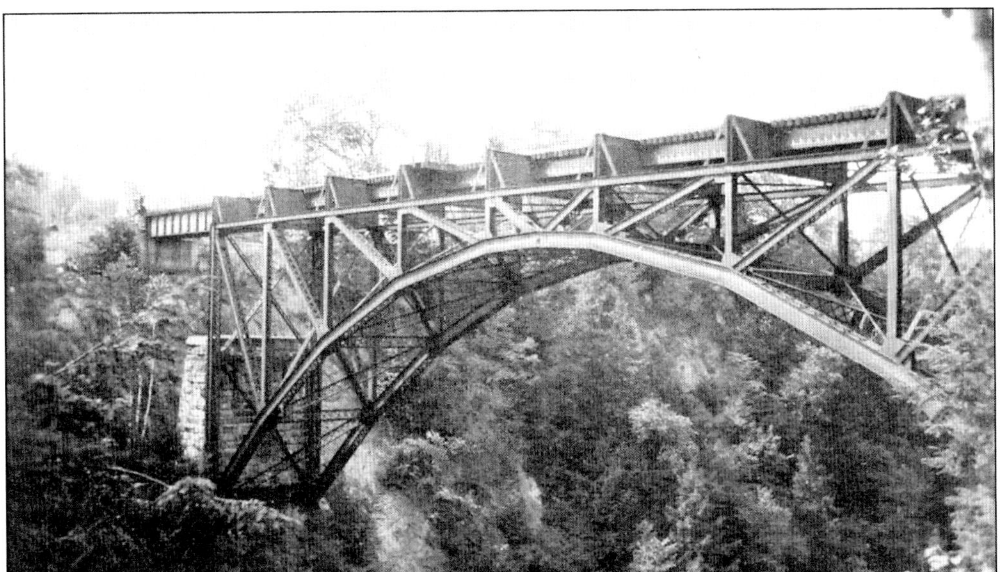

The new steel arched bridge cost the railroad about $26,000 and was capable of safely carrying the heaviest locomotives, freight, and Pullman cars that might appear in White River Junction, bound for Woodstock. By this time, Woodstock had achieved fame as a very desirable resort community, and it was not unusual to see heavy Pullman passenger cars and hopper cars loaded with coal in the yard at the Woodstock station.

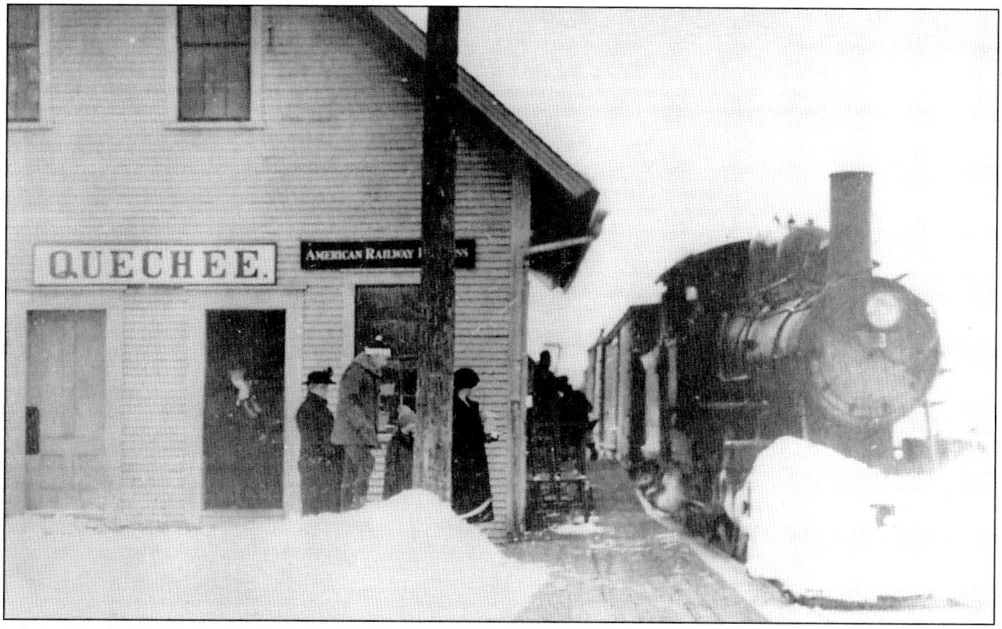

The schedule of train service, as of June 1906, from Monday through Saturday, lists four trains a day leaving Woodstock for White River Junction: train No. 6 at 5:30 a.m., No. 2 at 10:30 a.m., No. 8 at 12:30 p.m., and No. 4 at 3:30 p.m. On Sunday, there was only one train, No. 10, at 10:30 p.m. Here is the eastbound train, with the locomotive No. 3, the *J.G. Porter*, stopped at the station in Quechee on a wintry day in 1920.

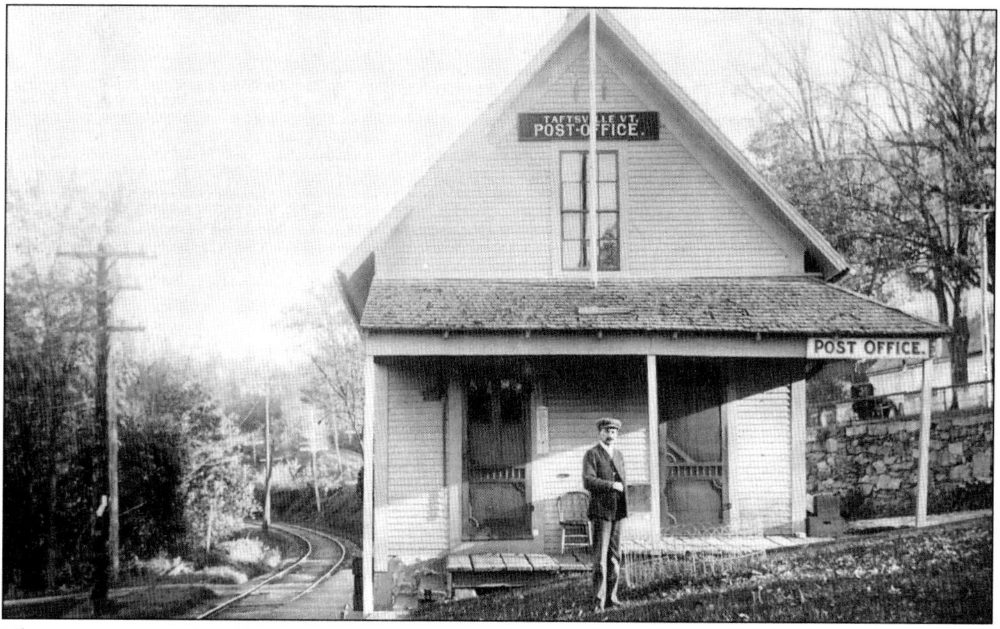

The station in Taftsville was an engaging piece of rural architecture, tightly situated between the tracks and the dirt highway. It also served as the village post office since, by the time when this early-20th-century photograph was taken, the nation's mail was primarily moved by rail. In 1933, after the Woodstock railway ceased to exist, this little building remained standing until the late 1960s.

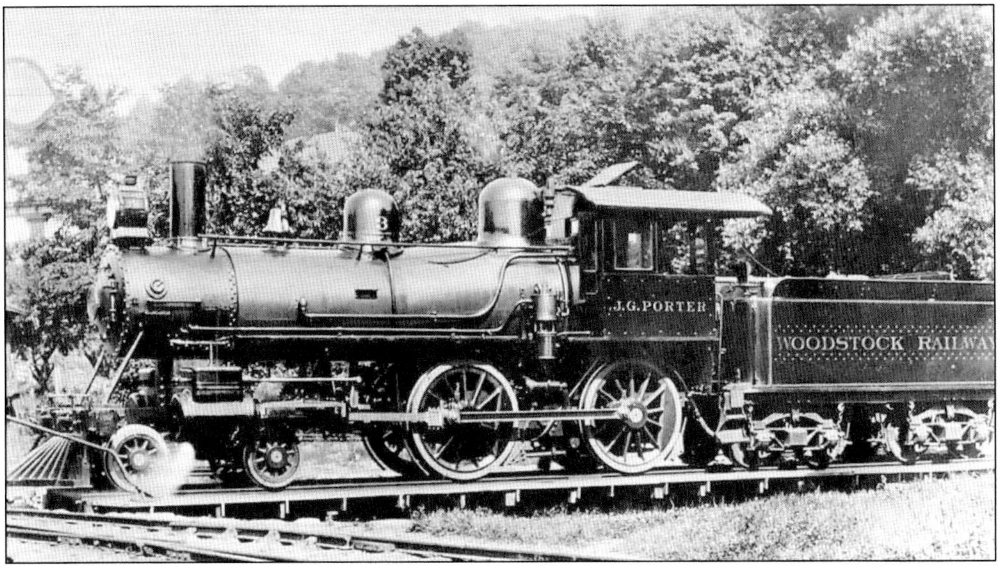

The first decades of the 20th century were good years for the Woodstock Railway. In 1905, the new *J.G. Porter* No. 3 was purchased from the ALCO locomotive works in Manchester, New Hampshire. Named for the railroads much beloved clerk, treasurer, general manager, and director, the $6,000 *Porter* had great pulling ability and was considered the best locomotive the road ever had. It was sold in June 1933 and retired in 1951.

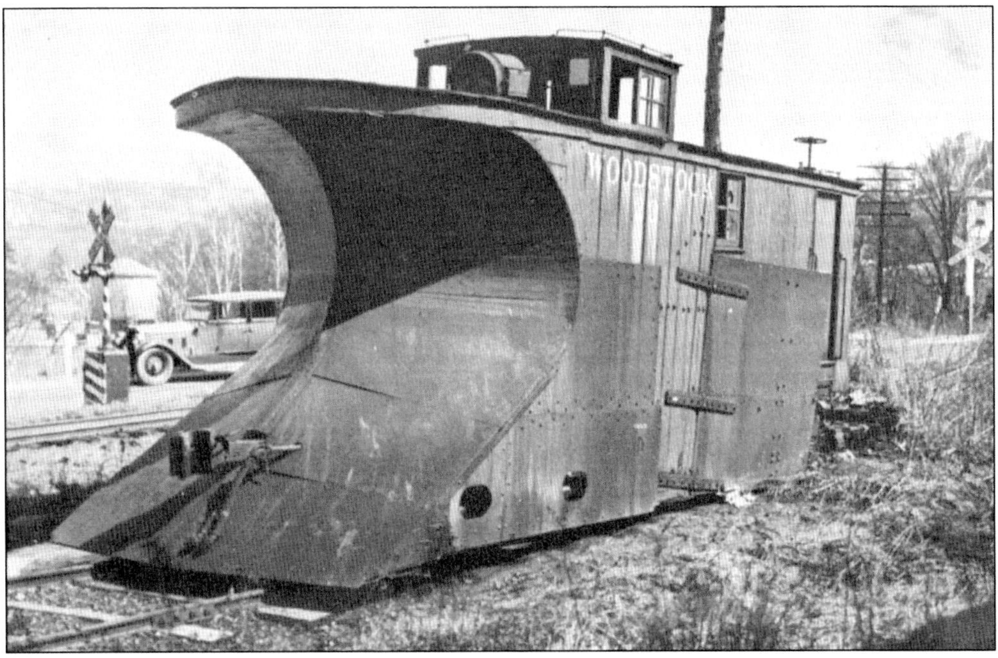

Although a small railroad, the Woodstock Railway was always well managed and properly equipped. To combat whatever a New England winter might throw at the road, this snowplow was kept on hand just in case. Acquired as a castoff from the much bigger Central Vermont Railroad, this piece of equipment was often seen laboring between Woodstock and White River Junction, keeping the line open and functioning during winter months.

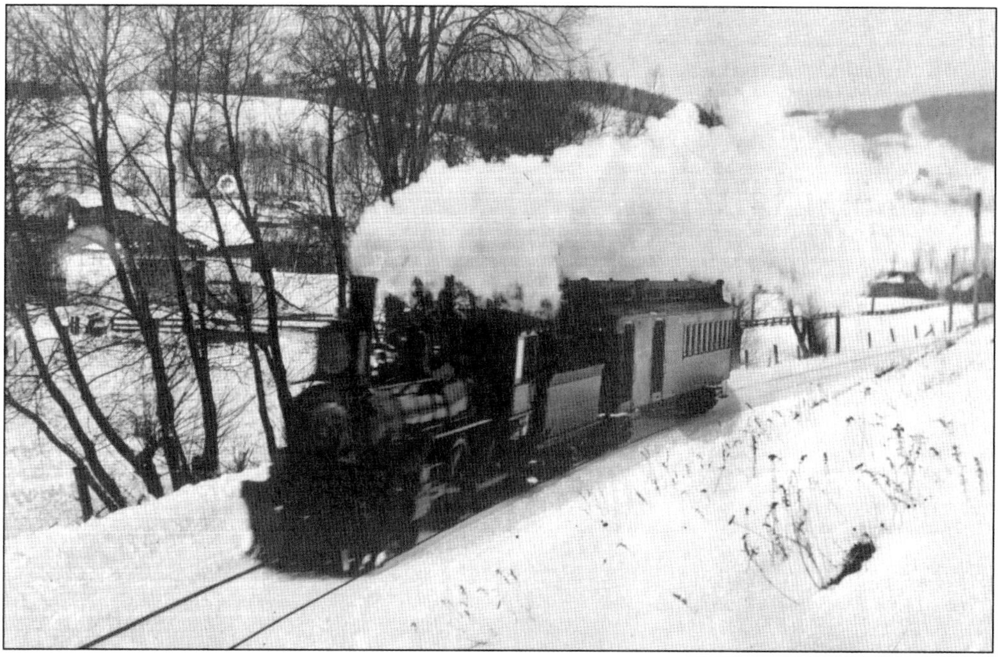

It is wintertime, perhaps about 1910, and the *E.H. Williams* is heading into Woodstock Village on a return run from White River Junction. On the draw bar is a single combine car, and it appears that the road's snowplow was recently through winging back the snowbanks. The snow-covered hills of the Ottauquechee River valley are visible beyond.

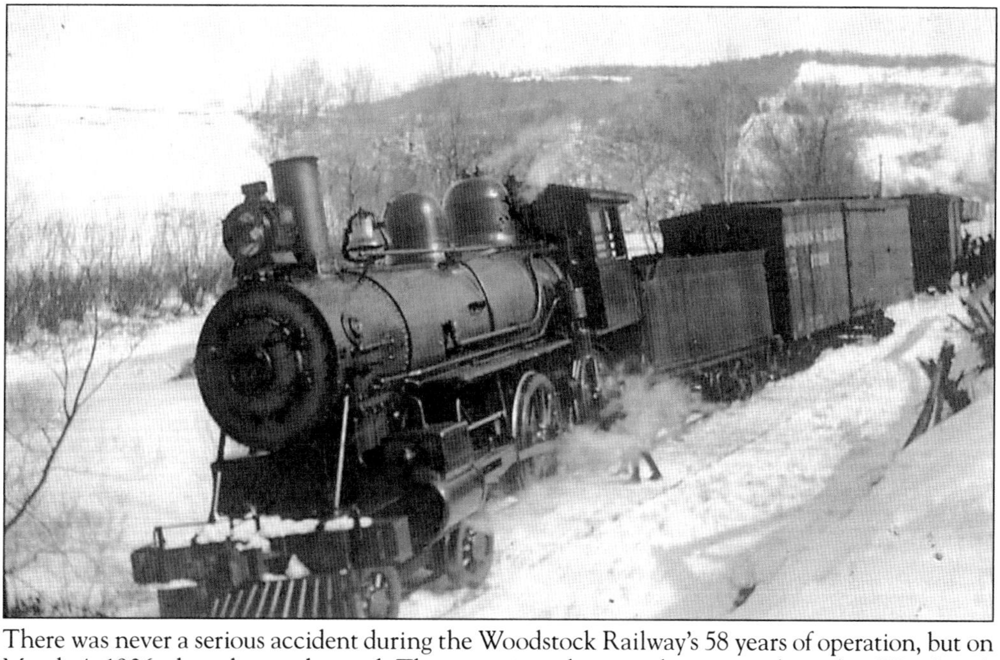

There was never a serious accident during the Woodstock Railway's 58 years of operation, but on March 4, 1906, that almost changed. That morning, the mixed train westbound to Woodstock derailed at an ice-packed crossing just east of the Taftsville station. Only the quick actions of skilled engineer Harry Payne saved the new locomotive *J.G. Porter*, three loaded freight cars, and a passenger car from plunging into the Ottauquechee River.

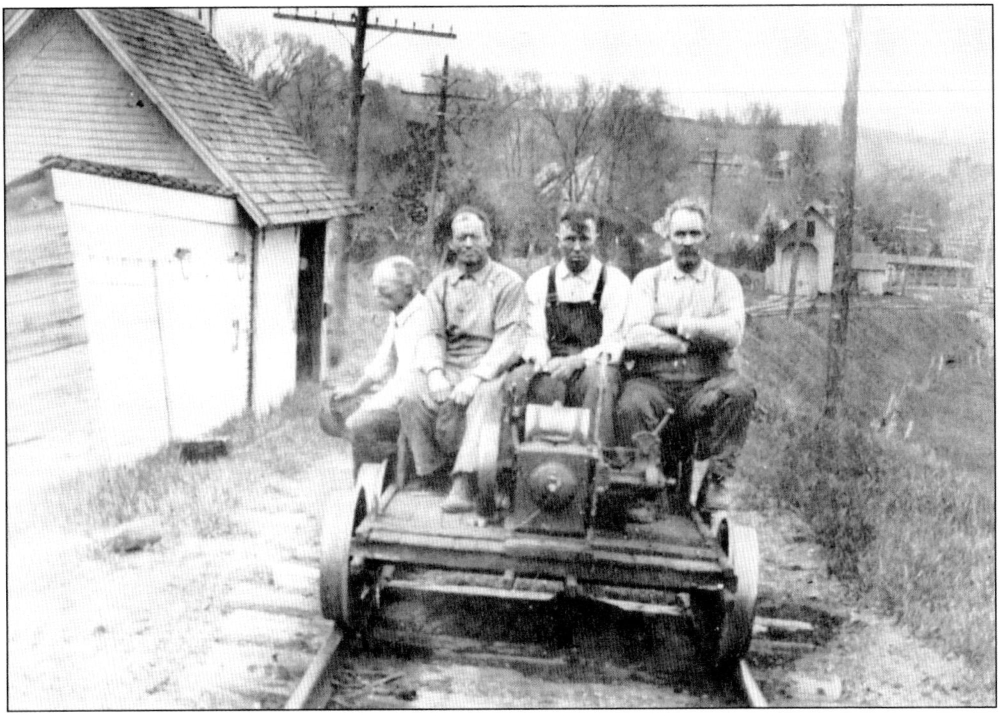

Railroads require maintenance, and the Woodstock Railway was no exception. Here, about 1920, is a section crew headed east out of Woodstock on a handcar powered by a single-cylinder gasoline engine. In the background are the single-stall enginehouse and the station platform. To the left is the section house where the handcar was kept.

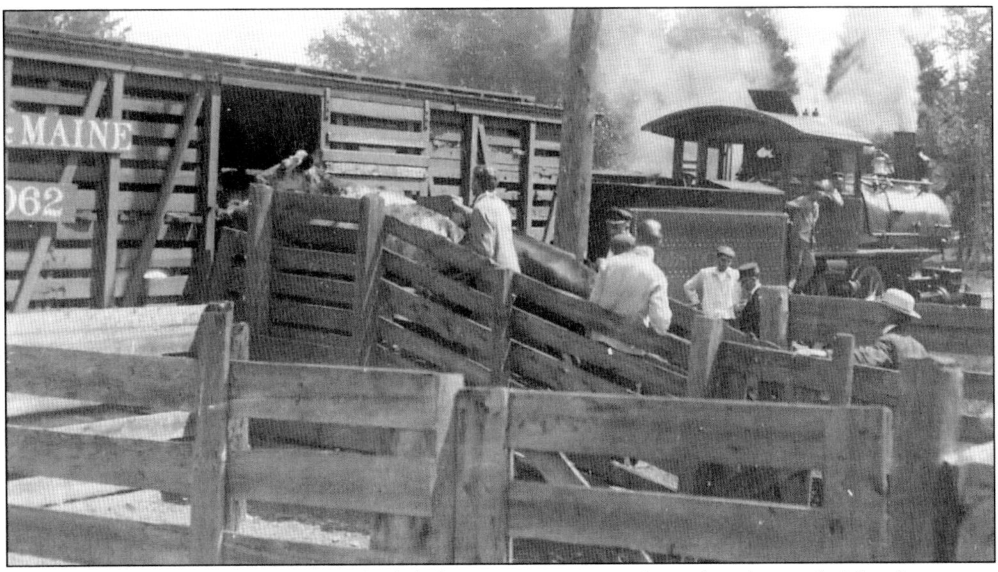

In addition to providing regularly scheduled passenger service, the railroad provided freight service for Woodstock area merchants, like F.A. Gillingham & Sons, and shipped farmers' livestock to urban markets. Here, about 1915, steers are being loaded from holding pens into cattle cars, behind the elderly A.G. *Dewey*. Although still working hauling unscheduled light-duty trains, the *Dewey* was sold in 1918 and retired and scrapped in 1934.

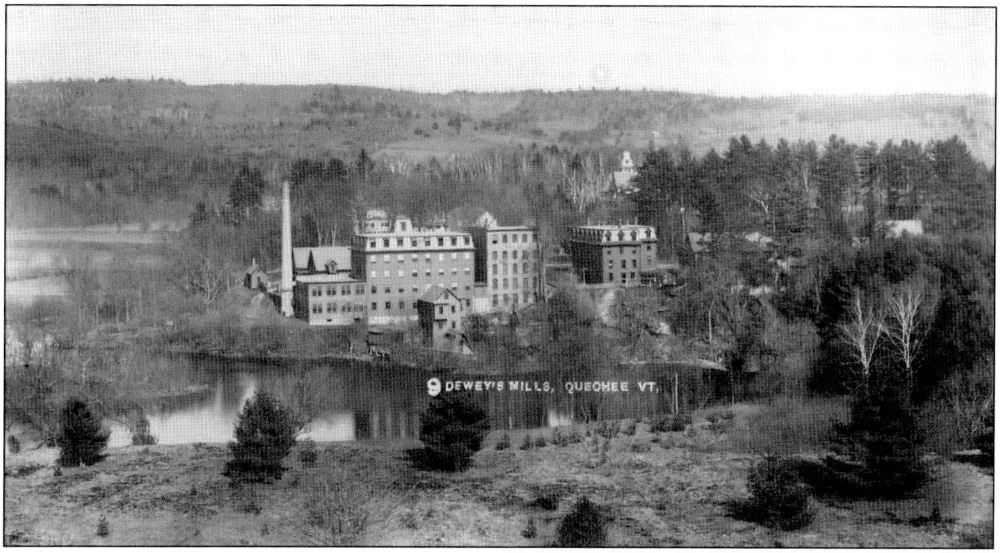

Established in 1836 at the head of Quechee Gorge, the Dewey family's woolen mills had grown to employ more than 100 persons, making 2,500 yards of cloth daily, by about 1910 when this image was made. The mill complex had a station stop on the Woodstock Railway appropriately named Dewey's Mills and remained a major shipper of wool, coal, and cloth on the railroad until the very end in 1933.

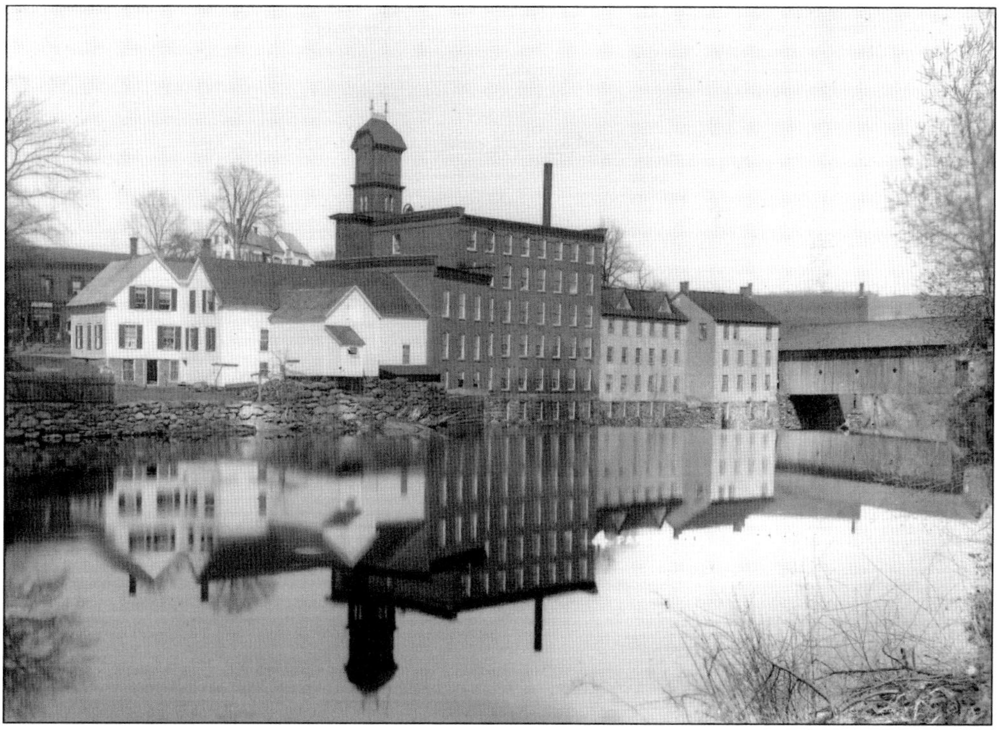

Several miles west of Dewey's Mill were the woolen mills at Quechee on the Ottauquechee River. Illustrated here is the J.C. Parker and Company complex about 1910. This was also an important freight customer for the Woodstock Railway. Bales of raw wool and coal for winter heat were shipped in, and finished cloth in bulk form was shipped out to markets worldwide.

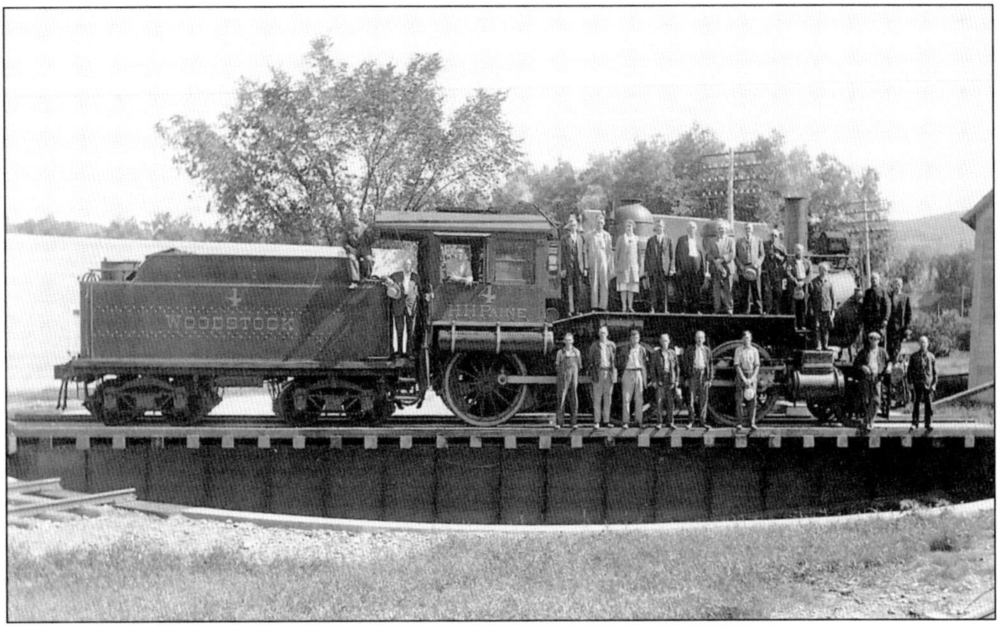

Although overall revenues were dropping by the late 1920s, the railroad purchased this used locomotive from the Bangor & Aroostook Railroad in Maine, for $6,100 in 1929. Given the number 4 and named for longtime senior engineer Harry H. Paine, the longer 62-ton locomotive required a new steel turntable to be built at Woodstock; both are seen here in 1930 with the railroad's employees and family members.

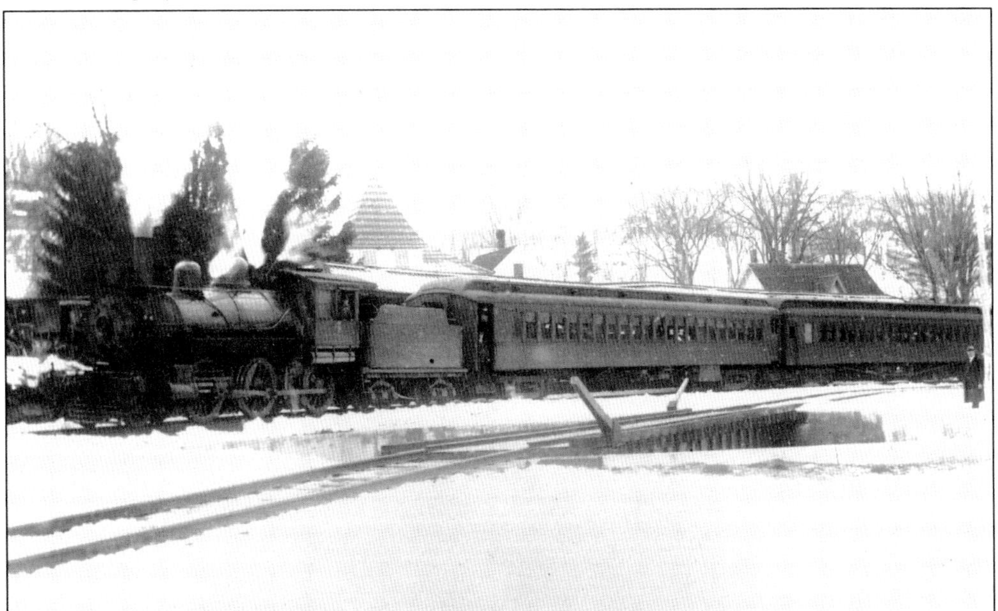

The early years of the Great Depression took a heavy toll on the Woodstock Railway, and it was clear that the end had come. As seen here on Saturday, April 15, 1933, the last run for the 58-year-old railroad was a commemorative trip from Woodstock into White River Junction for lunch and back. In the foreground is the turntable, and behind the train is the tower of the Woodstock station.

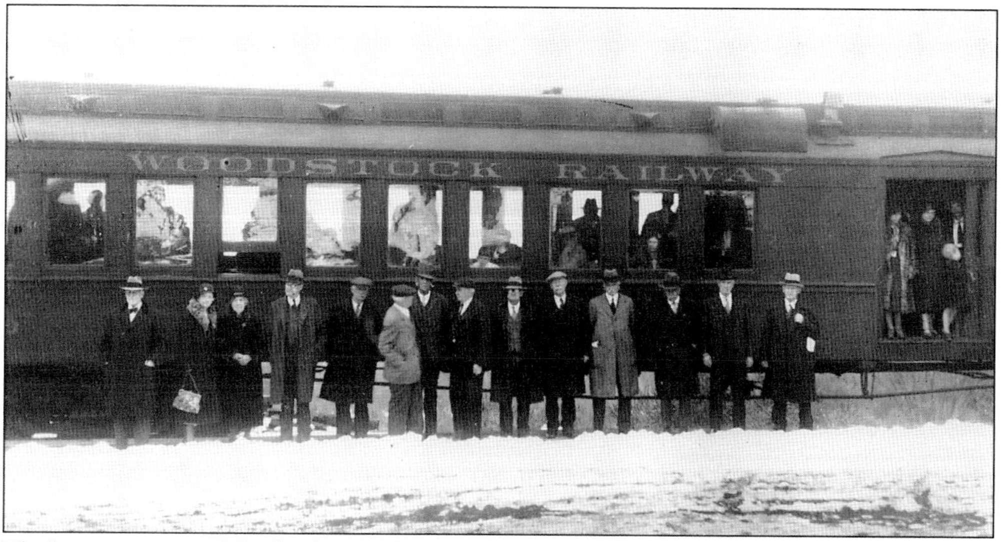

The last run was a sad day for the people of Woodstock. Of the 350 passengers who had purchased special tickets, 14 had also traveled on the first train into Woodstock 58 years earlier in 1875. The trip was uneventful except for greased tracks that caused the locomotive to spin getting over the incline at Sallies Hill between Quechee and White River Junction; the pranksters responsible were never identified.

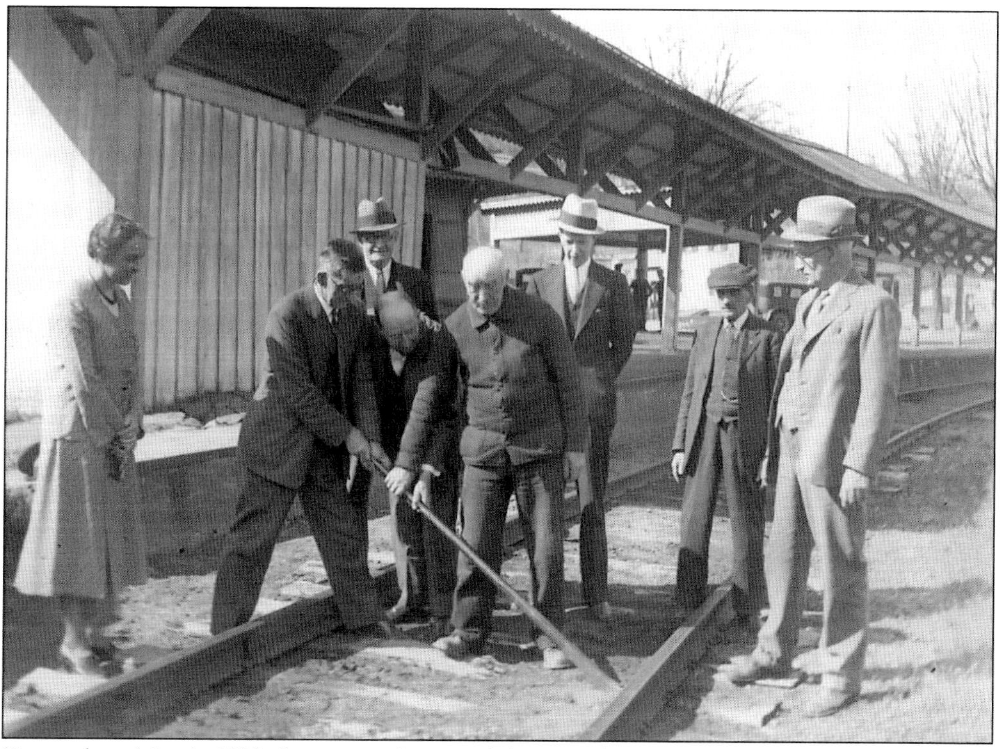

Pictured on May 1, 1933, former employees of the Woodstock Railway are at a sad ceremony to pull up the first spike to commence the dismantling of the entire railroad line during that summer. Above them is the long station platform roof under which, not too many years earlier, great numbers of joyous visitors had disembarked to enjoy Woodstock and its scenic environs.

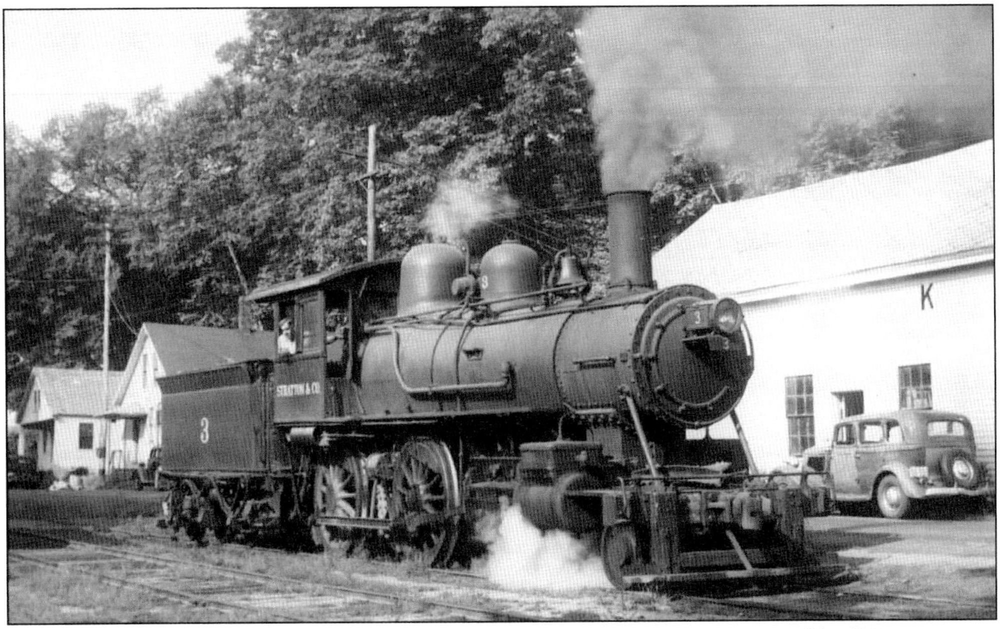

During the summer of 1933, the tracks were pulled up and the equipment sold off. Locomotive No. 4, the *H.H. Paine*, built in 1896, ended up unused and in a scrap heap in southern Vermont by 1941. No. 3, the *J.G. Porter*, was luckier—it lived on until 1951, leisurely moving freight cars of wheat and flour at the Stratton & Company mill in Penacook, New Hampshire.

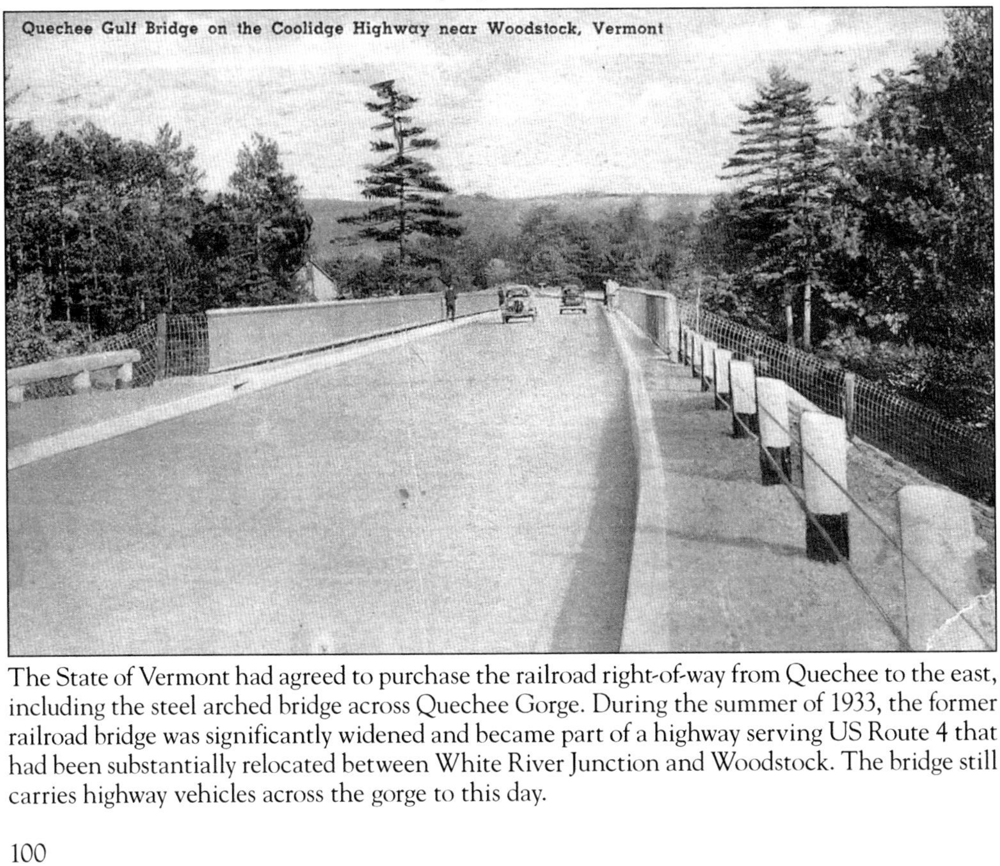

The State of Vermont had agreed to purchase the railroad right-of-way from Quechee to the east, including the steel arched bridge across Quechee Gorge. During the summer of 1933, the former railroad bridge was significantly widened and became part of a highway serving US Route 4 that had been substantially relocated between White River Junction and Woodstock. The bridge still carries highway vehicles across the gorge to this day.

Six

Resorts and Recreation

The years immediately preceding the American Civil War in the early 1860s saw the beginning of tourist-related businesses in areas like the White Mountains in New Hampshire and the Adirondacks in New York. In the decades after the war, aided by increased railroad development, this trade accelerated at a rapid rate to include many new vacation regions within the Northeast, including Woodstock and other areas of Vermont. The opening of the Woodstock Railway greatly facilitated the establishment of Woodstock as a desired vacation and resort destination. Those anxious to escape the summer heat and often disease-prone environments of large northeastern cities found the refreshing country air and scenic beauty of Woodstock a welcome break. By the early years of the 20th century, Woodstock had transformed into a truly year-round resort community, offering an appealing array of vacation-oriented activities, including horseback riding, golf, fishing, picnicking, and bicycle riding. During the winter months, skiing of all kinds flourished, and skating, tobogganing, and even dogsledding were popular with the visiting population, which included those who were somewhat local and others from far away.

As the century wore on, the Woodstock Railway was replaced by better roads and more automobiles. The ski industry that would later dominate in Vermont during the post–World War II years was very much identified with Woodstock. The establishment of the first ski tow in the United States quickly made Woodstock a mecca for New England skiers. In the 1960s, Laurance S. Rockefeller (1910–2004) and his wife, Mary Billings (French) Rockefeller (1910–1997), increased their deep interest in the community that her family had long ties to. And so, during that decade, the history of Woodstock as a full resort and historic community began a new and important chapter.

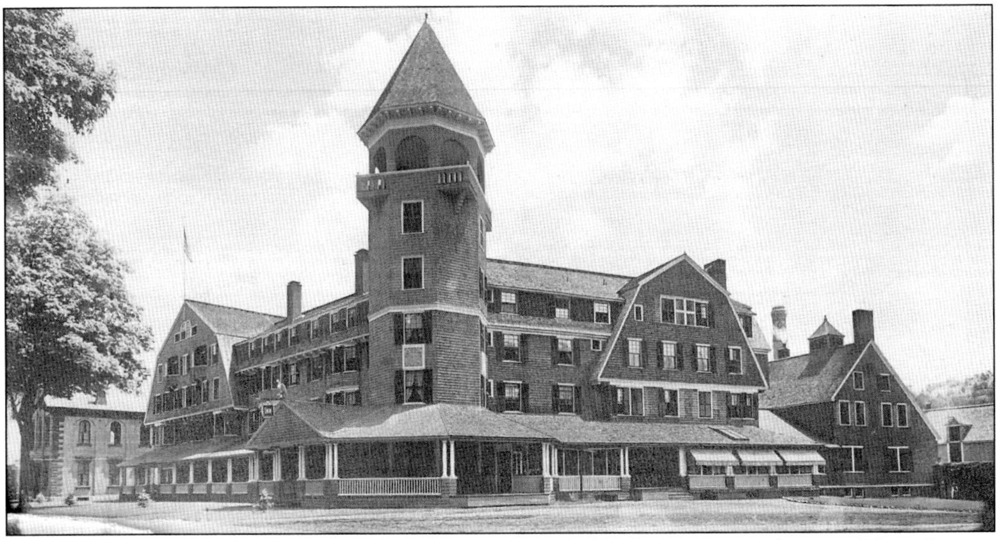

The great expansion in tourists to Woodstock demanded better accommodations. Therefore, in 1890, the Woodstock Hotel Company purchased the Eagle Hotel and razed the old building. In its place, the Woodstock Inn was opened in 1892. It was a modern resort building designed in the new and fashionable Shingle style that cost $120,000 to construct. Daily room rates ranged from $2.50 to $4, which included meals, or $12 for the week.

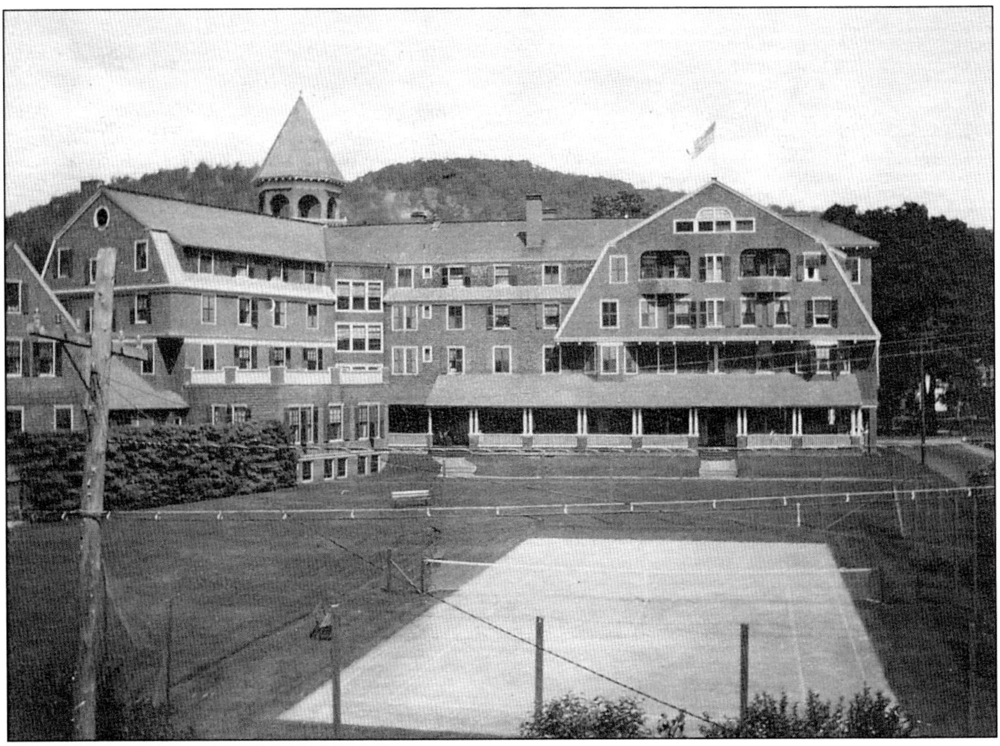

The rear of the new Woodstock Inn featured a sunny south-facing piazza and tennis courts. The new facility had more than 100 rooms, all with steam heat and gaslights. On each floor were toilet and bathing facilities. From the observation tower, one had a commanding view out over the village and adjacent countryside.

The sign and eagle that greeted visitors to the new inn were both salvaged from the former Eagle Hotel and had been carved by Moody Heath in 1830. Today, the eagle is perched above the entrance of the present Woodstock Inn and continues to "welcome the coming, and speed the departing guest." When the inn first opened in 1892, most of those guests arrived in town via the Woodstock Railway.

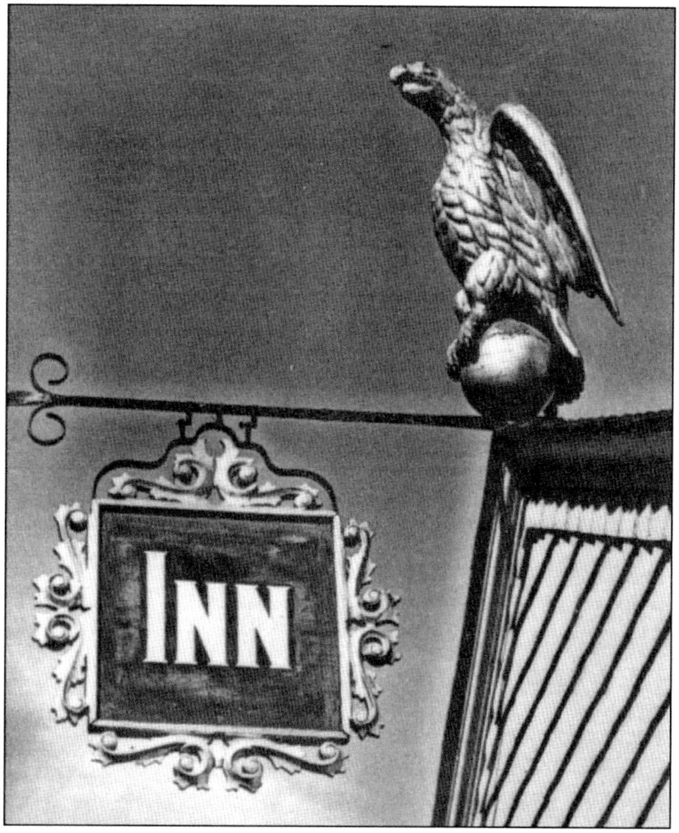

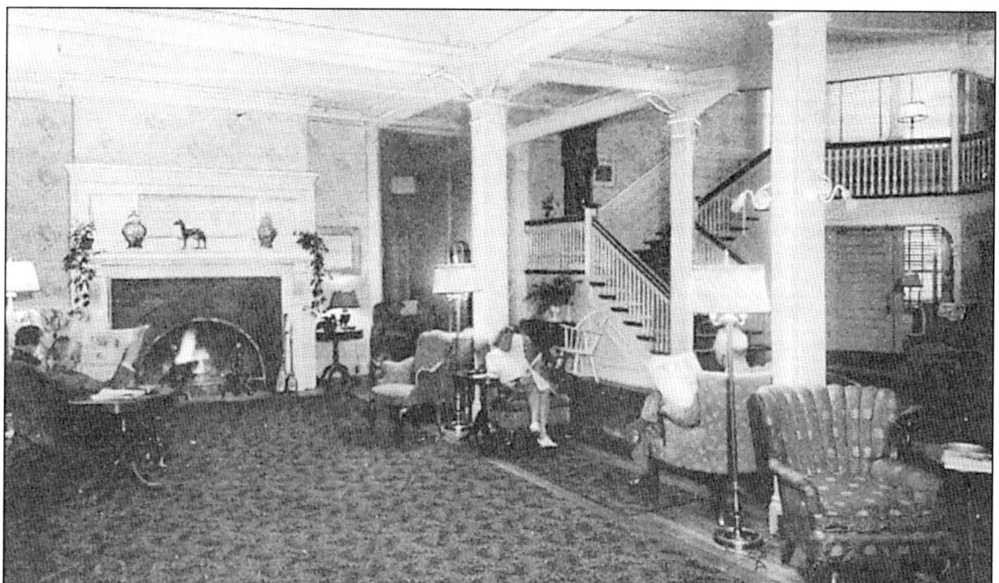

The comfortable and well-appointed front lobby of the new inn was where tea was served and guests were entertained by the Woodstock Inn Orchestra. Sunday evening concerts were open to the public. During the winter months, guests could warm themselves by relaxing before the open fireplace.

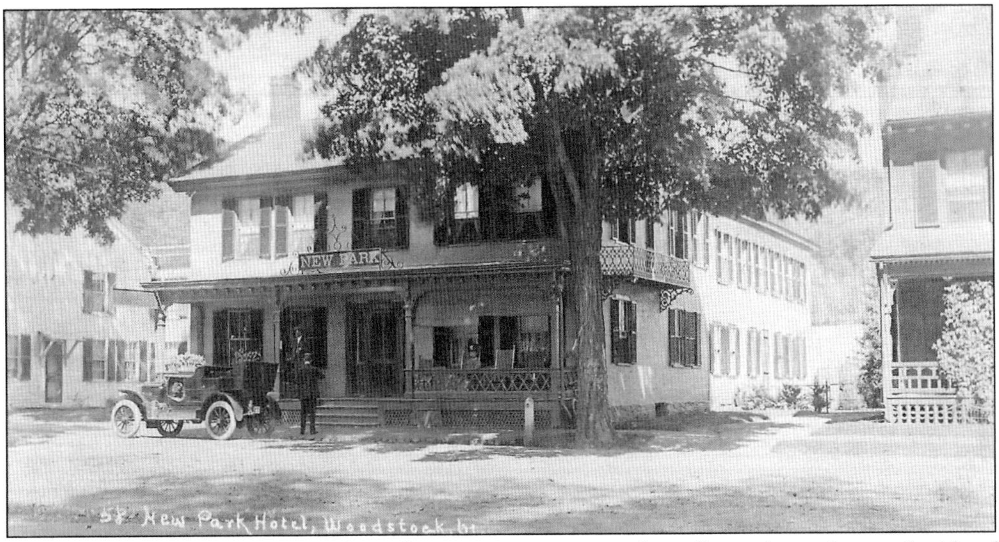

The Park Cottage Hotel, although no longer operating as such, still stands on the north side of the green. It was originally constructed in 1807 as a combination store and residence. In 1884, when the tourist trade into Woodstock was increasing in large part due to the opening of the Woodstock Railway, Victorian-era embellishments were added and it became a hotel, serving as such until 1915.

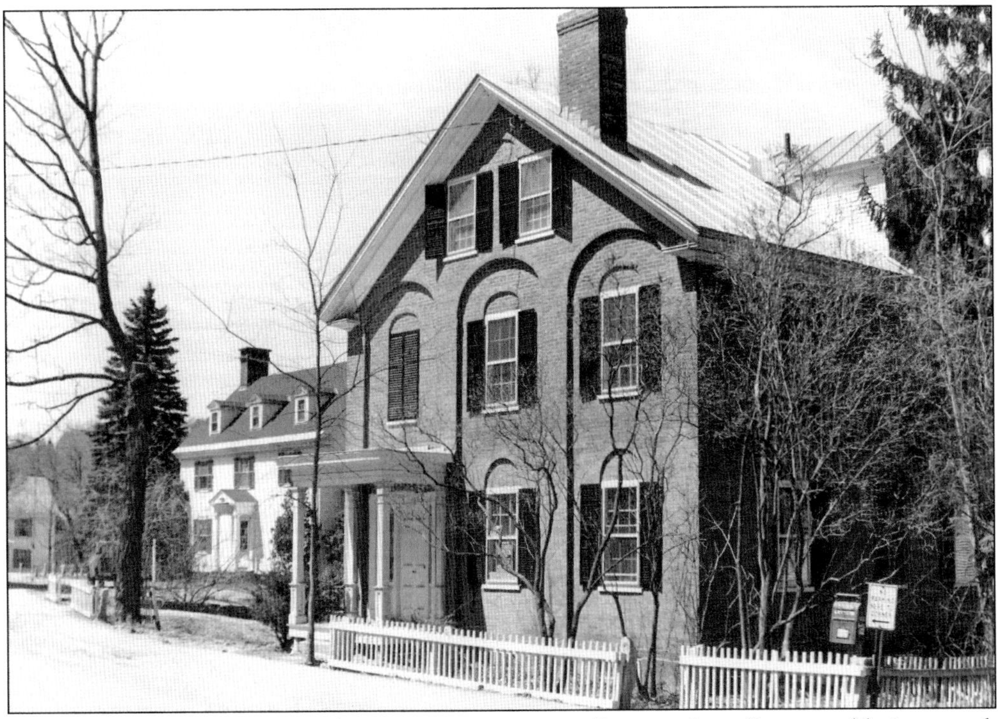

During the first half of the 20th century, as tourist traffic into the village steadily increased, some smaller, older buildings were made into inns, as seen here. For many years, the building was known as the Pember Inn at 11 Church Street. This striking Federal-style brick building was constructed in 1828 as a facility for the Clinical School of Medicine located on College Street (see page 79.)

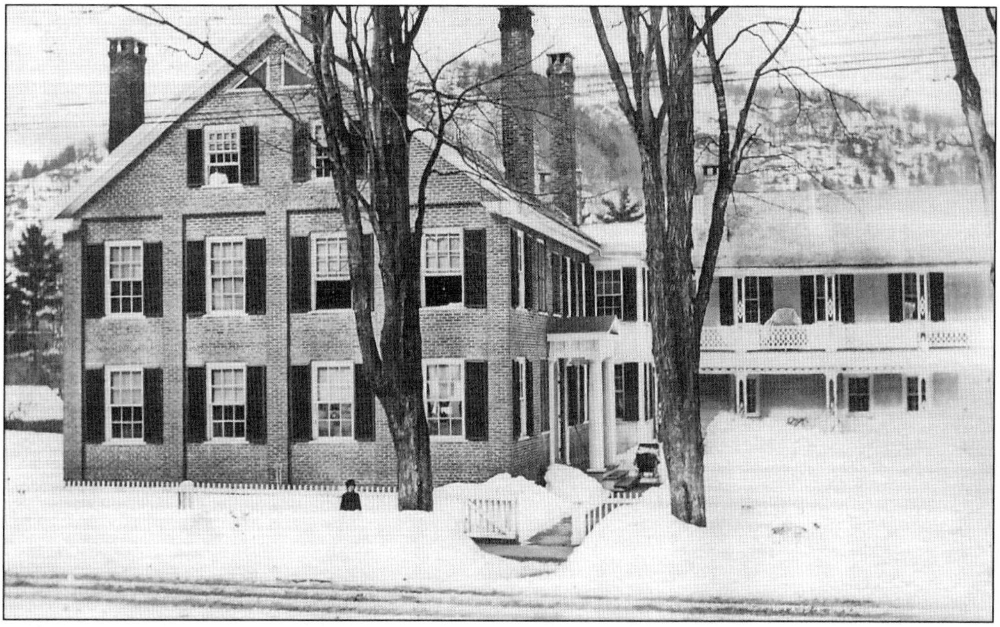

Joel Eaton was a longtime citizen and enterprising individual in Woodstock who, in 1831, constructed this sizable brick residence for his family, which still stands at 3 Church Street. Like the nearby Pember Inn, during the 20th century, the former Eaton residence became a small inn with a two-story wood-frame guest room annex added to the main building.

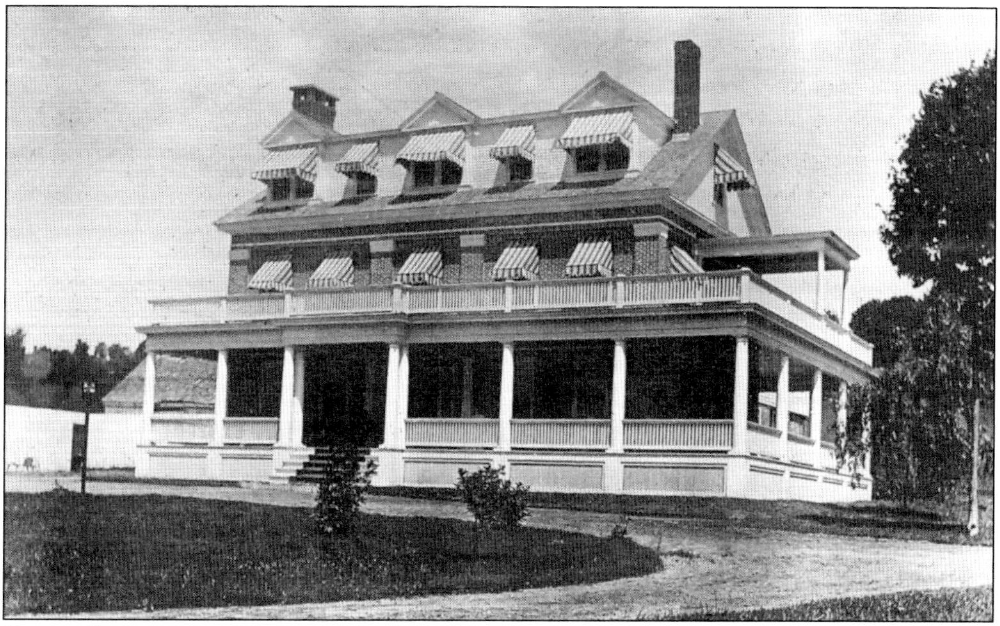

Originally catering to the stagecoach trade that passed through South Woodstock, Richard Ransom Jr. and Richard Mather, in 1826, constructed the National Hotel, which, in time, came to be called the Kedron Tavern (see page 32). In 1910, the building was extensively remodeled in the Colonial Revival style and reopened as the Colonial Inn. The new clientele were primarily early sightseeing motorists, experiencing the beauty of the Green Mountain State.

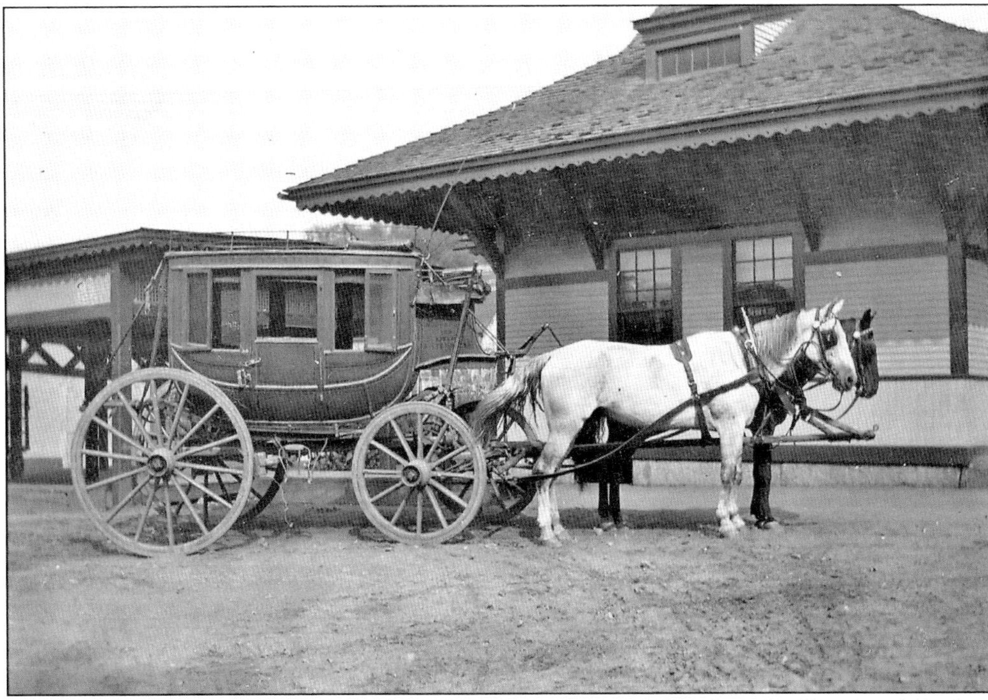

When the new Woodstock Inn opened in 1892, it sent a Concord Coach to the Woodstock Railway to pick up its guests, as seen here at the Woodstock station about 1900. By 1915, the horse-drawn coach had been replaced by a motorized bus; however, the coach continued to be used for taking visitors out to the nearby countryside for picnics and sightseeing tours.

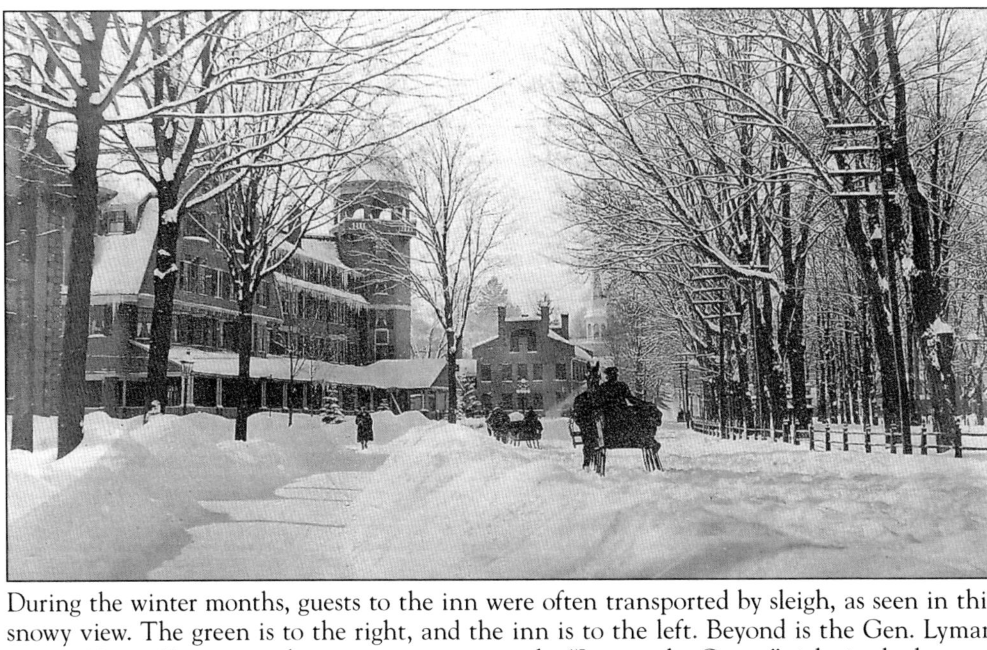

During the winter months, guests to the inn were often transported by sleigh, as seen in this snowy view. The green is to the right, and the inn is to the left. Beyond is the Gen. Lyman Mower House. For many urban visitors, staying at the "Inn on the Green," right in the heart of the historic village, was like a story from a mythically enchanted winter wonderland.

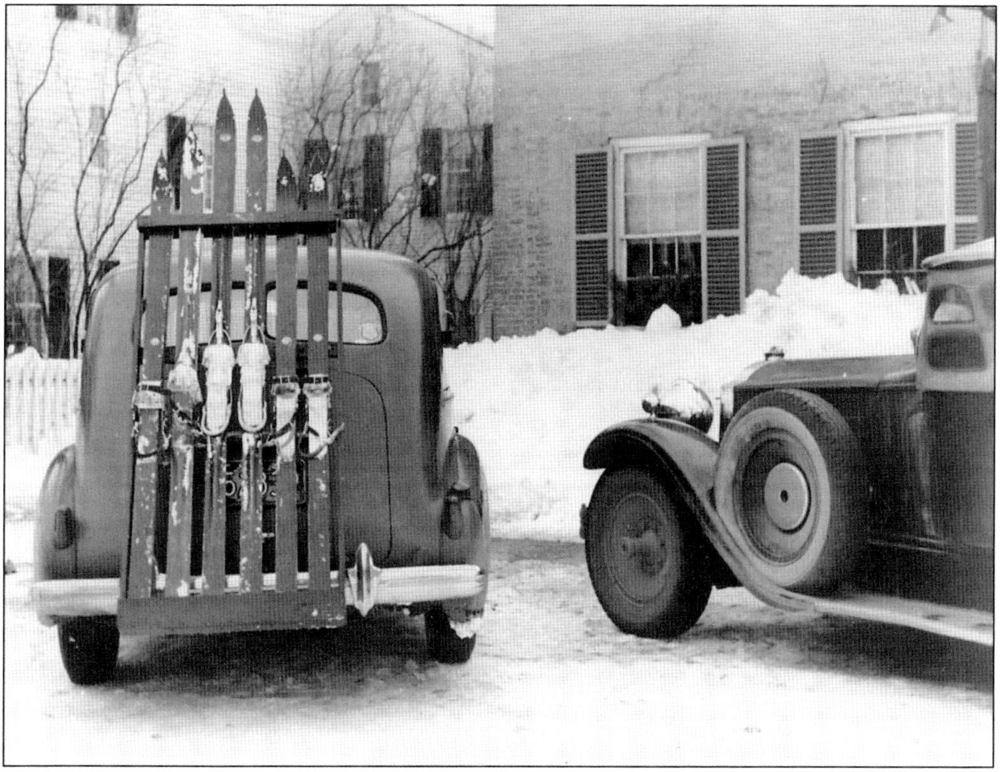

With better highways and the closing of the Woodstock Railway in April 1933, vacationing guests to Woodstock arrived in town driving their own automobiles throughout the year. Pictured in March 1940 parked in front of the White Cupboard Inn, a favorite of skiers, are a new family sedan complete with a ski rack on the left and an aging Packard touring car on the right.

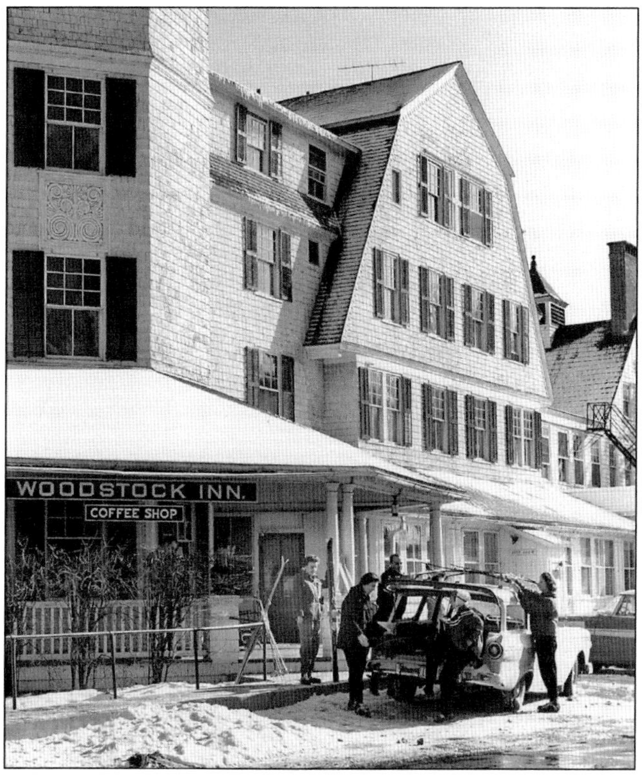

Driving a 1957 Ford station wagon, a family of skiers has pulled up in front of the coffee shop at the Woodstock Inn, either coming from or going to the ski slopes. By this time, skiing was an important business not only in Woodstock with the opening of two ski areas but also within the central Green Mountains of the state of Vermont.

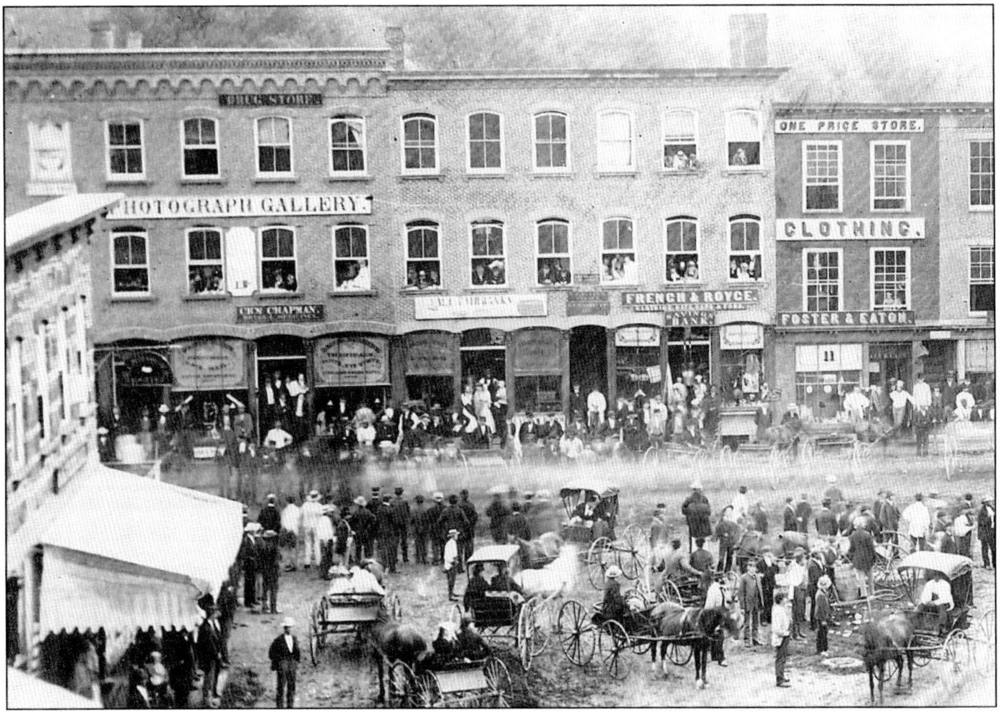

By the 1880s, equestrian-related activities had become popular in and around Woodstock. This was no doubt due in part to the yearly presence of the Windsor County Fair and, later, events sponsored by the Woodstock Inn. Here, in 1875, a horse race streaks through the square, too fast for the camera's shutter.

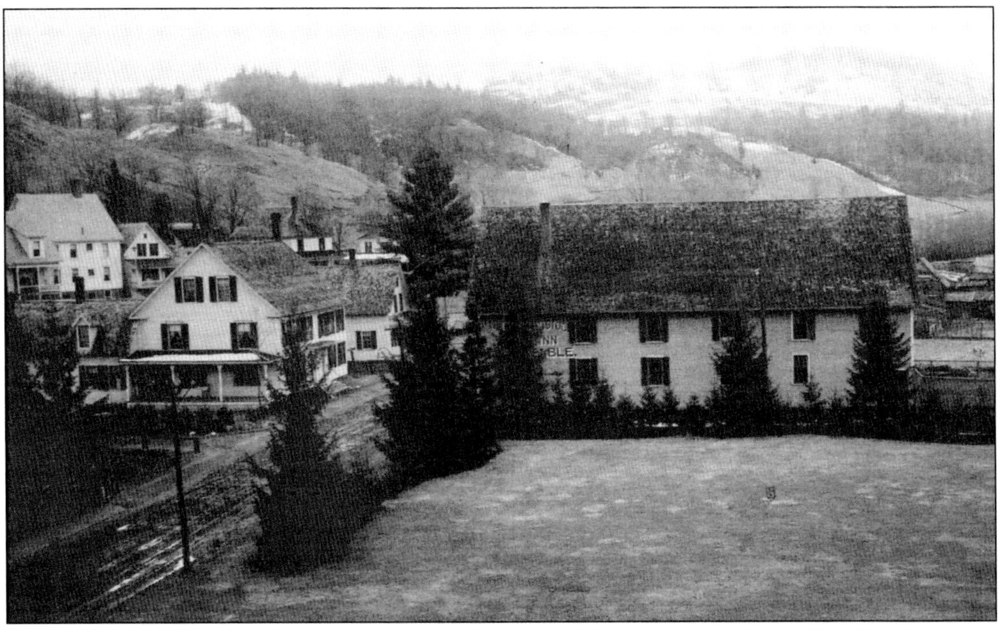

When the new Woodstock Inn opened in 1892, one of the many activities offered to its guests was horseback riding. The first stable that the inn kept, shown here in this c. 1900 view, burned in 1905 and was soon replaced by a far larger facility.

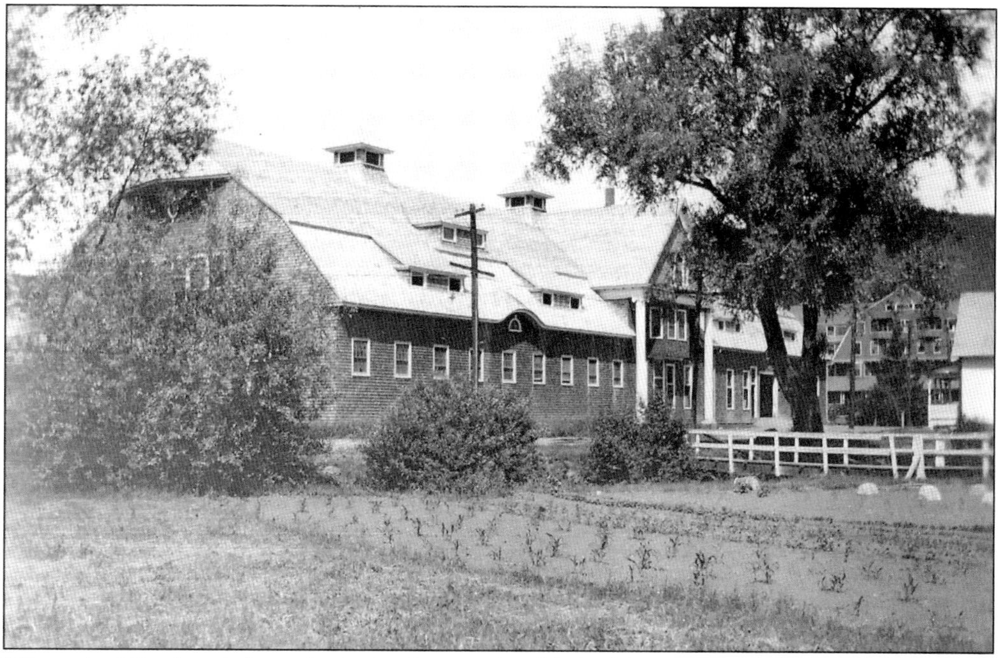

When the Woodstock Inn rebuilt the destroyed stable building, it was indeed considered to be the finest in the country. The new facility had a significantly greater architectural presence and offered heated waiting and powder rooms for the human clientele. Sixty horses could be comfortably stabled, and a lift allowed for ample carriage storage on the upper level. In the background, the new inn can be seen.

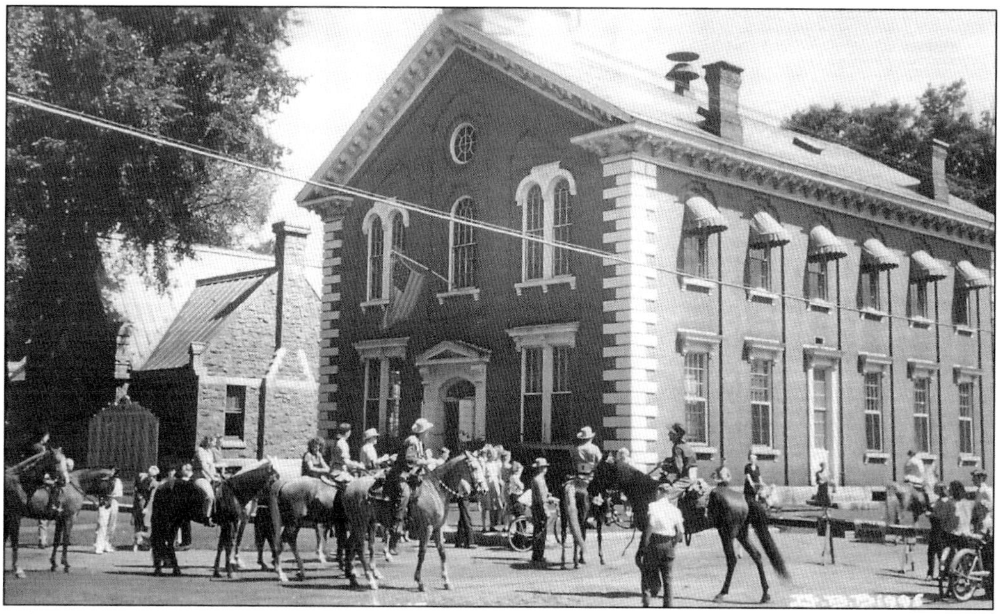

After World War II, and well into the 1950s, horseback riding remained very popular with Woodstock Inn guests. Here, a group of riders has assembled out on the street in front of the green and the courthouse and is eagerly awaiting the ride to come up into the hills surrounding the village. Some rides were 100 miles long. To the left is the Norman Williams Library.

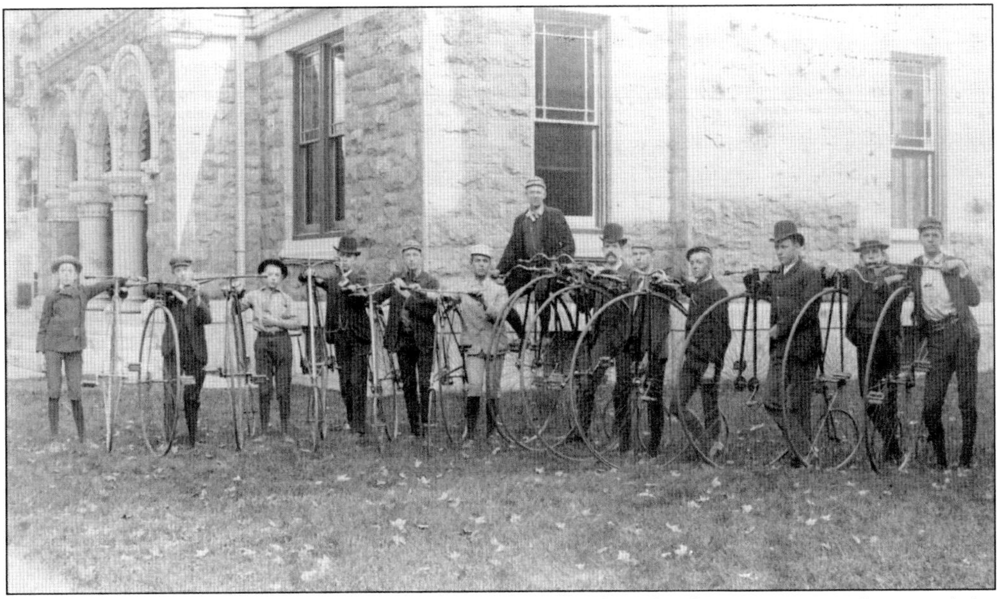

From the mid-1870s until the introduction of the safety bicycle about 1890 was the era of the high-wheeled bicycle craze in America—a craze dominated by daring men on their "boneshakers." Here is a group of such individuals beside the new Norman Williams Library, perhaps about to embark on a group ride out into the countryside along Woodstock's dirt roads.

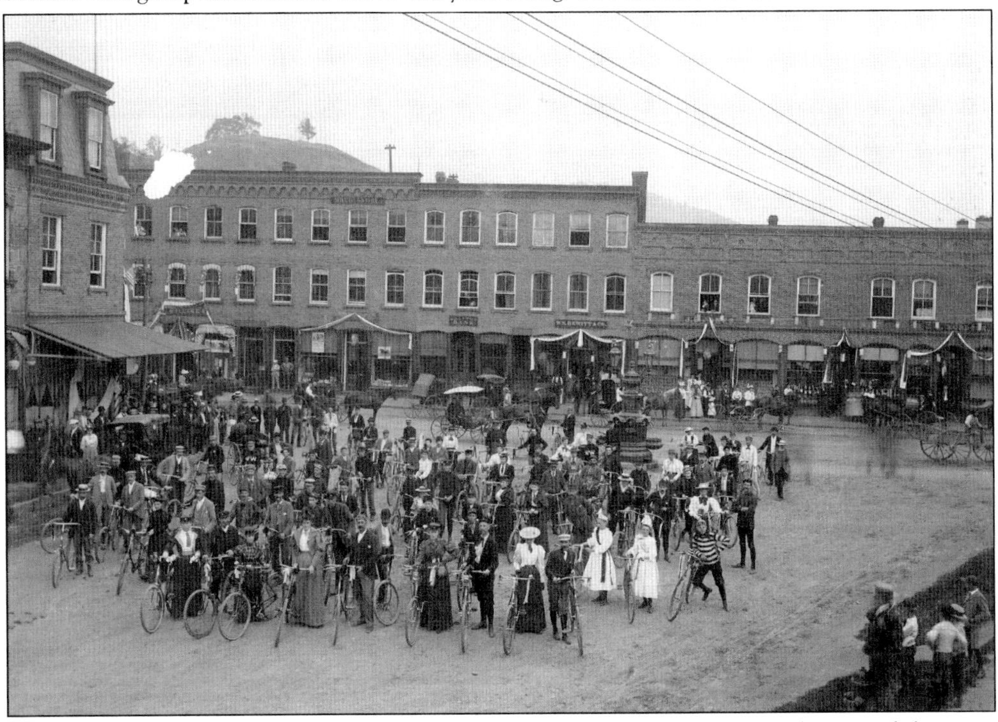

The introduction about 1890 and mass popularity of the so-called safety bicycle opened the sport of bicycle riding up to both men and women. This 1890s view shows a group of bicycle riders, probably staying at the new Woodstock Inn, assembled in the square and about to head down Elm Street and out of town on a tour around the Mount Tom area.

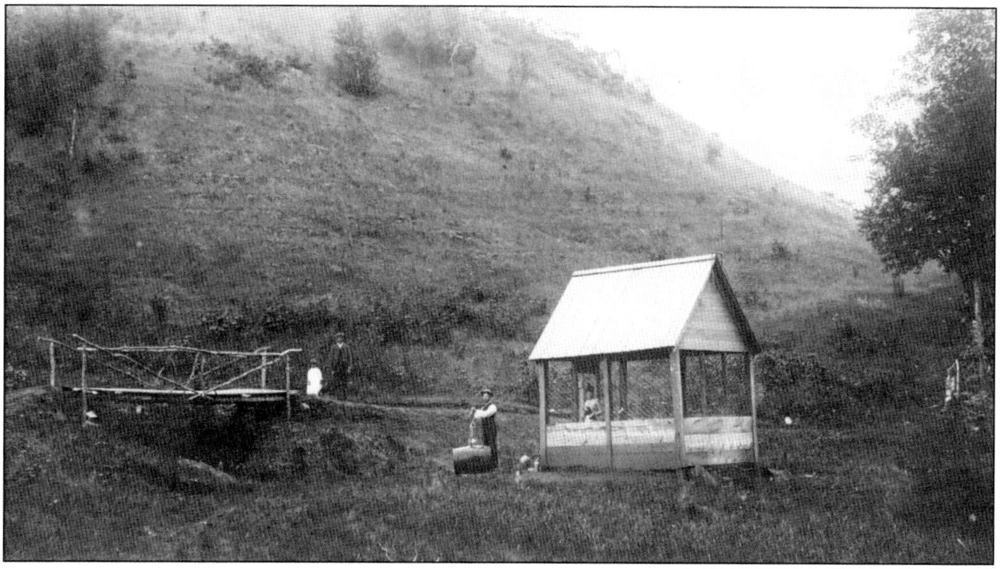

The new Woodstock Inn realized that it had much to offer, but no medicinal waters like at so many other late-18th-century resort communities. Therefore, what locals called Sanderson's Spring, located just south of the village on Dunham Hill, came to be advertised by entrepreneur Walter Dearborn for the healing properties of its waters. By the 1890s, what had been a local springhouse became, at times, a mob scene.

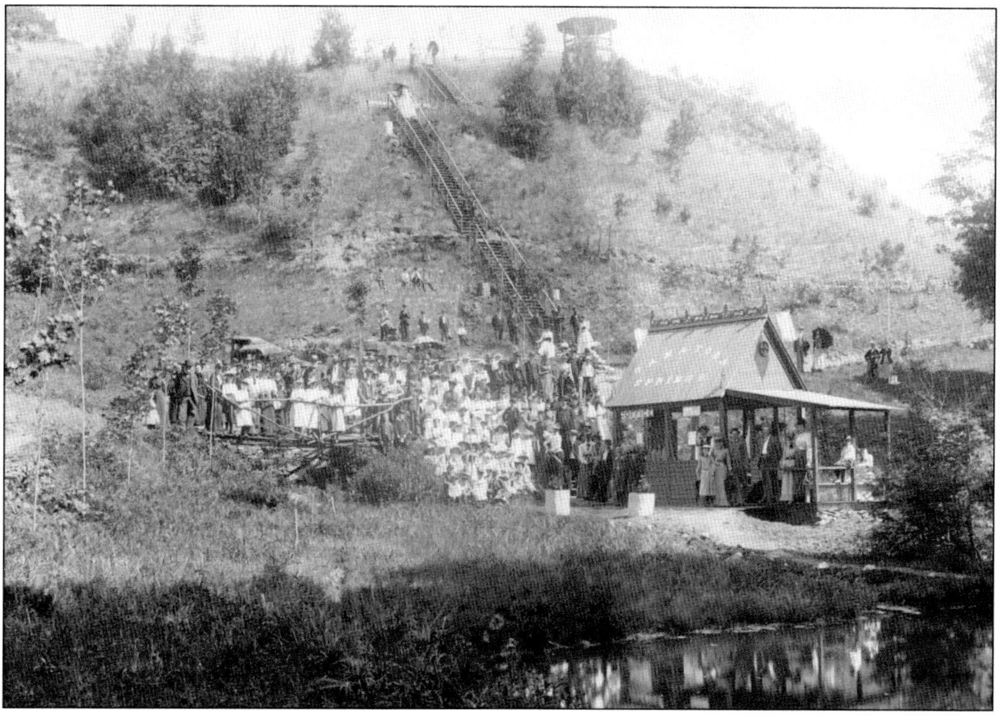

Walter Dearborn changed the name to Sanatoga Springs, dressed up the former springhouse, and created a 15-acre park complete with trails, rustic bridges, bridle paths, and pavilions. Dearborn claimed that the spring's water was beneficial for one's kidneys and skin ailments and, generally, was "miraculous." Meanwhile, the Woodstock Inn did a booming business until the craze subsided.

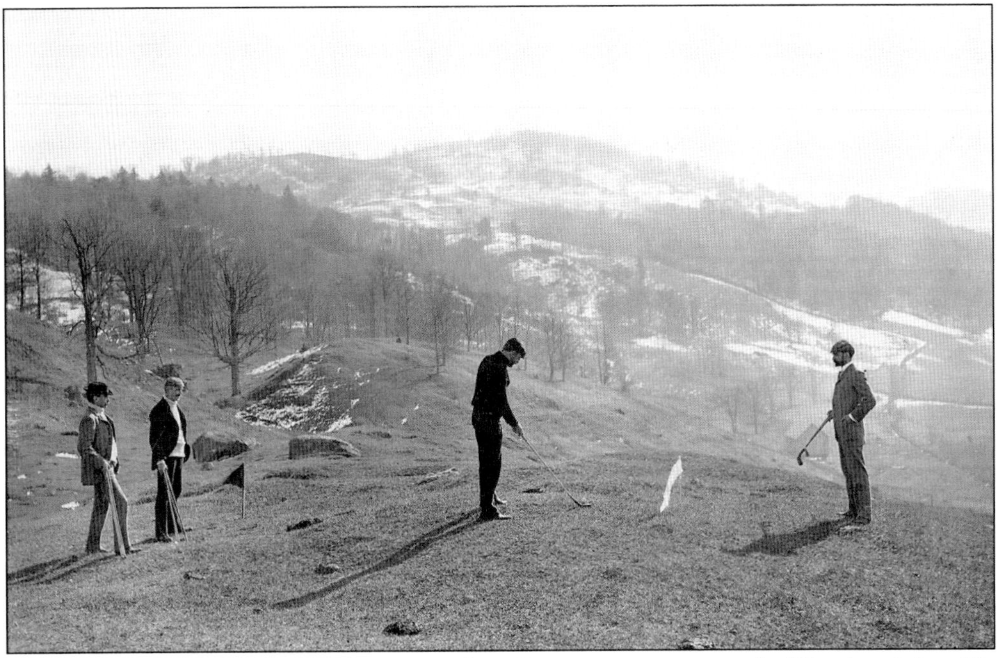

In October 1895, Dr. Francis B. Harrington from Boston was staying at the Woodstock Inn. He had brought along his golf clubs but was disappointed to learn from general manager Arthur Wilder that there were no golf links in Woodstock, let alone all of Vermont. That month, Dr. Harrington had Wilder up on the barren slopes of Mount Peg, where he demonstrated and sold Woodstock on the new sport.

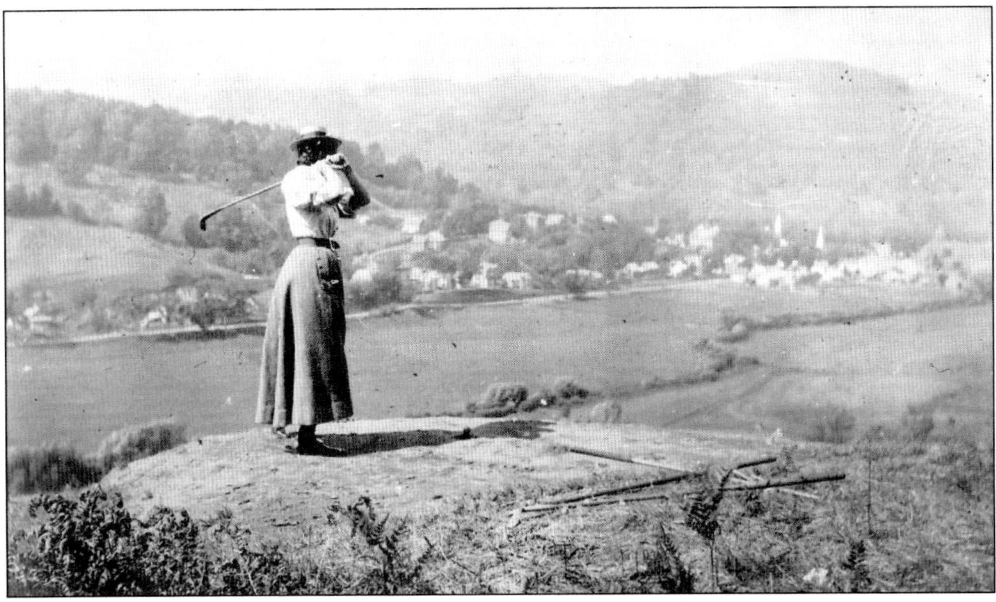

Golf immediately became popular in Woodstock, and as a result, the first golf course in Vermont was established late in 1895 and was called, appropriately enough, the Woodstock Country Club. Here, around 1900, Mary Montagu Billings French (1869–1951), daughter of Fredrick Billings tees off from high up on the slopes of Mount Peg. The Kedron Brook valley is below, and the village of Woodstock is shown beyond.

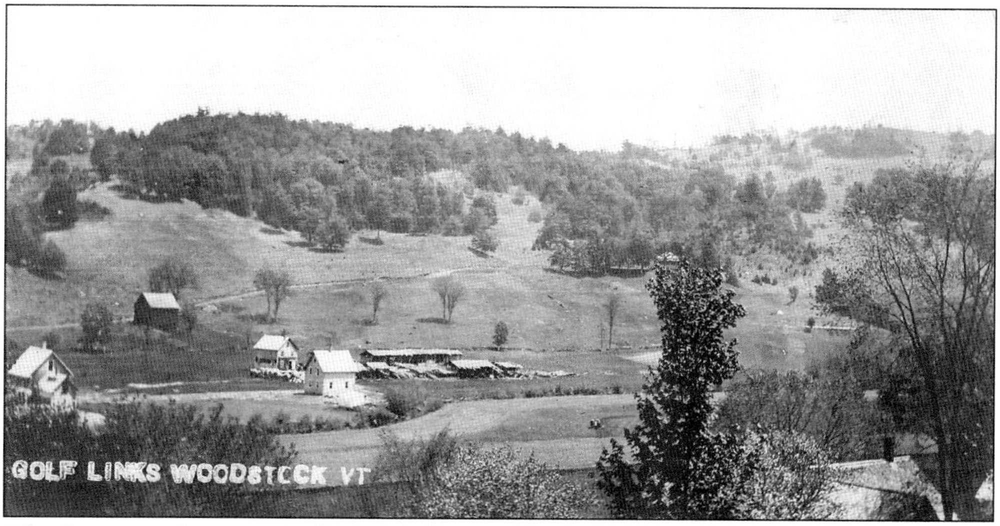

After becoming first organized in 1895, the Woodstock Country Club acquired land along both sides of Kedron Brook and further refined the layout of its links, as illustrated here with this c. 1915 real-photo postcard view. The somewhat rough nature of the former farmland is still apparent. In time, the links would become an 18-hole golf course.

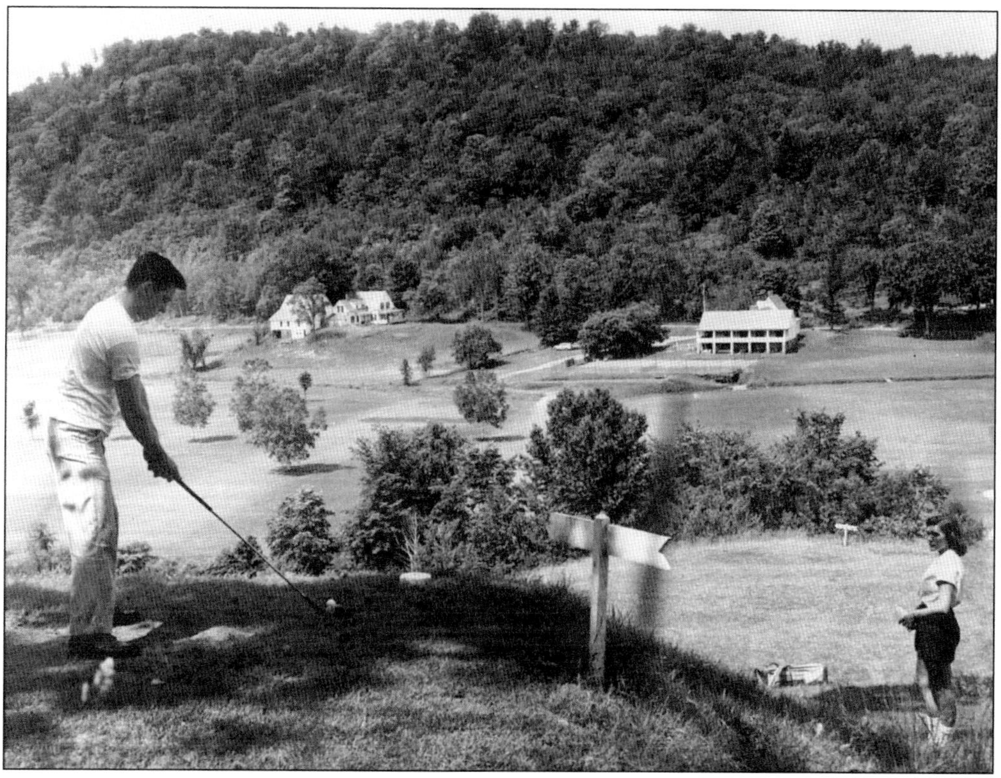

This 1950s photograph of a couple at the seventh tee, with the clubhouse visible beyond, illustrates how the golf course had become more manicured. In 1963, after having been acquired by Laurance S. Rockefeller's RockResorts enterprise, the course was substantially redesigned to be one of the finest in the Northeast region by noted golf course architect Robert Trent Jones Sr. (1906–2000).

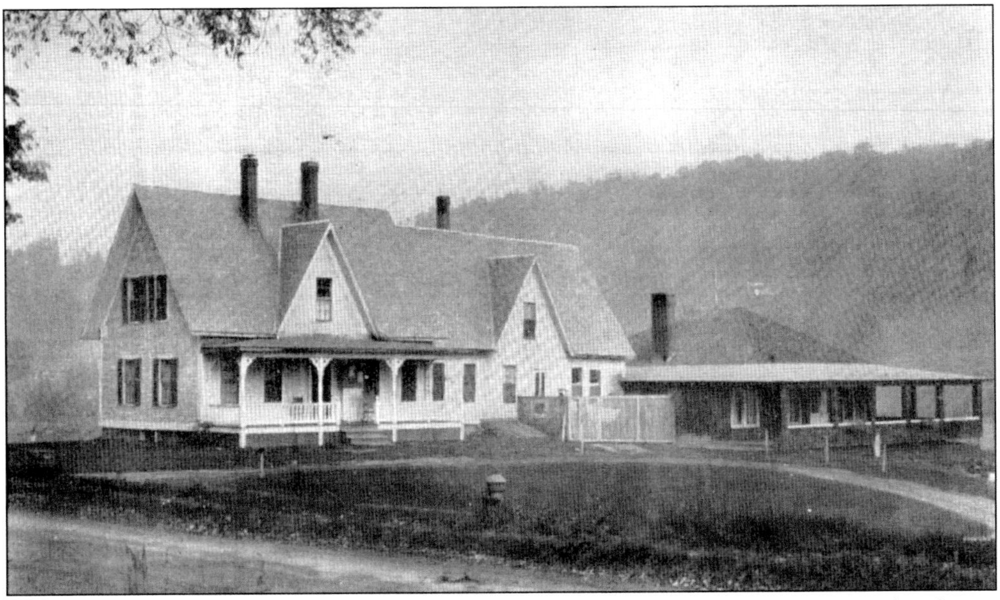

The first clubhouse of the Woodstock Country Club was simply a mid-19th-century farmhouse minimally converted to serve the needs of those playing the early golf links. However, early in the 20th century, a gracious and inviting covered porch addition was constructed in the Shingle style.

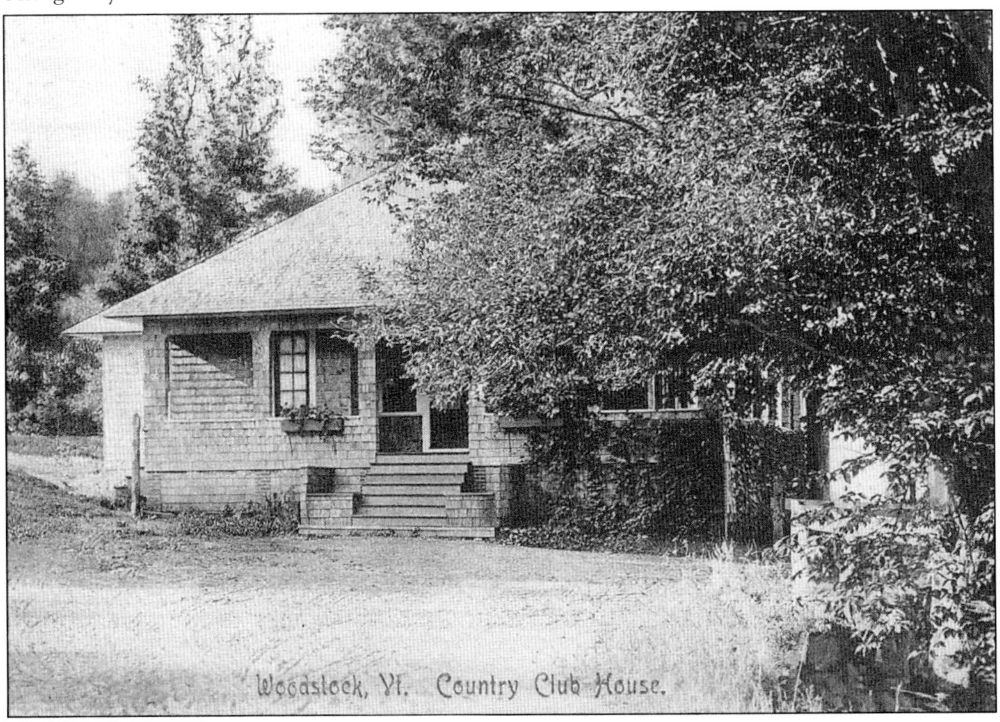

By the early years of the 20th century, the former farmhouse that had been converted to serve as a clubhouse was no more. In its place was a new facility designed in the Shingle style, popular at the time for resort and summer cottage architecture in New England. This building too would later be replaced as part of the upgrades to the overall golf course made by RockResorts.

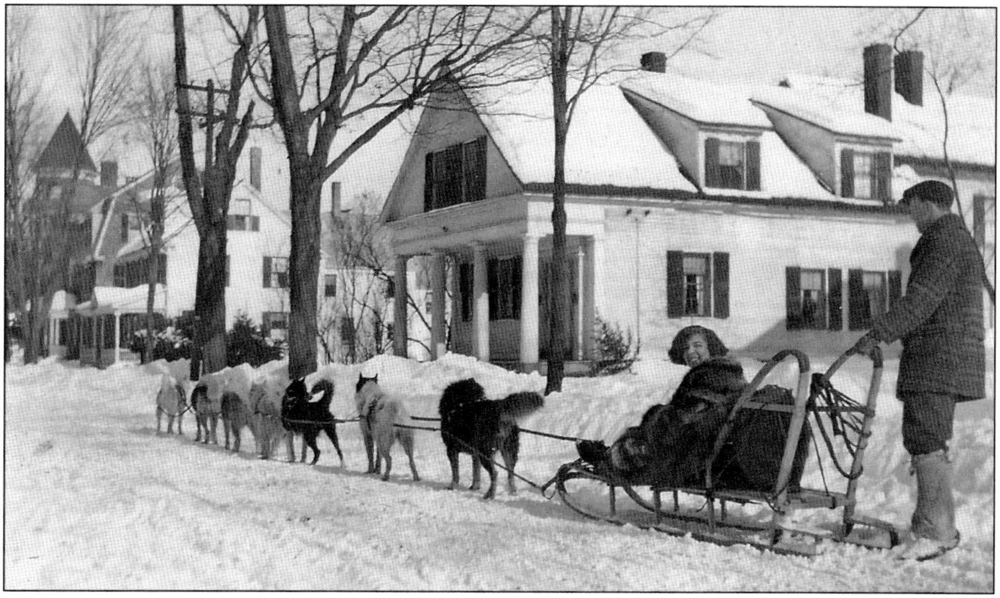

Wintertime dogsledding events around the green and into the side streets of the village remained popular into the 1950s, as seen here in this snowy scene. Note the observation tower of the Woodstock Inn visible in the background. The dogs do not seem to be working very hard, or even paying any attention to commands being made by the musher. Regardless, the young woman appears to be enjoying herself.

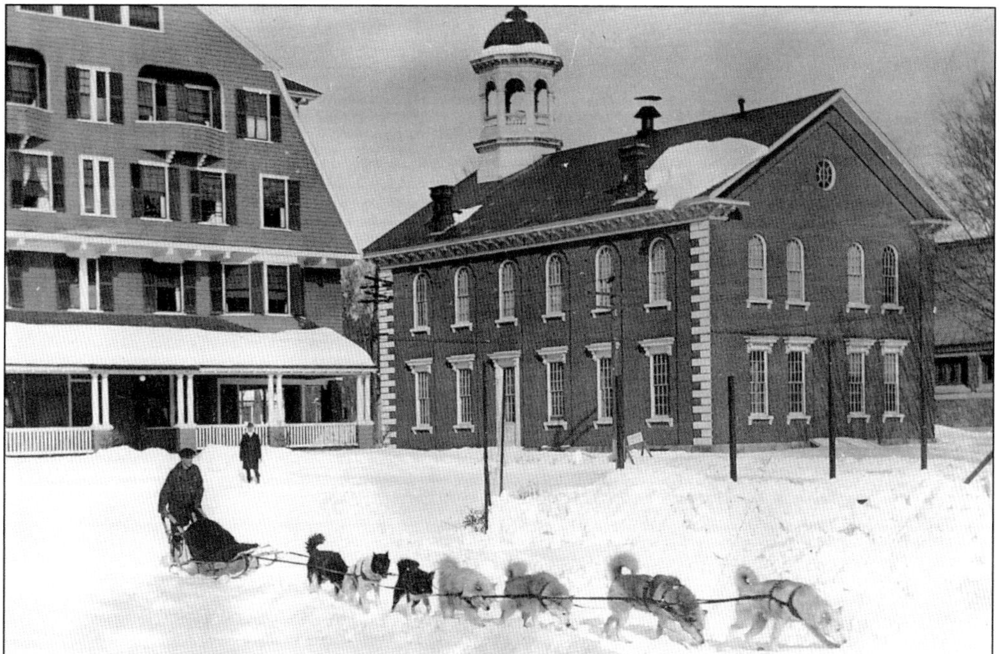

This photograph of a dog team setting out from the Woodstock Inn is also an excellent view of the side and rear of the Windsor County Courthouse, constructed in 1854. The dogs appear to be more interested in picking up the scent of perhaps a previous team than providing the passenger on the sled a good run.

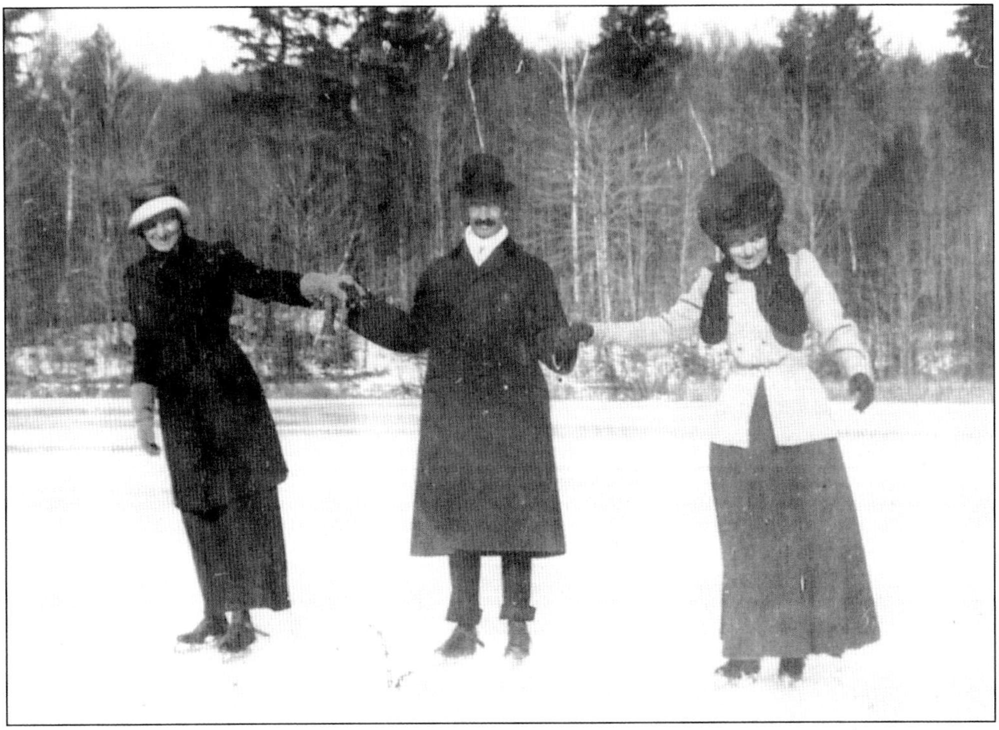

The Pogue is a 14-acre man-made pond created in the 1880s near the summit of Mount Tom. Reached by scenic carriage roads, it had become a popular spot for ice-skaters staying at the Woodstock Inn by the early years of the 20th century. Here, a gentleman, who was probably employed by the inn as an activities director, is escorting two ladies out onto the ice.

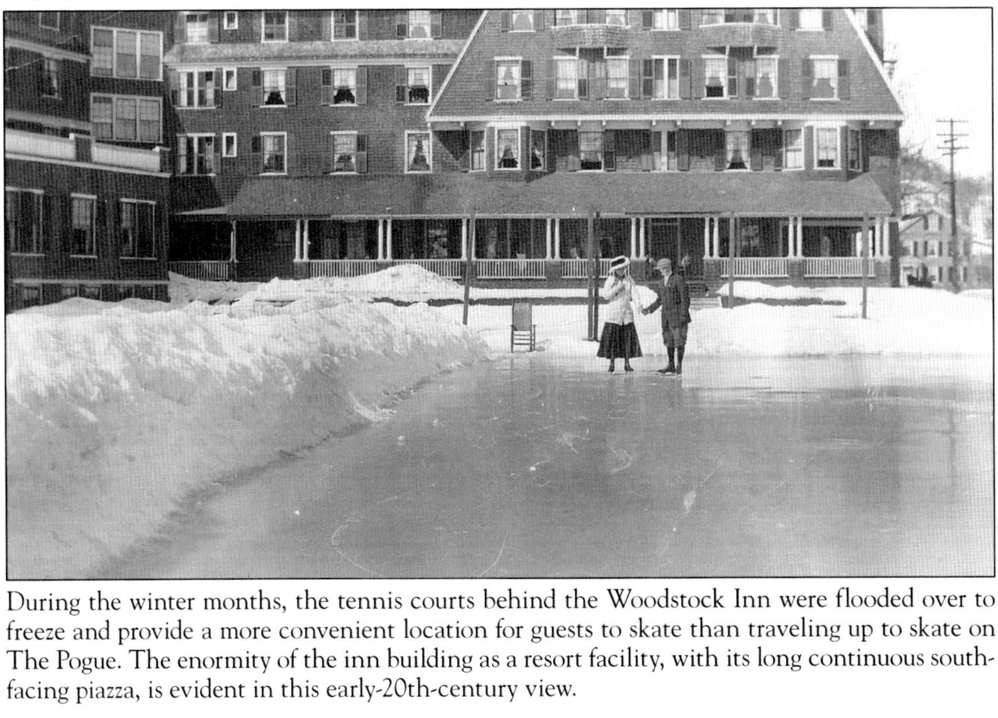

During the winter months, the tennis courts behind the Woodstock Inn were flooded over to freeze and provide a more convenient location for guests to skate than traveling up to skate on The Pogue. The enormity of the inn building as a resort facility, with its long continuous south-facing piazza, is evident in this early-20th-century view.

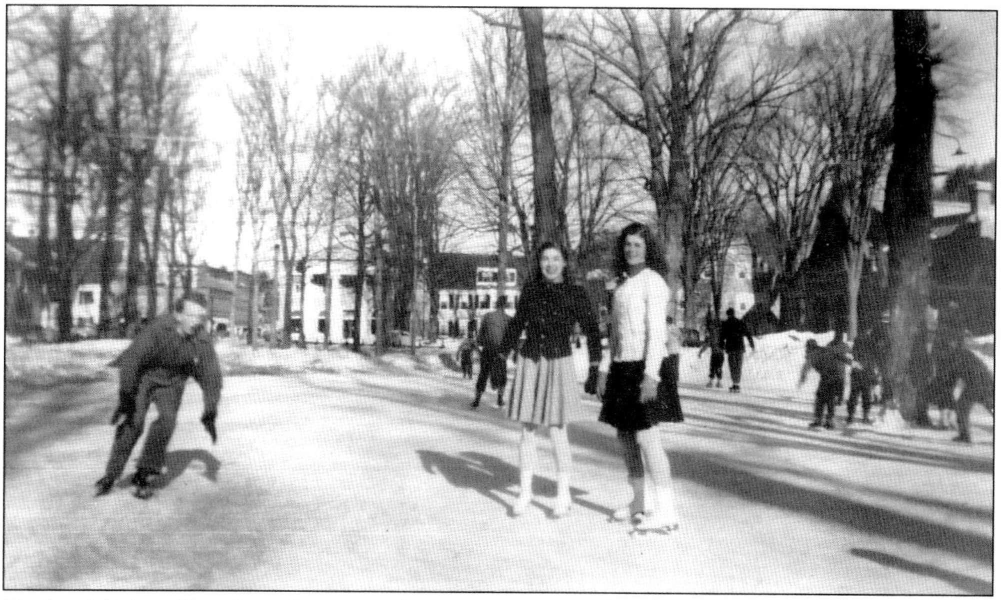

To the delight of locals and visitors, during winter months, the green was flooded and left to freeze, transforming it to a temporary skating rink. The young man to the left appears to be trying mightily to impress the two girls, perhaps from the city and guests at the inn, with his speed-skating techniques. The Ottauquechee Savings Bank building is in the background.

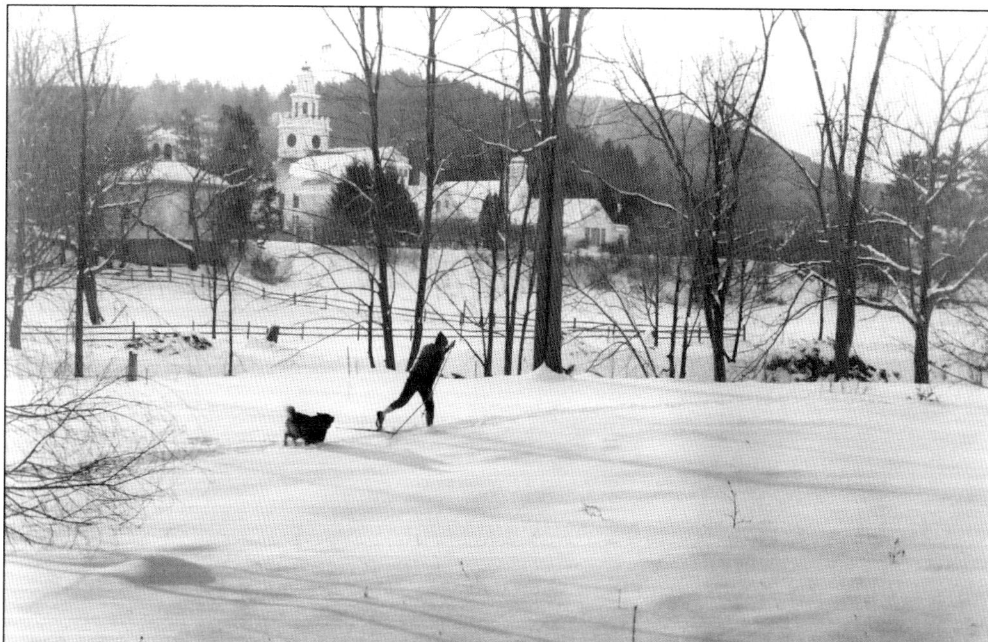

The back side of the First Congregational Church and related buildings along the river side of Elm Street provide a beautiful village backdrop for a cross-country skier and his dog out for a morning run. Woodstock became a popular destination for cross-country skiers, even when the sport was in its infancy in the United States, with warm accommodations in the village and trails immediately at the village's edge.

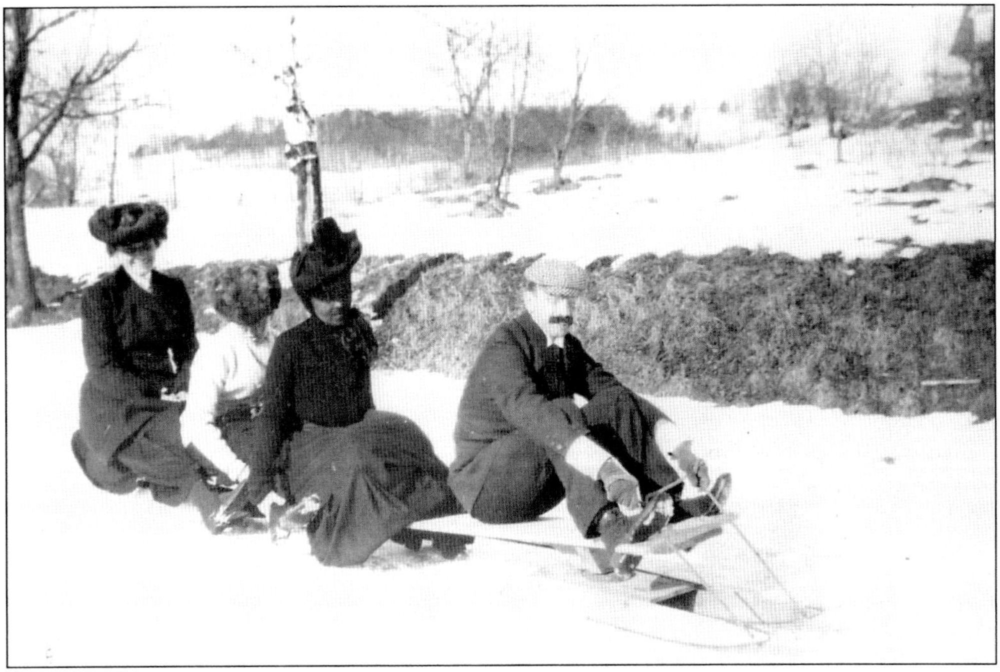

Sledding was a popular winter activity at the turn of the century. The same gentleman shown helping women skaters in the view on page 116 appears ready to guide the sled with three out-of-town ladies aboard on a breathtaking run down a steep hill. This and the image on page 116 might be promotional photographs taken by the Woodstock Inn.

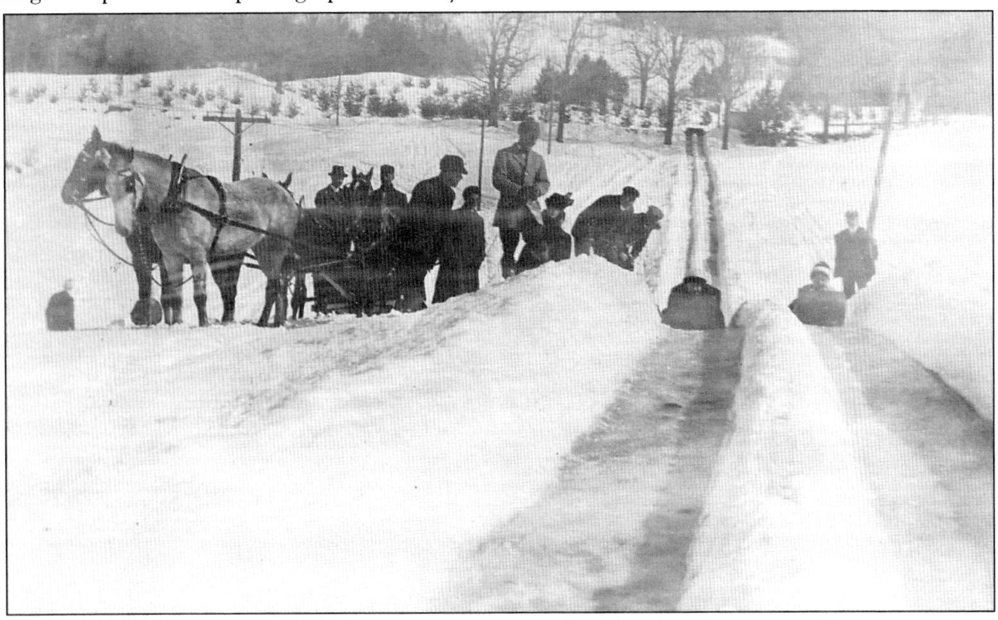

Also, tobogganing was a popular wintertime sport for Woodstock visitors. Here, a two-lane toboggan run has been carefully constructed and iced over in this c. 1910 view. Teams of horses from the Woodstock Inn's stables were used to pull the toboggans and their passengers back up the hill for another run. By 1910, the inn was featuring a 1,000-foot-long electrically lit toboggan chute out on the golf course.

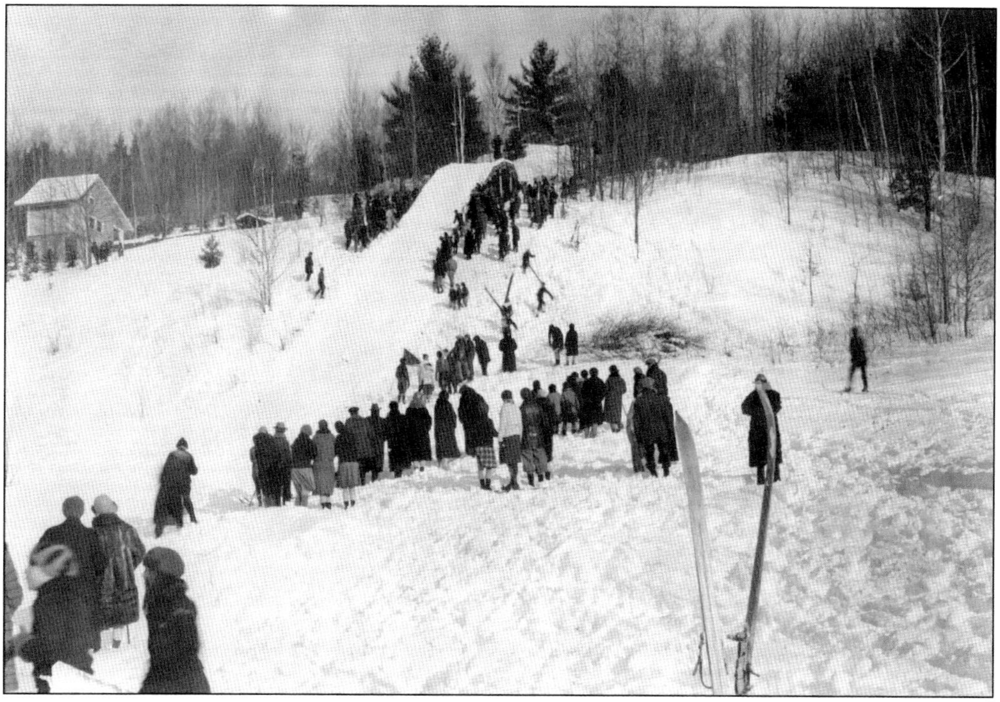

Winter carnival had, by February 22, 1930, when this photograph was taken, become a major annual event in Woodstock, in large part sponsored and organized by the Woodstock Inn. One of the many winter sports and activities available to visitors was ski jumping. Note that, before the days of ski tows, skiers had to climb back up the hill they had just come down, through the deep snow.

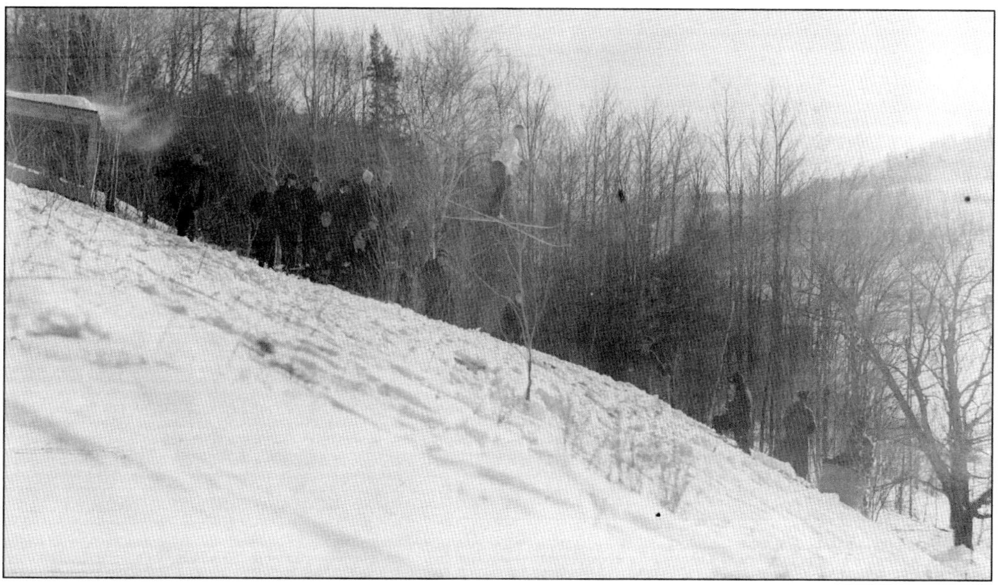

Taken up on the side of Mount Peg, this photograph shows an early ski jumper airborne. Before ski trails were developed on the back side of Mount Tom in the mid-1930s, winter recreational events, organized by the Woodstock Inn and other groups, took place on the slopes of Mount Peg and on the snow-covered land of the Woodstock Country Club.

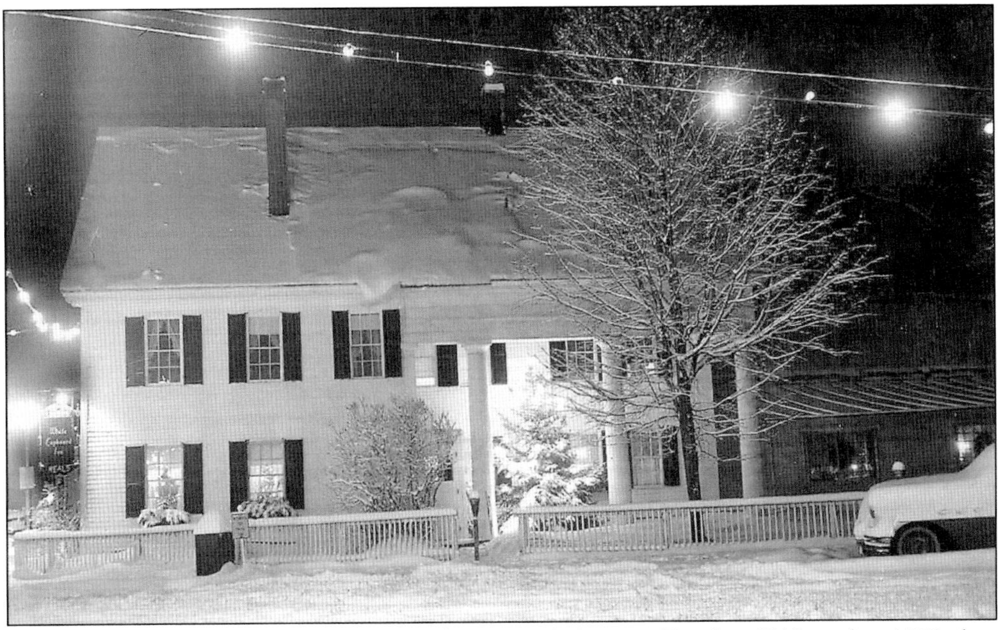

Robert and Elizabeth Royce acquired the former Park Cottage Hotel in 1918, and in 1925, they added the Hutchinson house that prominently faces the square. That year, utilizing the combined real estate, they opened the White Cupboard Inn, which soon became a popular place for skiers from afar. People were drawn to Woodstock's open and hospitable countryside. The inn certainly offers a warm and inviting presence in this c. 1960 view.

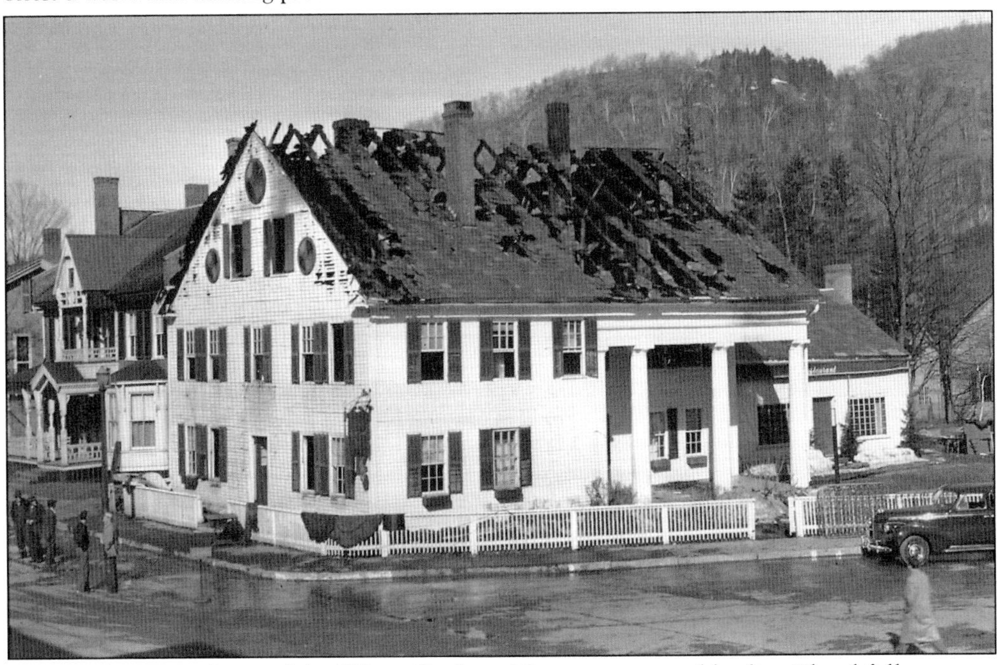

In 1941, the upper floors of the White Cupboard Inn were ravaged by fire. Thankfully, no one was injured and the Woodstock Fire Department saved the building from complete ruin. Within short order, the building was repaired to its former appearance, and business resumed as before. In the earlier years of the hospitality business, fire was always a constant fear.

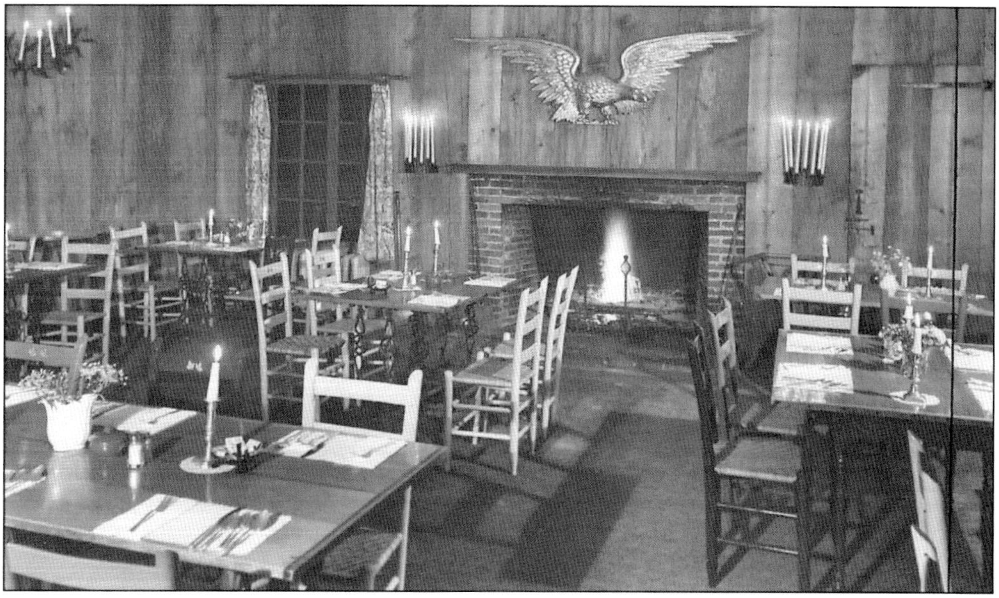

Pictured is the warm and hospitable dining room of the White Cupboard Inn. Little is known about the wooden eagle with an eight-foot wingspan above the fireplace. It may well have been in this room that, in January 1934, the idea for constructing the first ski tow in the United States was suggested to the Royces by three avid skiers that were staying at the inn.

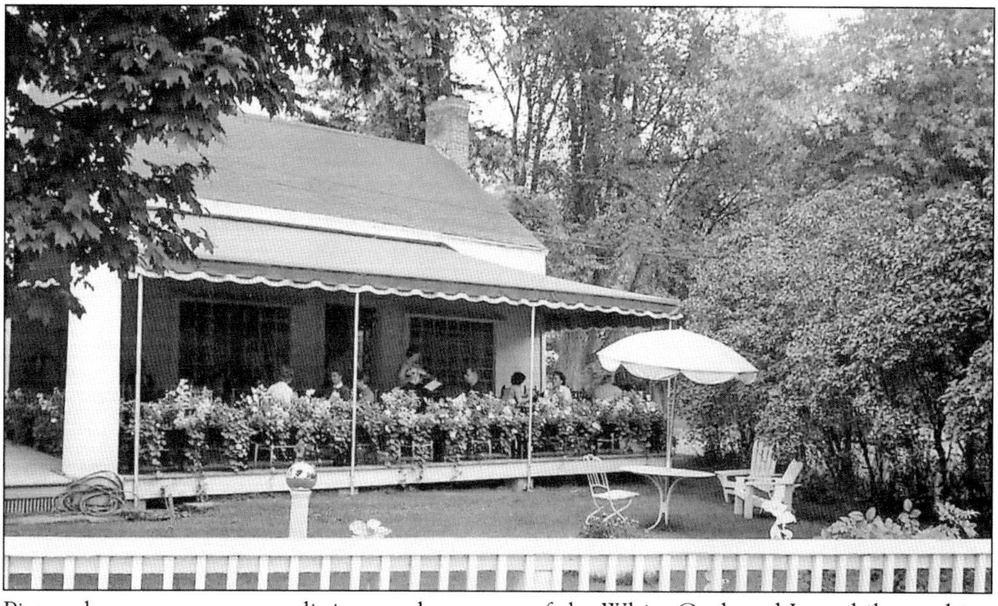

Pictured are summer guests dining on the terrace of the White Cupboard Inn while watching village life pass by. The Royces sold the inn to Mary and Nelson Lee, who, in 1953, hired George and Georgina Williamson from Scotland to manage it. Despite having 17 rooms available and a loyal clientele, by 1967, the inn was forced to close as the economics in a fast-changing world were working against it.

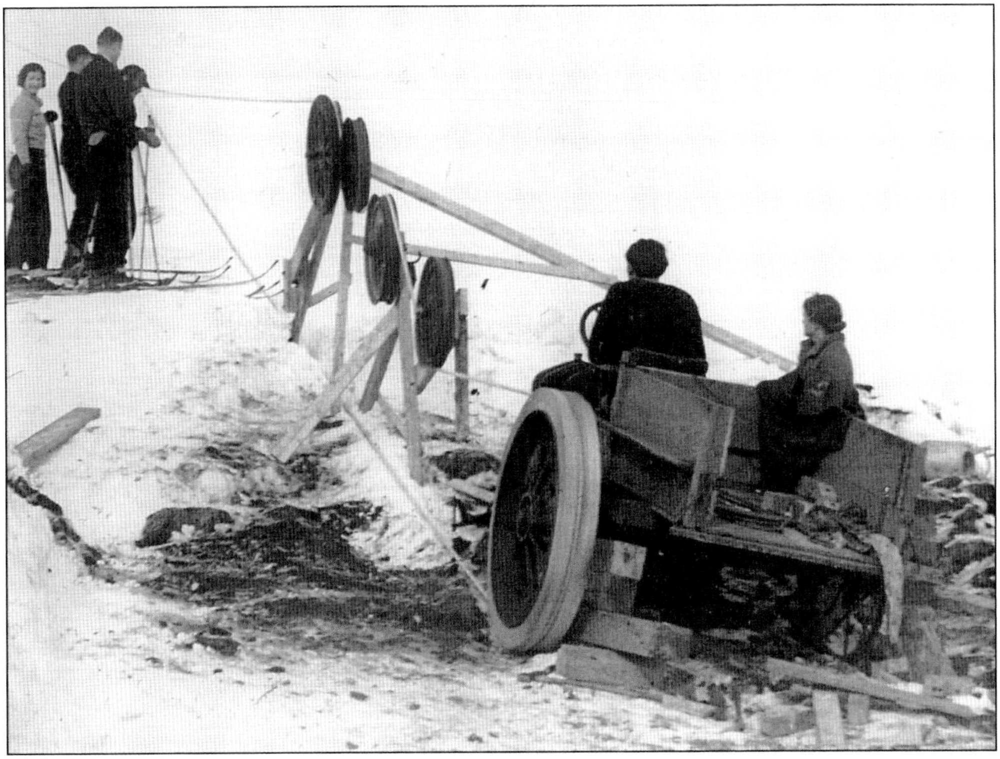

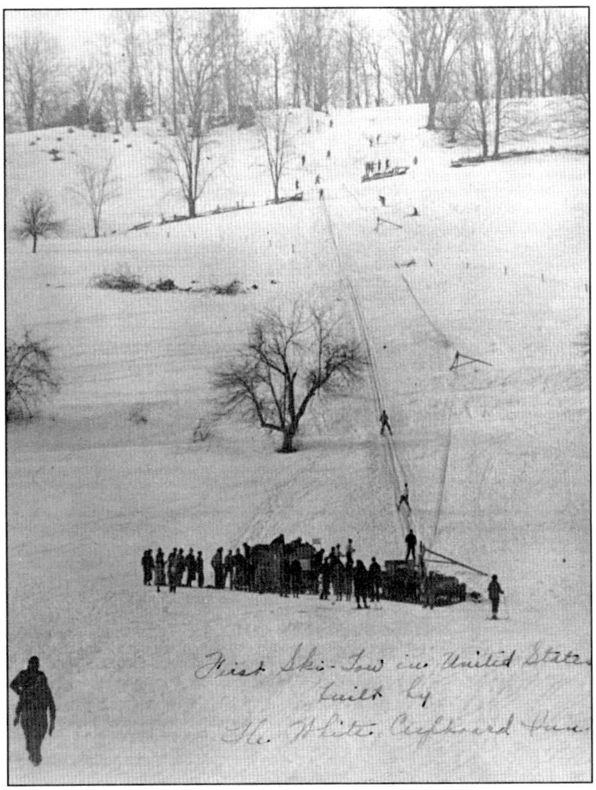

An after-dinner discussion between the owners of the White Cupboard Inn and three guests led to assembling the first ski tow in the United States. Located out on Clint Gilbert's hill, 1,800 feet of rope and a Ford Model T with a Montgomery Ward Pulford tractor conversion supplied the power on opening day, January 29, 1934. A new era in skiing in Woodstock, and well beyond, had begun.

Clint Gilbert's hillside was part of his farm located a short distance out of the village and near Mount Tom. This view shows the newly operational rope tow pulling skiers uphill in the winter of 1934. William Koch, Elizabeth Royce's brother, and his friend David Dodd were the ones who designed and assembled the ski lift for the Royces.

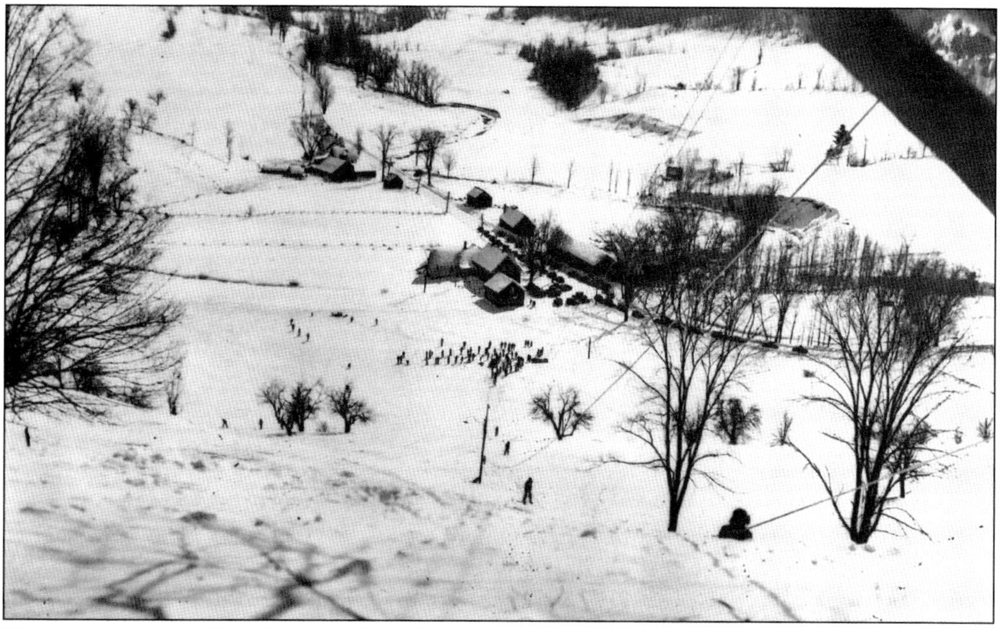

That same winter, this photograph with a view looking downhill from the top of the famous ski tow was taken. Clint Gilbert's farm buildings are seen at the base, while anxious skiers are gathering to await their turn for a lift back up the hill. Douglas Burden, Tommy Gammack, and Barklie Henry were the three skiers who recommended the idea to the Royces.

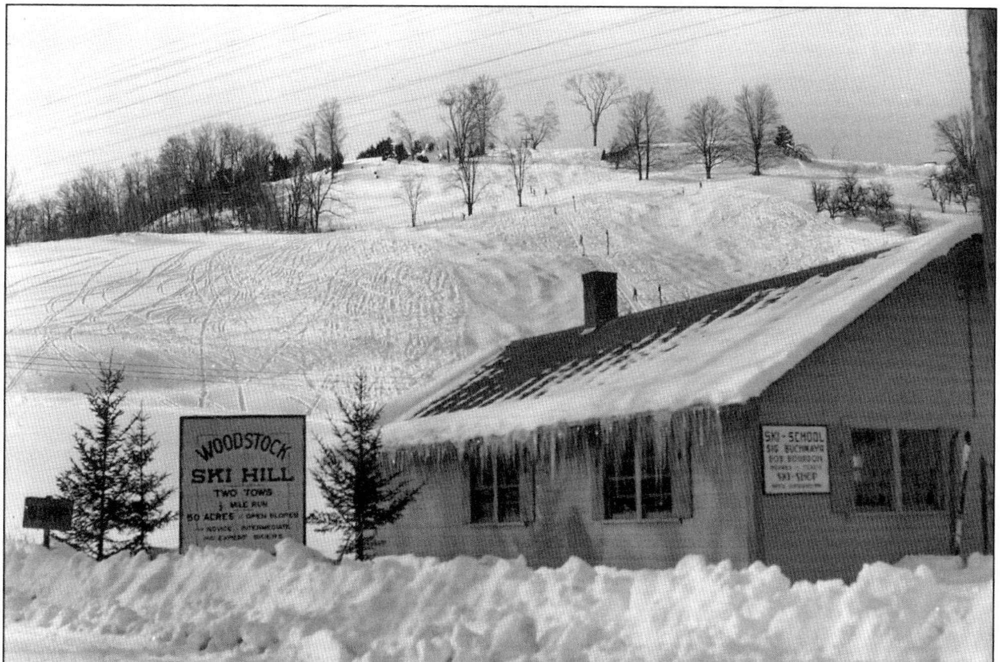

By 1940, a more refined rope tow had replaced the first job, and operations at Gilbert's hill, now called Woodstock Ski Hill, numbered two lifts, a warming hut, and a ski school. Clearly, Woodstock was in the forefront of what would develop into a major industry in Vermont and elsewhere in the country following World War II. In the 1950s, this became known as the Mount Tom ski area.

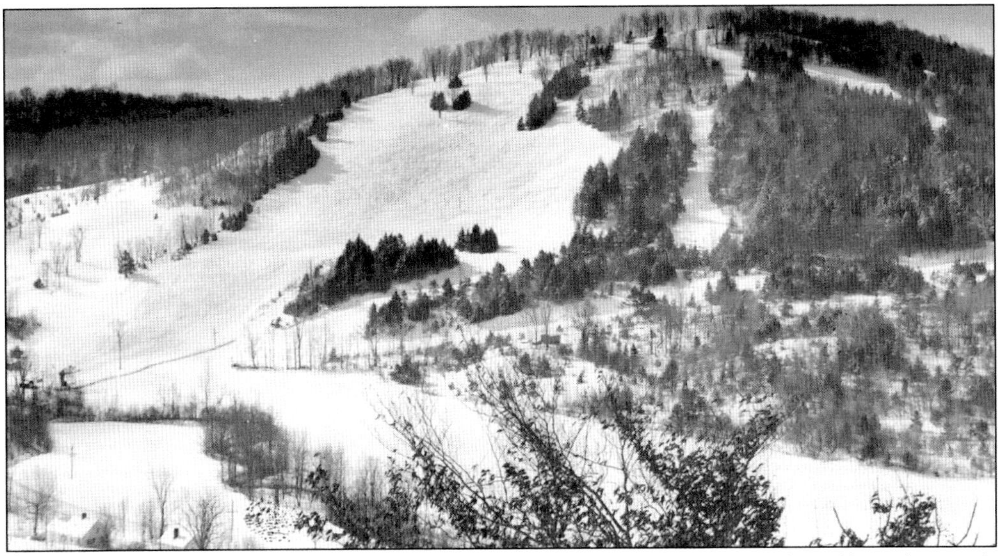

After the initial success on the slope of Gilbert's hill in 1934, Dartmouth College ski coach Wallace "Bunny" Bertram opened a second ski area nearby on what was known as Hill No. 6 during the 1936–1937 ski season. Bertram joked that it would be suicide to ski straight down its face, and hence, Woodstock's second ski area was born. In 1961, Bertram sold the operation to Laurance S. Rockefeller.

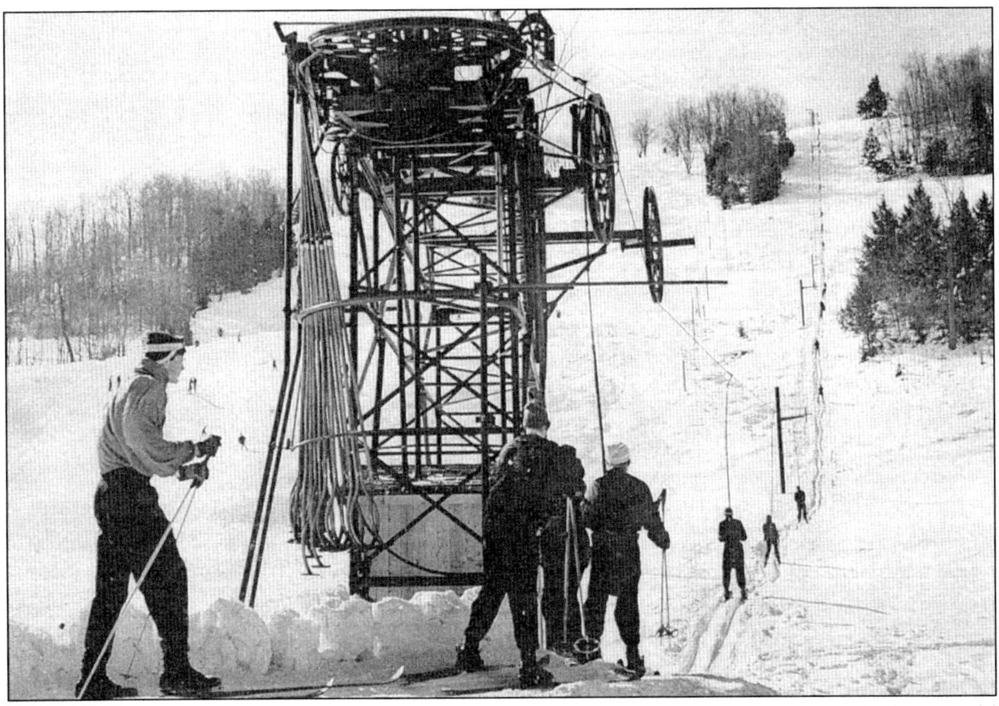

The T-bar and J-bar lifts were a great improvement over the simple rope tow, and after World War II, the so-called Poma lift, first developed in Europe, became another option for ski areas. For the 1953–1954 ski season, a modern Poma lift was installed at Suicide Six, and before the days of chairlifts, it proved very popular. Skiing in Woodstock was staying current with changing times.

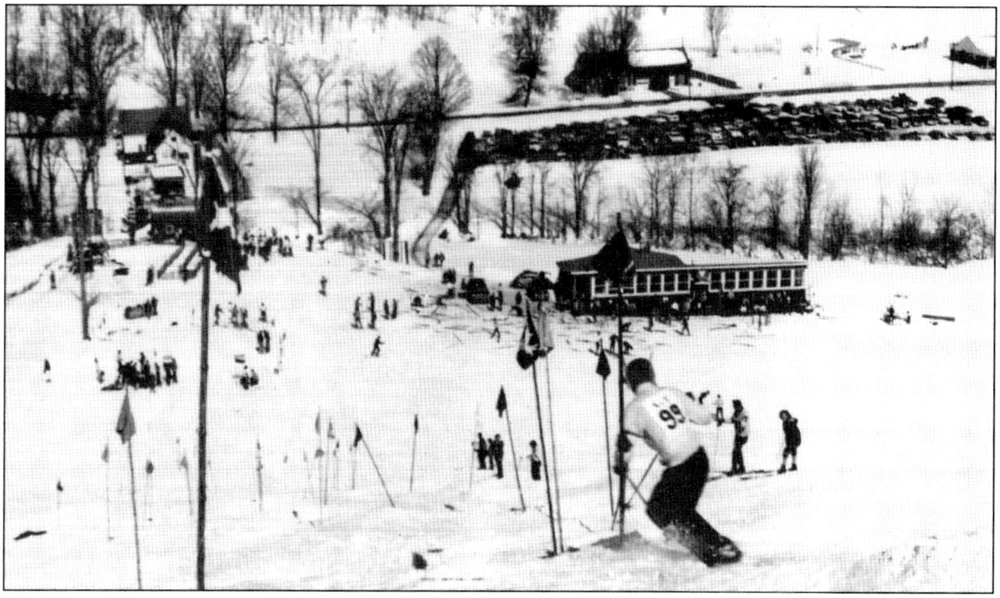

With humble origins in 1934 on Gilbert's hill, by the 1951–1952 ski season, the operation known as Mount Tom was becoming well developed and much loved. In the 1960s, the 500-foot vertical drop ski area featured seven trails and two Poma lifts. About 1961, Laurance S. Rockefeller also acquired Mount Tom, as well as Suicide Six, as part of his expanding RockResorts holdings, established in 1956.

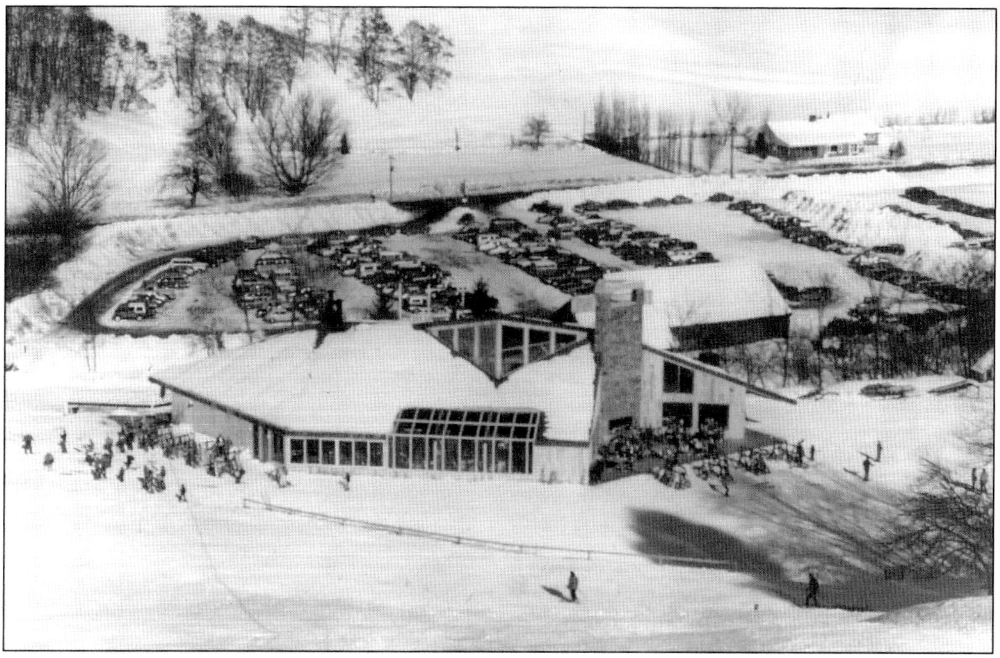

Under the ownership of RockResorts, the Suicide Six ski area, with added trails to its 650-foot vertical drop operation, was upgraded and expanded. Improvements, costing more than $1 million, were completed by the time of the 1977–1978 ski season. Renovations and upgrades included a new 10,000-square-foot lodge facility and a new double chairlift, a new J-bar lift in 1977, and a second chairlift in 1978.

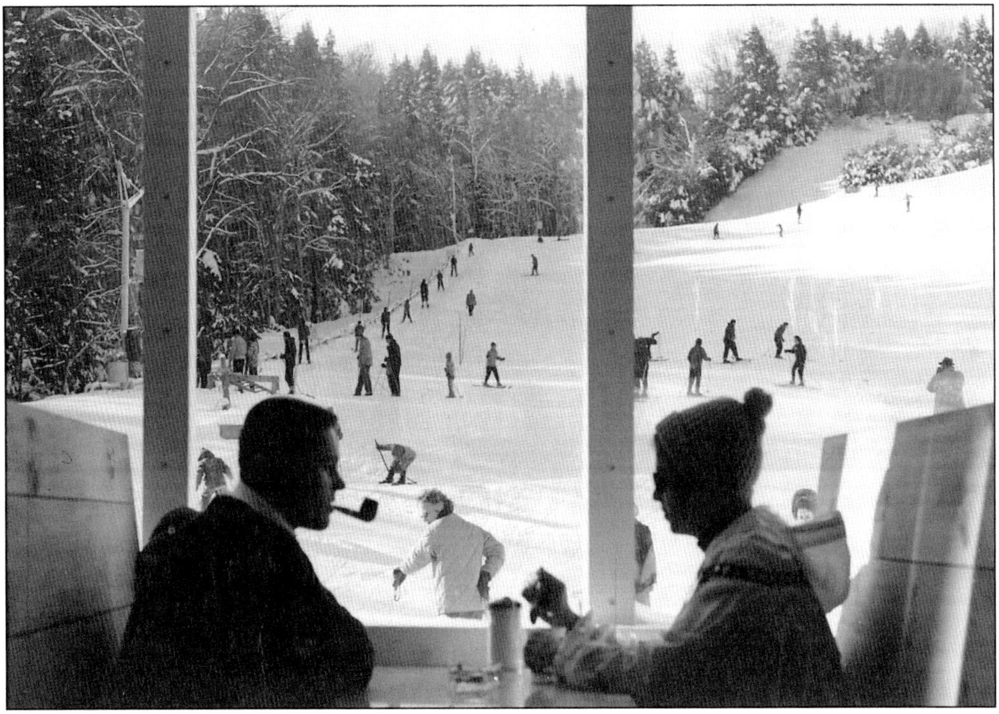

Mount Tom remained a very popular area, especially for family skiing activities, through the 1960s and into the 1970s. Visible beyond the lodge windows is the "baby Poma," a lift for very young skiers. However, by the 1970s, the cost of running two adjacent ski areas for RockResorts was proving difficult to justify. Hence, the 1977–1978 ski season was the last year of operation.

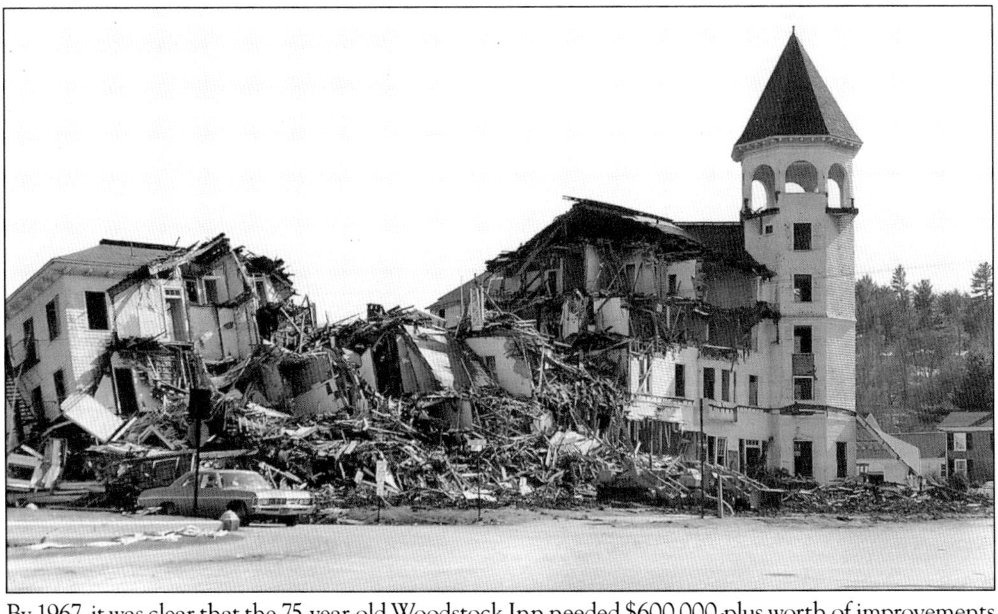

By 1967, it was clear that the 75-year-old Woodstock Inn needed $600,000-plus worth of improvements and modernization. As a result, that year, the property was acquired by Laurance S. Rockefeller as part of his RockResorts holdings. On March 22, 1969, as a new inn was under construction, a grand final ball was held in the old inn. Soon after, the old building was razed.

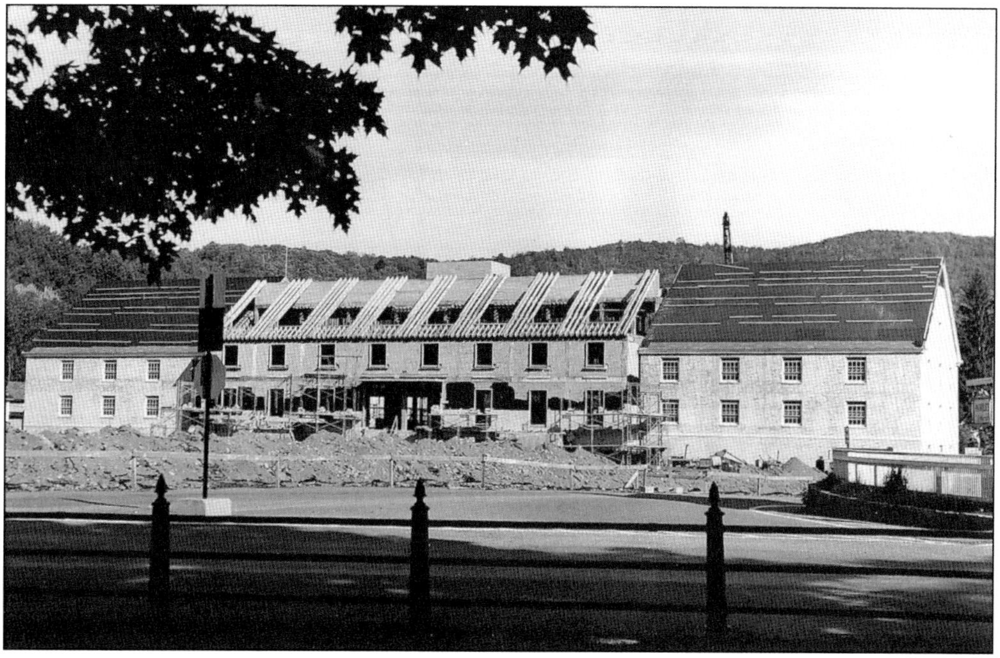

Out behind the old building, ground was broken for the new inn, designed by noted hotel architect William Tabler, in July 1968. For a period of time, the old inn remained in operation. This view looking from the green shows the new building under construction after the 1892 wood-frame facility, referred to as the "last of the big inflammables," had been removed.

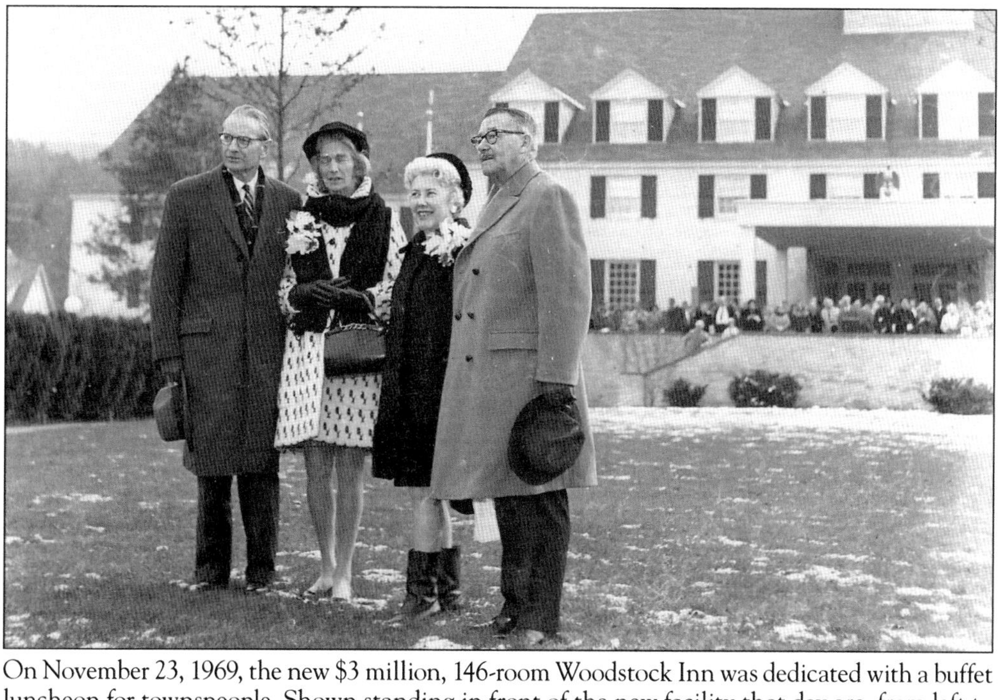

On November 23, 1969, the new $3 million, 146-room Woodstock Inn was dedicated with a buffet luncheon for townspeople. Shown standing in front of the new facility that day are, from left to right, Laurance S. Rockefeller, Mary Billings (French) Rockefeller, Marjorie Smith Conzelman Davis, and the governor of Vermont, Dean C. Davis (1900–1990).